Kotlin Coroutines by Tutorials

Mastering Coroutines in Kotlin and Android

By Filip Babić & Nishant Srivastava

Kotlin Coroutines by Tutorials

By Filip Babić and Nishant Srivastava

Copyright ©2019 Razeware LLC.

Notice of Rights

All rights reserved. No part of this book or corresponding materials (such as text, images, or source code) may be reproduced or distributed by any means without prior written permission of the copyright owner.

Notice of Liability

This book and all corresponding materials (such as source code) are provided on an "as is" basis, without warranty of any kind, express of implied, including but not limited to the warranties of merchantability, fitness for a particular purpose, and noninfringement. In no event shall the authors or copyright holders be liable for any claim, damages or other liability, whether in action of contract, tort or otherwise, arising from, out of or in connection with the software or the use of other dealing in the software.

Trademarks

All trademarks and registered trademarks appearing in this book are the property of their own respective owners.

ISBN: 978-1-942878-95-7

Dedications

"To my friends and family. And mostly to my loved one. Thank you for being patient and understanding, when I couldn't grab a cup of coffee or tea and catch up. Huge thanks to everyone who's supported me throughout the entire process, with positive and motivational encouragement. This wouldn't have gone as nearly as smooth without you."

— *Filip Babić*

"I would like to thank the many people who have made this book possible. To my father, who gave me the desire to be a curious soul and learn more. To my mom, who has supported me all along whenever I have had doubts about my own capabilities as a writer. To my friends, Saachi Chawla and Kirti Dohrey, who have always believed in me during my ups and downs. To people who have directly or indirectly been my mentor and helped me through understanding technology at a deeper level whenever I found myself stuck. And lastly, to the team at raywenderlich.com, my co-author, editors and everyone involved in making this book a reality."

— *Nishant Srivastava*

About the Authors

Nishant Srivastava is an author on this book. Nishant is a Sr.Android Engineer at Soundbrenner in Berlin, Germany and an open source enthusiast who spends his time doodling when not hacking on Android. He is a caffeine-dependent life-form and can be found either talking about android libraries or advocating that coffee is the elixir of life at community gatherings. He has been part of two startups in the past (Founding Team Member at OmniLabs, Inc. and one of the first employees at Silverpush) with experience in Android SDK Engineering and Audio Digital Signal Processing(DSP) on Android. While working at his past company (Silverpush), he developed the company's patented UAB (Unique Audio Beacon) Technology.

Filip Babić is an author of this book. He is an experienced Android developer from Croatia, working at the Five Agency, building world-known applications, such as the RosettaStone language-learning application and AccuWeather, the globally known weather reporting app. Previously he worked at COBE d.o.o., a German-owned mobile agency, which is partners with the biggest German media company. He's enthusiastic about the Android ecosystem, focusing extensively on applying Kotlin to Android applications, and building scalable, testable and user-friendly applications. Passionately building up good spirit in local development groups in Croatia, focusing on lectures, education, and engagement of new, aspiring developers in the Croatian IT community. But also pursuing global conferences, meetups, and IT fests. Altruistic when it comes to consulting and mentoring, trying to give help to everyone, whenever possible, motivated by the ideology that the Android ecosystem we live in is only as good as we make it.

About the Editors

Eric Crawford is a technical editor of this book. Eric is a Senior Software Developer at John Deere, where he bounces between iOS and Android development. Before coming to Deere he did freelance mobile development and serverside web development utilizing Java. In his free time he likes to dabble into other platforms like IOT and cloud computing.

Kevin Moore is a technical editor for the book. He has been developing Android apps for over 9 years and at many companies. He's written several articles at www.raywenderlich.com and created the "Programming in Kotlin" video series. He enjoys creating apps for fun and teaching others how to write Android apps.In addition to programming, he loves playing Volleyball and running the sound system at church.

Massimo Carli is the final pass editor of this book. Massimo has been working with Java since 1995 when he co-founded the first Italian magazine about this technology (http://www.mokabyte.it). After many years creating Java desktop and enterprise application, he started to work in the mobile world. In 2001 he wrote his first book about J2ME. After many J2ME and Blackberry applications, he then started to work with Android in 2008. The same year he wrote the first Italian book about Android; best seller on Amazon.it. That was the first of a series of 8 books. he worked at Yahoo and Facebook and he's actually Engineering Tech Lead at Lloyds. He's a musical theatre lover and a supporter of the soccer team S.P.A.L.

About the Artist

Vicki Wenderlich is the designer and artist of the cover of this book. She is Ray's wife and business partner. She is a digital artist who creates illustrations, game art and a lot of other art or design work for the tutorials and books on raywenderlich.com. When she's not making art, she loves hiking, a good glass of wine and attempting to create the perfect cheese plate.

Table of Contents

What You Need 13
Book License 15
Book Source Code & Forums 17
Book Updates 19
About the Cover 21
Introduction 23
   About Kotlin 23
   About Coroutines 24
   How to read this book 24

Section I: Introduction to Coroutines 25

Chapter 1: What Is Asynchronous Programming? 27
   Providing feedback 27
   Why multithreading? 29
   Interacting with the UI thread from the background 30
   Handling work completion using callbacks 34
   Indentation hell 35
   Using reactive extensions for background work 36
   Diving deeper into the complexity of Rx 38
   A blast from the past 39
   Explaining coroutines: The inner works 39
   Variations through history 40
   Key points 41
   Where to go from here? 42

Chapter 2: Setting Up Your Build Environments 43
   Choosing the build environments 43
   Installing the IntelliJ IDEA 44

    Building the Android environment 49
    Importing a project 51
    Key points 55
    Where to go from here? 55

Chapter 3: Getting Started with Coroutines 57
    Executing routines 57
    Launching a coroutine 58
    Building coroutines 59
    Explaining jobs 61
    Canceling Jobs 62
    Digging deeper into coroutines 63
    Posting to the UI thread 67
    Key points 68
    Where to go from here? 69

Chapter 4: Suspending Functions 71
    Suspending vs. non-suspending 71
    Elaborating continuations 82
    Creating your own suspendable API 86
    Key points 88
    Where to go from here? 88

Chapter 5: Async/Await 89
    The async/await pattern 89
    Learning from the past 90
    Using async/await 94
    Deferring values 98
    Combining multiple deferred values 99
    Being cooperative and structured 102
    Key points 107
    Where to go from here? 109

Chapter 6: Coroutine Context 111

Contextualizing coroutines 111
  Providing contexts. 114
  Key points 116

Chapter 7: Coroutine Contexts & Dispatchers 117
  Work scheduling 117
  Coroutine dispatcher types 121
  Using dispatchers 123
  Key points 126

Chapter 8: Exception Handling. 127
  Exception propagation 127
  Handling exceptions 128
  Callback wrapping 135
  Key points 138
  Where to go from here? 138

Chapter 9: Manage Cancellation 139
  Cancelling a coroutine 139
  Key points. 148
  Where to go from here? 149

Section II: Channels & Flows 151

Chapter 10: Building Sequences & Iterators with Yield . . . 153
  Getting started with sequences 153
  Enter: Sequence. 156
  Generators and Sequences 159
  SequenceScope is here to stay 162
  Yield and YieldAll at your service 163
  Key points 167
  Where to go from here? 167

Chapter 11: Channels. 169
  Getting started with channels 170

Pipelines 177
  Buffered channel 188
  Comparing send and offer 190
  Comparing receive and poll 192
  Error handling.. 193
  Comparing Channels to Java Queues........................... 196
  Key points.. 199

Chapter 12: Broadcast Channels 201
  Getting started with broadcast channels..................... 202
  ConflatedBroadcast channel 207
  ReactiveX vs. BroadcastChannel.............................. 210
  Key points.. 215
  Where to go from here?...................................... 215

Chapter 13: Producer & Actors 217
  Producing and consuming data................................ 217
  Producer-consumer problem................................... 218
  Acting upon data.. 224
  Key points.. 232
  Where to go from here?...................................... 233

Chapter 14: Beginning with Coroutines Flow 235
  Streams of data 235
  Limitations of streams...................................... 238
  A new approach to streams 239
  Flow Constraints 242
  Key Points 245

Chapter 15: Testing Coroutines 249
  Getting started... 250
  Writing tests for Coroutines 251
  Setting up the test environment............................. 253
  Summing it up 258

    Key points 258

Section III: Coroutines & Android 261

Chapter 16: Android Concurrency Before Coroutines 263
    Getting started 264
    Does Android need coroutines? 266
    Coroutines 297
    Introducing Anko 299
    Key points 300
    Where to go from here? 302

Chapter 17: Coroutines on Android - Part 1 303
    Getting started 304
    What's in the context? 308
    Converting existing API call to use coroutines 315
    Coroutines and Android lifecycle 318
    Key points 325
    Where to go from here? 325

Chapter 18: Coroutines on Android - Part 2 327
    Getting started 328
    Debugging coroutines 330
    Exception handling 333
    Don't forget testing 338
    Anko: Simplified coroutines 345
    Key points 349

Conclusion 351

What You Need

To follow along with this book, you'll need the following:

- **IntelliJ IDEA Community Edition 2019.1.x**: Available at https://www.jetbrains.com/idea/. This is the environment in which you'll develop most of the sample code in this book.

- **Jave SE Development Kit 8.**: Most of the code in this book will be run on the Java Virtual Machine or JVM, for which you need a Java Development Kit or JDK. The JDK can be downloaded from Oracle at http://www.oracle.com/technetwork/java/javase/downloads/index.html.

- **Android Studio 3.x.**: For the examples about Android described in Section 3, you can use the IDE available at https://developer.android.com/studio/.

If you haven't installed the latest versions of IntelliJ IDEA Community Edition and JDK 8, be sure to do that before continuing with the book. Chapter 2: "Setting Up Your Build Environments" will show you how to get started with IntelliJ IDEA to run Kotlin coroutines code on the JVM.

Book License

By purchasing *Kotlin Coroutines by Tutorials*, you have the following license:

- You are allowed to use and/or modify the source code in *Kotlin Coroutines by Tutorials* in as many apps as you want, with no attribution required.

- You are allowed to use and/or modify all art, images and designs that are included in *Kotlin Coroutines by Tutorials* in as many apps as you want, but must include this attribution line somewhere inside your app: "Artwork/images/designs: from *Kotlin Coroutines by Tutorials*, available at www.raywenderlich.com."

- The source code included in *Kotlin Coroutines by Tutorials* is for your personal use only. You are NOT allowed to distribute or sell the source code in *Kotlin Coroutines by Tutorials* without prior authorization.

- This book is for your personal use only. You are NOT allowed to sell this book without prior authorization, or distribute it to friends, coworkers or students; they would need to purchase their own copies.

All materials provided with this book are provided on an "as is" basis, without warranty of any kind, express or implied, including but not limited to the warranties of merchantability, fitness for a particular purpose and noninfringement. In no event shall the authors or copyright holders be liable for any claim, damages or other liability, whether in an action of contract, tort or otherwise, arising from, out of or in connection with the software or the use or other dealings in the software.

All trademarks and registered trademarks appearing in this guide are the properties of their respective owners.

Book Source Code & Forums

If you bought the digital edition

The digital edition of this book comes with the source code for the starter and completed projects for each chapter. These resources are included with the digital edition you downloaded from store.raywenderlich.com.

If you bought the print version

You can get the source code for the print edition of the book here:

https://store.raywenderlich.com/products/kotlin-coroutines-by-tutorials-source-code

Forums

We've also set up an official forum for the book at forums.raywenderlich.com. This is a great place to ask questions about the book or to submit any errors you may find.

Digital book editions

We have a digital edition of this book available in both ePUB and PDF, which can be handy if you want a soft copy to take with you, or you want to quickly search for a specific term within the book.

Buying the digital edition version of the book also has a few extra benefits: free updates each time we update the book, access to older versions of the book, and you can download the digital editions from anywhere, at anytime.

Visit our *Kotlin Coroutines by Tutorials* store page here:

- https://store.raywenderlich.com/products/kotlin-coroutines-by-tutorials.

And if you purchased the print version of this book, you're eligible to upgrade to the digital editions at a significant discount! Simply email support@razeware.com with your receipt for the physical copy and we'll get you set up with the discounted digital edition version of the book.

Book Updates

Since you've purchased the digital edition version of this book, you get free access to any updates we may make to the book!

The best way to get update notifications is to sign up for our monthly newsletter. This includes a list of the tutorials that came out on raywenderlich.com that month, any important news like book updates or new books, and a list of our favorite iOS development links for that month. You can sign up here:

- www.raywenderlich.com/newsletter

About the Cover

It would be difficult to think of an animal that cooperates more effectively and asynchronously with others of its kind than a bee. Beyond that, bees famously work with their environment to keep entire natural ecosystems and man-made industries thriving. Their community and industry has been well documented and celebrated throughout time, with references by philosopher Aristotle, economic theorist Karl Marx and even comedian Jerry Seinfeld.

Like the coroutines explored in this book, the various 16,000 known species of bees live harmoniously in their intricate colonies — an elegant network of productivity and execution of duties.

Developers can easily take great insight from the bee, working to architect code in an asynchronous way in which each part plays a critical role to contribute to the overall success of the project at hand.

Learn more about these important animals, here: https://en.wikipedia.org/wiki/Bee.

Introduction

Coroutines with Kotlin represents one of the most interesting and fasinating challenges in the software engineering world. It's an opportunity to implement complex concurrent tasks in an elegant and performant way. Reading this book will give you the opportunity to learn the basic concepts about multithreading and how concurrent programming can be simplified using Kotlin and Coroutines.

About Kotlin

Kotlin is a general purpose, open source, statically typed "pragmatic" programming language for the JVM that combines object-oriented and functional programming features. It originated at JetBrains, the company that drives IntelliJ IDEA, and has been open source since 2012.

At Google I/O 2017 Kotin was officially supported by Google as the main language for developing Android applications. It is a language focused on interoperability, safety, clarity, and tooling support.

It is also important to mention it's multiplatform support with JavaScript (ECMAScript 5.1) and native code (using LLVM).

About Coroutines

Asynchronous programming is often tedious and error-prone. The extensive usage of callbacks makes the code hard to read, debug and test. Coroutines define a different paradigm which introduces the concept of suspending functions. Coroutines generalize subroutines for non-preemptive multitasking, by allowing execution to be suspended and resumed. In this way, you can write asynchronous code as if it were synchronous. Coroutines are a recent solution in Kotlin and Android environment for writing concurrent and asynchronous code.

How to read this book

This book contains four sections.

The first section is an introduction to multithreading and concurrent programming with Kotlin. It explains how you can execute asynchronous tasks using the Kotlin language, what problems you may face and how coroutines can be a valid solution. You'll be introduced to the fundamental concepts of suspending functions, coroutine context and dispatching. You'll also learn how to manage exception and how to handle errors with coroutines.

The second section explains, in detail and with several examples, how to use very important API based on coroutine technology. You'll learn how to create sequences and iterators. Using channels, you'll learn how different coroutines can communicate and exchange data in thread safe way. Finally you'll learn all the details about coroutine flow which are a fundamental part of the last version.

In the first two sections, you learned everything about coroutines. If you need some specific knowledge about how to use them in the Android environment, this is the section for you. You'll create a complete Android application and you'll see how to use coroutines in order to create a very responsive application.

Kotlin can be used on JVM but also in other enviroments; this is called multiplatform. In this forth section you'll learn how to use coroutine with other languages like Java.

The best way to learn about Kotlin Coroutines is to roll up your sleeves and start coding. Enjoy the book!

Section I: Introduction to Coroutines

In the first chapter, you'll learn about the problems related to multithreading and how coroutines can be an elegant solution. After setting up your development environment in IntelliJ or Android Studio, you'll start writing your first coroutine to understand what suspending functions are and how to define them. You'll finish this section learning how to use **async** and **await** functions for efficient use of resources.

- **Chapter 1: What Is Asynchronous Programming?**: In this very first chapter, you'll learn what asynchronous programming means and why a modern developer should understand it. You'll see the basics of multithreading like queue and shared memory, and you'll understand how to solve the "Indentation Hell Problem."

- **Chapter 2: Setting Up Your Build Environments**: Learning through example is one of the most efficient ways to gain more skills. To do this, you need to set up your build environment and learn how to load the starting projects with IntelliJ or Android Studio. This chapter describes all you need to start writing your code.

- **Chapter 3: Getting Started with Coroutines**: This is the chapter where you'll learn the main concepts about coroutines like builders, scope and context. You'll see for the first time the Job object and learn how to manage dependencies between coroutines. You'll understand and write code to manage one of the most important features of asynchronous tasks: cancellations.

- **Chapter 4: Suspending Functions**: To understand how to use coroutines, you need to learn what a suspending function is and how to implement it. In this chapter, you'll learn all you need to create and use your suspending functions. You'll also learn how to change your existing functions to use them in a coroutine.

- **Chapter 5: Async/Await**: In multithreading and asynchronous development in Java, you often use Runnable, Callable and Future. With coroutines, you can use Deferred instead. These are objects that you can manage using the async/await functions. In this chapter, you'll write code to understand when and how to use this pattern most effectively.

- **Chapter 6: Coroutine Context**: This chapter is about one of the most important concepts about coroutines: Coroutine Context. You'll learn what it is and how this is related to the dependencies between different coroutine jobs. You'll also learn how to create your context.

- **Chapter 7: Context Switch & Dispatching**: In this chapter, you'll learn how to run different Jobs into the proper thread. You'll learn how to configure and use the proper thread to display information on the UI or to invoke different services on the network.

- **Chapter 8: Exception Handling**: Using functions with a callback is not difficult only because of the indentation hell problem but also for error and exception handling. In this very important chapter, you'll learn, with several examples, all the techniques you can use to handle exceptions.

- **Chapter 9: Manage Cancellation**: One of the most important topics to master when you deal with multithreading is a cancellation. Starting a thread is very easy compared to the techniques used to cancel it leaving the system in a consistent state. In this very important chapter, you'll learn, with several examples, all the techniques you can use to manage cancellations.

Chapter 1: What Is Asynchronous Programming?

By Filip Babić

The **UI (user interface)** is a fundamental part of almost every application. It's what users see and interact with in order to do their tasks. More often than not, applications do **complex work**, such as talking to external services or processing data from a database. Then, when the work is done, they show a **result**, mostly in some form of a message.

The UI must be **responsive**. If the work at hand takes a lot of time to complete, it's necessary to provide **feedback** to the user so that they don't feel like the application has frozen, that they didn't click a button properly — or perhaps that a feature doesn't work at all.

In this chapter, you'll learn how to provide useful information to users about what's happening in the application and what different mechanisms exist for working with multiple tasks. You'll see what problems arise while trying to do complex and long-running synchronous operations and how asynchronous programming comes to the rescue.

You'll start off by analyzing the flow of a function that deals with data processing and provides feedback to the user.

Providing feedback

Suppose you have an application that needs to upload content to a network. When the user selects the Upload button, loading bars or spinners appear to indicate that something is ongoing and the application hasn't stopped working. This information is crucial for a good user experience since no one likes unresponsive applications.

But what does providing feedback look like in code?

Consider the following task wherein you want to upload an image but must wait for the application to complete the upload:

```
fun uploadImage(image: Image) {
  showLoadingSpinner()
  // Do some work
  uploadService.upload(image)
  // Work's done, hide the spinner
  hideLoadingSpinner()
}
```

At first glance, the code gives you an idea of what's happening:

- You start by showing a spinner.
- You then upload an image.
- When complete, you hide the spinner.

Unfortunately, it's not exactly that simple because the spinner contains an animation, and there must be code responsible for that. showLoadingSpinner() must then contain code such as this:

```
fun showLoadingSpinner() {
  showSpinnerView()
  while(running) {
    rotateSpinnerImage()
    delay()
  }
}
```

showSpinnerView() displays the actual View component, and the following cycle manages the image rotation. But when does this function actually return?

In uploadImage(), you assumed that the spinner animation was running even after the completion of showLoadingSpinner(), so that the uploading of the image could start. Looking at the previous code, this is not possible. If the spinner is animating, it means that showLoadingSpinner() has not completed. If showLoadingSpinner() has completed, then the upload has started. This means that the spinner is not animating anymore. This is happening because when you invoke showLoadingSpinner() you're making a **blocking call**.

Blocking calls

A **blocking call** is essentially a function that only returns when it has completed. In the example above, `showLoadingSpinner()` prevents the upload of an image because it keeps the **main thread** of execution busy until it returns. But when it returns (because `running` becomes `false`), the spinner stops rotating.

So how can you solve this problem and animate the spinner even while the `upload` function is executing?

Simply put, you need additional threads on which to execute your long-running tasks.

The **main thread** is also known as the **UI thread**, because it's responsible for rendering everything on the screen, and this should be **the only thing it does**. This means that it should manage the rotation of the spinner but not the upload of the image — that has nothing to do with the UI. But if the **main thread** cannot do this because that isn't its job, what can execute the upload task? Well, quite simply, you need **a new thread** on which to execute your long-running tasks!

Computers nowadays are far more advanced than they were 10 or 15 years ago. Back in the day computers could only have one thread of execution making them freeze up if you tried to do multiple things at once. But because of technological advancements, your applications support a mechanism known as **multi-threading**. It's the art of having multiple threads, where each can process a piece of work, collectively finishing the needed tasks.

Why multithreading?

There's always been a hardware limit on how fast computers could be — that's not really about to change. Moreover, the number of operations a single processor in a computer can complete is reaching the law of diminishing returns.

Because of that, technology has steered in the direction of increasing the number of cores each processor has, and the number of threads each core can have running **concurrently**. This way, you could logically divide any number of tasks between different threads, and the cores could prioritize their work by organizing them. And, by doing so, multithreading has drastically improved how computer systems optimize work and the speed of execution.

You can apply the same idea to modern applications. For example, rather than spending large amounts of money on servers with better hardware, you can speed up the entire system using **multithreading** and the smart application of **concurrency**.

Comparing the main and worker threads

The **main thread**, or the **UI thread**, is the thread responsible for managing the UI. Every application can only have one main thread in order to avoid a classical problem called **deadlock**. This can happen when many threads access the same resources — in this case, UI components — in a different order. The other threads, which are not responsible for rendering the UI, are called **worker threads** or **background threads**. The ability to allow the execution of multiple threads of control is called **multithreading**, and the set of techniques used to control their collaboration and synchronization, is called **concurrency**.

Given this, you can rethink how `uploadImage()` should work. `showLoadingSpinner()` starts a new thread that is responsible for the rotation of the spinner image, which interacts with the main thread just to notify a refresh in the UI. Starting a new thread, the function is now a **non-blocking call** and can return immediately, allowing the image upload to start its own worker thread. When completed, this background thread will notify the main thread to hide the spinner.

Once the program launches a background thread, it can either forget about it or expect some result. You will see how background threads process the result, and communicate with the main thread, in the following section.

Interacting with the UI thread from the background

The upload image example demonstrates how important managing threads is. The thread responsible for rotating the spinner image needs to communicate with the main thread in order to refresh the UI at each frame. The worker thread is responsible for the actual upload and needs to communicate with the UI thread which handles the animation when it completes in order to stop it, and to hide the spinner. All of this must happen without any type of blocks. Knowing how threads *communicate* is key to achieving the full potential of concurrency.

Sharing data

In order to communicate, different threads need to share data. For instance, the thread responsible for the rotation of the spinner image needs to notify the main thread that a new image is ready to be displayed. Sharing data is not simple, and it needs some sort of synchronization, which is one of the main benefits of well written concurrency code.

What happens, for instance, if the main thread receives a notification that a new image is available and, before displaying it, the image is replaced? In this case, the application would skip a frame and a **race condition** would happen. You then need some sort of a **thread safe** data structure. This means that the data structure should work correctly even if accessed by multiple threads at the same time.

Accessing the same data from multiple threads, maintaining the correct behavior and good performance, is the real challenge of **concurrent programming**.

There are special cases, however. What if the data is only accessed and never updated? In this case, multiple threads can read the same data without any race condition, and your data structure is referred to as **immutable**. Immutable objects are always thread safe.

As a practical example, take a coffee machine in an office. If two people shared it, and it wasn't thread safe, they could easily make bad coffee or spill it and make a mess. As one person started making a mocha latte and another wanted a black coffee, they would ultimately ruin the machine — or worse, the coffee.

What are the data structures that you can use in order to safely share data in a thread? The most important data structures are **queues** and, as a special case, **pipelines**.

Queues

Threads usually communicate using **queues**, and they can act on them as **producers** or **consumers**. A producer is a thread that puts information into the queue, and the consumer is the one that reads and uses them. You can think of a queue as a list in which producers append data to the end, and then consumers read data from the top, following a logic called FIFO (First In First Out). Threads usually put data into the queue as objects called **messages**, which encapsulate the information to share.

A queue is not just a **container**, but it also provides synchronization in order to allow a thread to consume a message only if it is available. Otherwise, it waits if the message is not available. If the queue is a **blocking queue**, the consumer can block and wait for a new message — or just retry later.

The same can happen for the producer if the queue is full. Queues are thread safe, so it is possible to have multiple producers and multiple consumers.

A great real-life example of queues are fast food lines.

Imagine having three lines at a fast food restaurant. The first line has no customers, so the person working the line is blocked until someone arrives. The second has customers, so the line is slowly getting smaller as the worker serves customers. However, the last line is full of customers, but there's no one to serve them; this, in turn, blocks the line until help arrives.

In this example customers form a queue waiting to consume what the fast food workers are preparing for them. When the food is available, the customer consumes it and leaves the queue. You could also look at the customers as produced work, which the workers need to consume and serve, but the idea stays the same.

Pipelines

If you think about pipes or faucets and how they work, it's a fairly simple concept. When you release the pressure by turning the valve, you're actually **requesting** water. On the other side of that request, there's a system that **regulates the flow** of water. As soon as you make a request, it is blocked until the water comes running — just like a blocking call.

The same process is used for **pipelines** or **pipes** in programming. There's a pipe that allows **streams of data** to flow, and there are **listeners**. The data is usually a stream of bytes, which the listeners parse into something more meaningful.

As an example, you can also think about factory lines. Just like in a factory line, if there's too much product, the line has to stop until you process everything. That is, if there's **too much** data that you haven't yet processed, the pipeline is blocked until you consume some of the data and make room for more to flow. And, alternatively, if there's not enough product, the person processing it sits and waits until something comes up.

In other words, if there's **not enough** data to flow — the pipe is empty — you're blocked until some data emerges. Because you're either trying to send data to an overflowed stream, or trying to get data from an empty stream, the mechanism doesn't know how to react but to block until the conditions are met.

You can think of pipes as blocking queues wherein you don't have messages, but chunks of bytes.

Handling work completion using callbacks

Out of all the asynchronous programming mechanisms, **callbacks** are the most often used. This consists of the creation of objects that encapsulate code that somebody else can execute later, like when a specific task completes . This approach can also be used in real life when you ask somebody to push a button when they have completed some task you have assigned to them. When using **callbacks**, the button is analogous to code for them to execute; the person executing the task is a **non-blocking function**.

How can you put some code into an object to pass around? One way is by using **interfaces**. You can create the interface in this way:

```
interface OnUploadCallback {

  fun onUploadCompleted()
}
```

With this, you are passing an implementation of the interface to the function that is executing the long-running task. At completion, this function will invoke onUploadCompleted() on the object. The function doesn't know what that implementations does, and it's not supposed to know.

In modern programming languages like Kotlin, which support functional programming features, you can do the same with a **lambda** expression. In the previous example, you could pass the lambda to the upload function as a callback. The lambda would then contain the code to execute when the upload task completes:

```
fun uploadImage(image: Image) {
  showLoadingSpinner()

  uploadService.upload(image) { hideLoadingSpinner() }
}
```

Looking back at the very first snippet, not much has changed. You still show a loading spinner, call upload() and hide the spinner when the upload is done. The core difference, though, is that you're not calling hideLoadingSpinner() right after the upload. That function is now part of the **lambda block**, passed as a parameter to upload(), which will be executed at completion. Doing so, you can call the wrapped function anytime you're done with the connected task. And the lambda block can do pretty much anything, not just hide a loading spinner.

In case some value is returned, it is passed down into the lambda block, so that you can use it from within. Of course, the inner implementation of the `uploadService` depends on the service and the library that you're using. Generally, each library has its own types of callbacks. However, even though callbacks are one of the most popular ways to deal with asynchronicity, they have become notorious over the years. You'll see how in the next section.

Indentation hell

Callbacks are simpler than building your own mechanisms for thread communication. Their syntax is also fairly readable, when it comes to simple functions. However, it's often the case that you have **multiple function calls**, which need to be **connected or combined** somehow, mapping the results into more complex objects.

In these cases, the code becomes extremely difficult to write, maintain and reason about. Since you can't return a value from a callback, but have to pass it down the lambda block itself, you have to **nest callbacks**. It's similar to nesting `forEach` or `map` statements on collections, where each operation has its own ambda parameter.

When nesting callbacks, or lambdas, you get a large number of braces '{}', each forming a **local scope**. This, in turn, creates a structure called **indentation hell** — or **callback hell** (when it's specific to callbacks). A good example would be the fetching, resizing and uploading images:

```
fun uploadImage(imagePath: String) {
  showLoadingSpinner()

  loadImage(imagePath) { image ->
    resizeImage(image) { resizedImage ->
      uploadImage(resizedImage) {
        hideLoadingSpinner()
      }
    }
  }
}
```

You show the upload spinner before the upload itself, as before. But, after you load the image from a file, you proceed to resize it. Next, when you've resized the image successfully, you start uploading it. Finally, once you manage to upload it, you hide the loading spinner.

The first thing you notice is the amount of braces and indentation that form a **stair-like** code structure. This makes the code *very hard* to read, and it's not even a complex operation. When building services on the web, nesting can easily reach 10 levels, if not more. Not only is the code hard to read, but it's also extremely hard to maintain such code. Because of the structure, you suffer from cognitive load, making it harder to reason about the functionality and flow. Trying to add a step in between, or change the lambda-result types, will break *all* the subsequent levels.

Additionally, some people find callbacks really hard to grasp at first. Their steep learning curve, combined with the cognitive load and the lack of extensibility, make people look elsewhere for a solution to asynchronous programming. This is where **reactive extensions** come to life. You'll see how they solve the nesting problem in the next section.

Using reactive extensions for background work

The most significant issue of a callback-based approach is passing the data from one function to another. This results in **nested callbacks**, which are tough to read and maintain.

If you think about the queues and pipes, they operate with **streams** of data, wherein you can **listen** to the data as long as you need. Reactive extensions, or Rx, are built upon the idea of having asynchronous operations wrapped up in streams of events.

Rx incorporates the **observer pattern** into helpful constructs. Furthermore, there are a large number of **operators** that extend the behavior of **observable streams**, allowing for clean and expressive data processing. You can **subscribe** to a **stream of events**, map, filter, reduce and combine the events in numerous ways, as well as handle errors in the entire **chain of operations**, using a *single* lambda function.

> Reactive extensions resolve the problem of unreadable code of blocks with streams

The previous example of loading, uploading and resizing an image, using Rx, can be represented as:

```
fun uploadImage(imagePath: String) {
  loadImage(imagePath)
    .doOnSubscribe(::showLoadingSpinner)
    .flatMap(::resizeImage)
    .flatMapCompletable(::uploadImage)
    .subscribe(::hideLoadingSpinner, ::handleError)
}
```

At first, this code might look weird. In reality, it's a stream of data modified by using a bunch of operators. It begins with the flatMap operator, which takes some data — the image from loadImage() — and passes it to another function, creating a new stream. Then, the new stream sends events in the form of resizedImage, which gets passed to uploadImage(), using flatMapCompletable(), and operator chaining.

Finally, the uploadImage stream doesn't pass data but, rather, **completion events**, which tell you to hide the loading spinner when the upload has finished.

These streams of data and operations don't actually get executed until someone **subscribes** to them, using subscribe(onComplete, onError).

Additionally, doOnSubscribe() takes an action that the stream executes whenever you subscribe to it. There are also functions like doOnSuccess and doOnError, which propagate their respective events.

Further, it's important to know that, if any error or exception occurs in any of the operations in a chain, *it's not thrown*, and the application doesn't crash. Instead, the stream passes it down the chain, finally reaching the onError lambda. Callbacks do not have this behavior; they just throw the exception and you have to handle it yourself, using try/catch blocks.

Reactive extensions are cleaner than callbacks when it comes to asynchronous programming, but they also have a steeper learning curve.

With dozens of operators, different types of streams and a lot of edge cases with switching between threads, it takes a large amount of time to fully understand them.

The learning curve, and a few other issues, will be discussed in the next section.

Diving deeper into the complexity of Rx

Since this book isn't about Rx, you'll only have a narrow overview of its positive and negative features. As seen before, Rx makes asynchronous programming clean and readable. Further, in addition to the operators that allow for data processing, Rx is a powerful mechanism. Moreover, the error handling concept of streams adds extra safety to applications.

But Rx is not perfect. It has problems like any other framework, or paradigm, some of which are showing up in the programming community lately.

To start, there is the learning curve. When you start learning Rx, you have to learn a number of additional concepts, such as the **observer pattern** and **streams**. You will also find that Rx is not just a framework; it brings a completely new paradigm called **reactive programming**. Because of this, it's very hard to start working with Rx. But it's even harder to grasp the finesse of using its operators. The amount of **operators**, types of **thread scheduling**, and the combinations between the two, creates so many options that it's nearly impossible to know the full extent of Rx.

Another problematic issue with using Rx is the *hype*. Over the years, people have moved towards Rx as a silver bullet for asynchronous operations.

This eventually led to such programming being Rx-driven, introducing even more complexity to existing applications. Finding workarounds and using numerous design patterns, just to make Rx work, introduced new layers of unwanted complexity. Because of this, in Android, the Rx community has been debating if programmers should represent things like network requests as streams of data versus just a single event that they could handle using callbacks or something even simpler.

The same debate transitions to navigation events, as an example. Should programmers represent clicks as streams of events, too? The community opinion is very divided on this topic.

So, with all this in mind, is there a better or simpler way to deal with asynchronicity? Oddly enough, there's a concept dating back decades, which has recently become a hot topic.

> co-routines are part thread and part-callbacks which us systems power of the suspending and scheduling work

A blast from the past

This is a book about **coroutines**. They're a mechanism dating back to the 1960's, depicting a unique way of handling asynchronous programming. The concept revolves around the use of **suspension points**, **suspendable functions** and **continuations** as first-class citizens in a language.

They're a bit abstract, so it's better to show an example:

```
fun fetchUser(userId: String) {
  val user = userService.getUser(userId) // 1

  print("Fetching user") // 2
  print(user.name) // 3
  print("Fetched user") // 4
}
```

Using the above code snippet, and revisiting what you learned about blocking calls, you'd say that the execution order was 1, 2, 3 and 4. If you carefully look at the code, you realize that this is not the only possible logical sequence. For instance, the order between 1 and 2 is not important, nor is the order between 3 and 4. What is important is that the user data is fetched before it is displayed; 1 must happen before 3. You can also delay the fetching of the user data to a convenient time before the user data is actually displayed. Managing these issues in a transparent way is the black magic of **coroutines**!

They're a part-thread, part-callback mechanism, which use the system's power of scheduling and suspending work. This way, you can immediately return a result from a call *without* using callbacks, threads or streams. Think of it this way, once you start a coroutine, or call a suspendable function, it gets nicely wrapped up and prepared like a taco. But, until you want to eat the taco, the code inside might not get executed.

> It is like a nicely wrapped up taco which is ready but code does not get executed until you want to eat

Explaining coroutines: The inner works

It's not really black magic — only a smart way of using low-level processing. getUser() is marked as a **suspendable function**, meaning the system prepares the call in the background, and you get an unfinished, wrapped taco. But it might not execute the function yet. The system moves it to a **thread pool**, where it waits for further commands. Once you're ready to eat the taco and you request the result, the program can block until you get a ready-to-go snack, or suspend and wait for it within the coroutine.

Knowing this, the program can skip over the rest of the function code, until it reaches the first line of code on which it uses the user. This is called **awaiting** the result. At that point, it executes getUser() and if it hasn't already, suspends the program.

This means you can do as much processing as you want, in between the call itself and using its result. Because the compiler knows suspension points and suspendable functions are asynchronous and treats their execution sequentially, you can write understandable and clean code. This makes your code very extensible and easy to maintain.

Since writing asynchronous code is so simple with coroutines, you can easily combine multiple requests or transformations of data. No more staircases, strange stream mapping to pass the data around, or complex operators to combine or transform the result. All you need to do is mark functions as suspendable, and call them in a coroutine block.

Another, extremely important thing to note about coroutines is that they're not threads. They are a low-level mechanism that utilizes **thread pools** to shuffle work between multiple, existing threads. This allows you to create millions of coroutines, without overflowing memory. A million threads would take so much memory, even today's state-of-the-art computers would crash.

Although many languages support coroutines, each has a different implementation.

Variations through history

As mentioned, coroutines are a dated but powerful concept. Throughout the years, several programming languages have evolved their versions of the implementation. For example, in languages like Python and Smalltalk, coroutines are first-class citizens, and can be used without an external library.

A **generator** in Python would look like this:

```
def coroutine():
    while True:
        value = yield
        print('Received a value:', value)
```

This code defines a function, which loops forever, listening and printing any arguments you send to it. The concept of an infinite loop, which listens for data is called a generator. The keyword yield is what triggers the generator, receiving the value. As you can see, there's a `while True` statement in the function. In regular code, this would create a standard infinite loop, effectively blocking the program, since there's no exit condition. But this is a coroutine-powered call, so it waits in the background until you send some value to the function, which is why it doesn't block.

Another language with first-class coroutines is C#. In C#, there's support for the `yield` statement, like in Python, but also for `async` and `await` calls, like this:

```
MyResult result = await AsyncMethodThatReturnsAResult();
await AsyncMethodWithoutAResult();
```

By adding the `await` keyword, you can return an asynchronous result, using normal, sequential code. It's pretty much what you saw in the example above, where you first learned about coroutines.

Both Python and C# have first-class support for coroutines. By including them in the language itself, it allows you to make asynchronous calls without including a third-party framework. Many other programming languages utilize external libraries in order to support programming with coroutines. Kotlin also has coroutine support in its standard library. Additionally, the way Kotlin coroutines are built using global and extension functions with receivers, makes them very **extensible**. You can also create your own APIs by building on top of the existing functions.

You'll see how to do this in the next chapters of the book.

Key points

- **Multithreading** allows you to run multiple tasks in parallel.
- **Asynchronous programming** is a common pattern for thread communication.
- There are different **mechanisms** for sharing data between threads, some of which are queues and pipelines.
- Most mechanisms rely on a **push-pull** tactic, blocking threads when there is too much, or not enough data, to process
- **Callbacks** are a complex, hard-to-maintain and cognitive-load-heavy mechanism.
- It's easy to reach **callback hell** when doing complex operations using callbacks.
- **Reactive extensions** provide clean solutions for data transformation, combination and error handling.

- Rx can be too complex, and doesn't fit all applications.
- **Coroutines** are an established, and reliable concept, based on low-level scheduling.
- Too many **threads** can take up a lot of memory, ultimately crashing your program or computer.
- **Coroutines** don't always create new threads, they can reuse existing ones from thread pools.
- It's possible to have asynchronous code, written in a clean, **sequential** style, using coroutines.

Where to go from here?

Well that was a *really brief* overview of the history and theory behind asynchronous programming and coroutines.

If you're excited about seeing some code and Kotlin's coroutines, in the next section of the book you'll learn about **suspendable functions** and **suspension points**. Moreover, you'll see how coroutines are created in Kotlin, using **coroutine builders**. Next, you'll build asynchronous calls, which return some data with the **async** function, and see how you await the result. And, finally, you'll learn about **jobs** and their children, in coroutines.

You'll cover the entire base API for Kotlin Coroutines, learn how to wrap asynchronous calls into async blocks, how to combine multiple operations and how to build Jobs which have multiple layers of coroutines.

But before that, you have to set up your build environment, so let's get going!

Chapter 2: Setting Up Your Build Environments

By Filip Babić

To start learning about coroutines and suspending functions, you need a place to work. Throughout this book, you will utilize IntelliJ IDEA or Android Studio, which will serve as workstations for all the projects and challenges of this book.

Android Studio is based off of IntelliJ IDEA, so both tools will look and function similarly. Once you set up a good part of the first environment, the second one should be easier to do.

Choosing the build environments

IntelliJ IDEA is great when you have pure Kotlin or Java projects, but it also supports a variety of plugins to those projects, like the Spring framework. Android Studio, on the other hand, is the prime tool used for building Android applications, and it's crucial for the last section of this book.

Since both of these tools require a Java Virtual Machine (JVM) environment, you'll have to set that up first.

Configuring the Java development kit

When writing Kotlin, you're dependent upon the JVM and its build tools, unless you're using Kotlin/Native. This means that you have to set up the Java development Kit (JDK).

First, go to the JDK dowload site here: https://www.oracle.com/technetwork/java/javase/downloads/jdk8-downloads-2133151.html.

JDK download from oracle.com

Please note that there are newer versions of the JDK available, but Android only supports up to version 1.8, and some of the projects in this book are based in Android. This is why JDK 1.8 (or Java 8) is a safe bet for you to use. Once you download it, you can proceed with the installation, and that should be it regarding the Java dependencies.

Your next step is IntelliJ IDEA.

Installing the IntelliJ IDEA

To work with most of the projects in this book, you'll use IntelliJ. It's a powerful tool built by Jetbrains, and it helps with productivity using features such as smart autocomplete, code and project templates, and much more.

To install it, go to the Jetbrains website here: https://www.jetbrains.com/idea/download/.

IntelliJ download

Choose the free community edition, as it is sufficient enough for the projects that you'll work on. Download it and, once the download completes, run the installer. This chapter uses **MacOS**; if you're using **Windows** or **Linux**, make sure to pick the right version for you. The user interface for the installers might be a bit different, depending on which operating system you are using. When you finish installing it, you can run the program, and it will prompt you for settings like so:

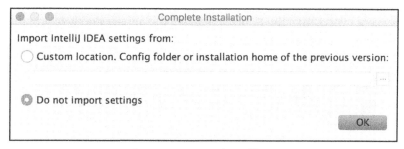

Import your settings if any

If you haven't worked with IntelliJ before, choose the default settings or the **Do not import settings** option. If you already have it installed, or have used it before, you can import your previous settings.

Next, you might be asked to read through and accept the license agreement and privacy policy, which should like like this:

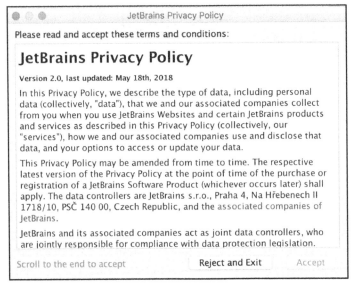

Read and accept JetBrains Privacy Policy

Once you accept everything, the home screen should appear and give you the option to create new projects or open existing ones.

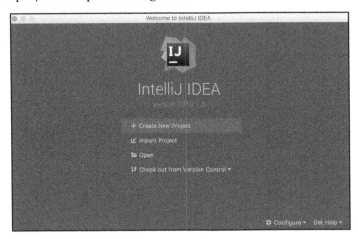

Create a new Project

To make sure everything works, try creating a simple Kotlin JVM project and see what happens.

You should see a window that asks you what type of a project you would like. Make
sure to select **Kotlin** and the **Kotlin/JVM** option.

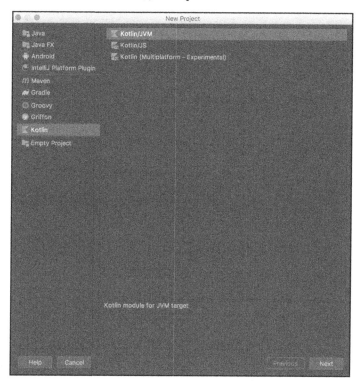

Select the Kotlin platform

When you press Next, you should see a project overview screen. This screen shows
you details like the **project name**, the type of **runtime** and the version of the Java
SDK.

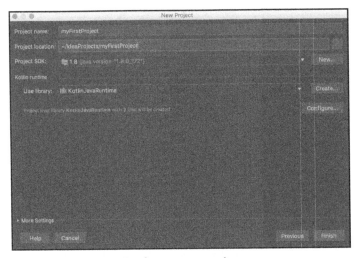

Configure your project

The program should find your Java SDK location, but, if it doesn't, you can manually add it by:

- Pressing **New**.

- Locating the JDK install directory on your computer.

- You can also go through the the **File ▸ Project Structure** menu.

- If you have newer versions of Java installed, this image might show JDK 10, but you should pick JDK 1.8, since the newer versions have some issues when building projects with the **Gradle** build system.

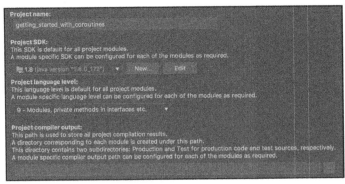

Setup your JDK configuration

If you have to set it up manually, pick the Java 1.8 SDK that you've installed and press **Apply** or **Accept**. Once the JDK path is set up, you should be able to build and run Kotlin and Java projects! When you open the project, you should see the default layout of an IntelliJ IDEA project.

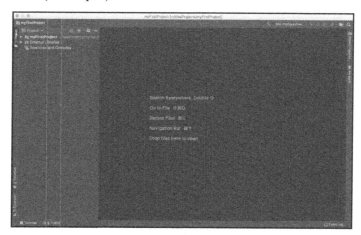

The structure of your project

On the left, you have the **project structure** view. You can change between different view types, but mostly you'll use the project overview, as it shows everything. There you can browse through all the files and libraries that you will use in the project.

On the bottom, there are a few things to note, such as the **Terminal** and the **Event log**. The bottom strip is reserved for system and build messages, logs, the terminal and the console. You can see any output-related data there. On the top, below the project name, there's another strip, but this one generally shows tools for the build system and debugging.

IntelliJ is filled with features, which you'll learn as you read through the book. You could also look up the official documentation to see everything the IDE offers. Now that you've set up IntelliJ, the only thing left is the Android Studio!

Building the Android environment

Later on in the book, you'll work on an Android project to see how coroutines can be implemented in a multi-threaded environment like Android. To do this, you first need Android Studio. Android Studio is an IDE built by Jetbrains, as well.

It also contains many helpful features, like autocomplete and various templates. However, the main benefit is the end-to-end Android build system, powered by Gradle.

To set Android studio up, first go to the download site here: https://developer.android.com/studio/.

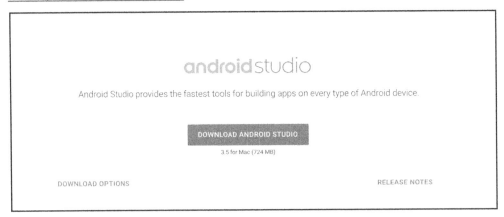

Download Android Studio

Download the latest stable version and run the installer. You'll be prompted for a few things, like the SDK you wish to download and the emulator settings. The default options should be alright, but if you wish you can tweak them.

Once you install it, you should see a window similar like this:

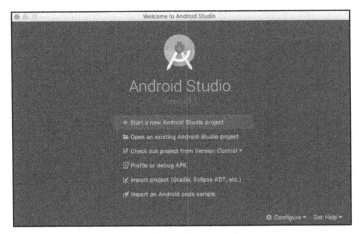

Android Studio Launcher

Starting a new project

You can start a new project.

- Select **Next** on the first step.
- On the second step, where you choose the target API level, pick API 21.
- Click **Next**, again.
- Finally, select the **Empty Activity** option.
- Press **Next** one final time, followed by a **Finish**.

This should set you up with an empty Android project. You'll find out about the settings for each Android project later on in the Android section of the book.

If the build system finishes without any errors, it means you have successfully configured Android Studio, and you'll be able to work on the Android section of the book. Don't worry about the time it takes for the project to build; the build system is doing a lot of work, so it may take a few minutes.

Importing a project

One of the things you'll be doing in this book is importing projects. This means that you're taking in an already-built project and adding it to your workspace. After adding it, the IDE builds it and connects any modules that should be connected in order for the project to work.

For example, if you're importing a Gradle project, the build environment will connect the scripts and load all the dependencies that you need. You'll do this in the following chapters, so let's walk through an example project import.

> **Note**: This is just an example of what it would look like to import a project. You don't actually have this project available yet; it's in the next chapter. You don't have to follow the steps yourself, but do remember to go back to this in case you forget how to import projects in the future.

To import a project in IntelliJ, you have to open it up, and then click the **Import project** button:

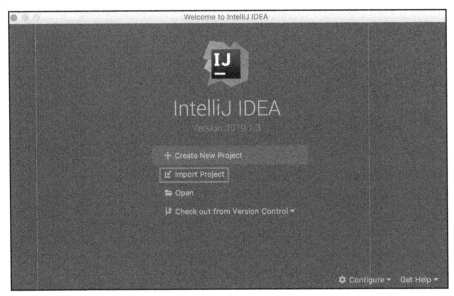

Import a Project in IntelliJ

Once you press it, a pop-up should appear, asking you which project you want to import.

Find the project you want — the image shows a project from the next chapter of the book, but you get the idea:

Select the project folder from your local file system

Once you pick the project, import by pressing **Open**; you'll get a pop-up asking you what type of project would you like to import it as. Usually, the IDE will understand which type it is, so here it knows it's a Gradle project:

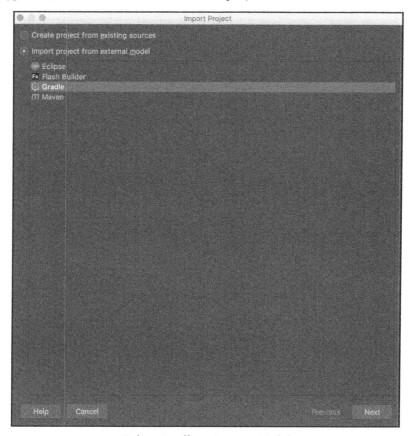

Select Gradle as Import Model

Then, once you choose the type of module you want to import and press **Next**, you'll see some general settings for the Gradle modules. But, in general, you can just press **Finish** and everything should work:

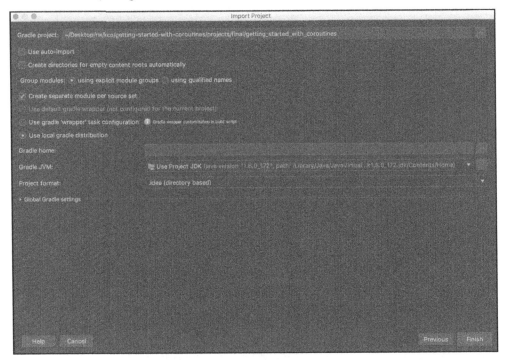

Accept the default configuration

For this chapter, you don't have a project; in the next chapter, you'll have to import a project with Gradle. Once you've done that, you'll see a new project, and you'll be ready to play around with coroutines!

Key points

- The **Build environments** that you'll use for the book require **Java**.
- **IntelliJ IDEA** is the most popular JVM development environment, and it is developed by Jetbrains.
- IntelliJ is powered by the IntelliJ platform, enabling features such as **autocomplete**, **templates**, **pre-baked projects** and many more.
- For Android projects, you'll use **Android Studio**, also developed by Jetbrains.
- Android Studio uses the **Gradle** build system, fully integrated into every project.
- **Importing project** connects all the gears that need to run fluently for you to work.

Where to go from here?

Now that you have environments set up, you can finally work on projects and write some Kotlin and coroutines code. Some of the chapters in the book might come with starter projects, which are already set up, so you don't have to do any extra work. Some might require you to complete a challenge. Without further ado, time to start writing practical code!

Chapter 3: Getting Started with Coroutines

By Filip Babić

So you've heard a lot about working with asynchronous or concurrent programming. It's time for you to learn a bit more about coroutines and how they work in the background (pun intended).

In this chapter, you will:

- Learn about **routines** and how a program controls its execution flow.
- Learn about suspendable functions and suspension points in code.
- **Launch** your first Kotlin coroutine, creating **jobs** in the background.
- Practice what you've learned by creating a few typical tasks, including posting to the **UI thread**.

Let's get started with **routines**!

Executing routines

Every time you start a process — launching an application, for instance — your computer creates something called a **main routine**. This is the core part of every program because it's where you set up and run all the other components in your code. As in the most basic learning samples, you often have a **main** function, which prints `Hello World`. That main function is the entry point of your program and is part of the main routine.

But as your programs gets bigger, so does the number of functions and the number of calls to other functions. Whenever you call some other function in the **main** block, you start something called a **subroutine**. A subroutine is just a routine, nested within another routine. The computer places all of these routines on the **call stack**, a construct that keeps track of what's currently running and how the current routine has been called. When a subroutine is finished running it is **popped** off the stack, and control is passed back to the caller routine. Lastly, if the stack is empty, and there's nothing else to run, the program finishes.

Invoking a subroutine is like doing a **blocking call**. A **coroutine** is then a subroutine that you can invoke as a **non-blocking call**. Because of this, the main difference between a standard subroutine and a coroutine is that the latter can run in parallel with other code. You can start and forget them, moving on to the rest of the program.

Launching a coroutine

To follow the code in this chapter, import this chapter's starter project, using IntelliJ, and selecting **Import Project**, and navigating to the **getting-started-with-coroutines/projects/starter** folder, selecting the **getting_started_with_coroutines** project.

When the project opens, locate and open **Main.kt**. There, you will find the following code:

```
fun main() {
  (1..10000).forEach {
    GlobalScope.launch {
      val threadName = Thread.currentThread().name
      println("$it printed on thread ${threadName}")
    }
  }
  Thread.sleep(1000)
}
```

Since launching your first coroutine is not *that* fascinating, you'll launch your first ten thousand coroutines! Now, launching ten thousand threads is a bit tedious for a computer, and most programs would get an `OutOfMemoryException`. But since coroutines are extremely lightweight, you're able to launch a large number of them, without any performance impact. If you run the program, you should see a lot of text, each line saying which number it is printing and on which thread.

There are a few important things to notice in the snippet above. The first is about the coroutine body that is represented by the block of code passed as the parameter to launch(), which is called a **coroutine builder**.

Second, when launching coroutines, you have to provide a CoroutineScope because they are background mechanisms which don't really care about the **lifecycle** of their starting point. What would happen if the program ended before the completion of the coroutine body? In this case, you use something called the GlobalScope, which makes explicit the fact that the coroutine lifecycle is bound to the **lifecycle of the application**. Because of this, you also need to put the current thread on hold, calling Thread.sleep(1000) in the end of main().

This is the basic explanation of what you're doing, but these concepts are more complex than that.

Building coroutines

You've heard the term **launching coroutines** quite a few times now. In truth, you first have to use a **coroutine builder**. The Coroutines library has several coroutine builder functions for you to use to start a new coroutine. In the previous example, you used launch() with the following signature:

```
public fun CoroutineScope.launch(
    context: CoroutineContext = EmptyCoroutineContext,
    start: CoroutineStart = CoroutineStart.DEFAULT,
    block: suspend CoroutineScope.() -> Unit
): Job
```

As you can see, launch() has a few arguments that you can pass in: a CoroutineContext, a CoroutineStart and a lambda function, which defines what's going to happen when you launch the coroutine. The first two are optional.

A CoroutineContext is a persistent dataset of contextual information about the current coroutine. This can contain objects like the Job and Dispatcher of the coroutine, both of which you will touch on later. Since you haven't specified anything in the snippet above, it will use the EmptyCoroutineContext, which points to whatever context the specified CoroutineScope uses. You can create custom contexts if you'd like, but for the most part, the existing ones are sufficient.

The `CoroutineStart` is the mode in which you can start a coroutine. Options are:

- **DEFAULT**: Immediately schedules a coroutine for execution according to its context. *(creates job in active state)*
- **LAZY**: Starts coroutine lazily.
- **ATOMIC**: Same as DEFAULT but cannot be cancelled before it starts.
- **UNDISPATCHED**: Runs the coroutine until its first suspension point. *— allows nested coroutine*

Last but not least, you specify a lambda block with the code that the coroutine will execute. If you check the previous definition of `launch()`, you will notice that this lambda block has a somewhat different signature than standard lambda blocks. Its signature is `block: suspend CoroutineScope.() -> Unit`. It's a lambda with a receiver of type `CoroutineScope`. This allows you to have nested jobs, as you can launch more coroutines from another `launch` block. Another thing that is specific is the `suspend` modifier. *— suspendable function*

As you've learned, coroutines build upon the concept of suspendable functions. You can use the modifier at hand to mark a lambda or another function suspendable. You'll learn a bit more about suspendable functions in the next chapter.

Scoping coroutines

As you've learned, coroutines can be launched in parallel with the main execution of a program. However, this doesn't mean that if the main program finishes, or stops, the coroutines will do the same. Or at least it didn't in the first few versions of the API. This behavior leads to subtle bugs in which applications would execute tasks even if you closed the application.

To mitigate these cases, the Coroutines API team created the `CoroutineScope`. Each scope instance knows which context it's related to, and each scope has its own lifecycle. If the lifecycle for your selected scope ends, while it's trying to run coroutines, all the work, even if in progress, will stop. This is why, if you try running the snippet without `Thread.sleep`, there may not be any output or there may be only some.

Since you have to call `launch()` on a `CoroutineScope`, there are two ways of doing this. You can use the `GlobalScope`, as you did so far, not caring about where exactly the coroutine is launched. Or you can implement the `CoroutineScope` interface, and provide an instance of the `CoroutineContext` in which you'll run coroutines. The former is easier, and it's a great option when you don't care about coroutine results, posting to the UI thread or about the job completion. The latter is crucial if you want to specify where you need to use the result (like the UI thread), and when you want to bind the jobs to the lifecycle of a certain object instance, like `Activity` instances in Android.

There are cases in which the lifecycle or manual cancellation don't necessarily cancel the coroutines. It's not only important that you provide cancellation mechanisms, but that you also have to write **cooperative code**. This means that your functions check whether or not their wrapping Job is running. You'll see how to do this later in the chapter.

You should have a better understanding of how coroutines work and what's important to define when launching them. In the next few sections, you'll learn a bit more about different functionalities coroutines have and, finally, you'll see how to combine jobs running a few different tasks using `launch()`.

Explaining jobs

If you've noticed, most things in coroutines refer to a **job**, which you create and run. A Job is also what `launch()` returns. But what is a Job and what can you do with it?

When you launch a coroutine, you basically ask the system to execute the code you pass in, using a lambda expression. That code is not executed immediately, but it is, instead, inserted into a queue.

A Job is basically **a handle** to the coroutine in the queue. It only has a few fields and functions, but it provides a lot of extensibility. For instance, it's possible to introduce a dependency relation between different Job instances using `join()`. If Job A invokes `join()` on Job B, it means that the former won't be executed until the latter has come to completion. It is also possible to set up a **parent-child** relation between Job instances using specific **coroutine builders**. A Job cannot complete if all its children haven't completed. A Job must complete in order for its parent to complete.

The Job abstraction makes this possible through the definition of **states**, whose transitions follow the workflow described by the diagram on the next page:

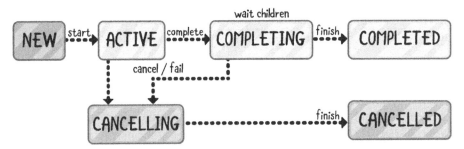

When you launch a coroutine, you create a Job, which is always in the **New** state. It then goes directly into the **Active** state by default, unless you've supplied the LAZY CoroutineStart parameter in the coroutine builder you've used. You can also move a Job from the New to the Active state using start() or join(). A running coroutine is always in the Active state. As you can see in the state diagram, the Job can complete or can be canceled.

It's very important to note how completion and cancellation work for dependent Job instances. In particular, you can see that a Job remains in the **Completing** state until all of its children complete. It's important to say that the Completing state is internal and, if queried from outside, the Job will result in the Active state.

States are fundamental because they give you information about what's going on with the coroutines and what you can do with them. You can also query the state of a Job or simply iterate over the children and do something with them.

Creating a Job is pretty easy and nesting isn't hard either. You've seen how they work with completion, but how do things work in the case of cancellation or errors?

Canceling Jobs

When you launch a coroutine and you create a Job, many things can happen. An exception can occur, or you might need to cancel the Job because of some new conditions in the application. Consider, for instance, a list of images that you download from the network. Every time you need to display an image in a list item, you start a coroutine for the download. This download might fail because there's no connection, and you have to handle the related exception. Or the download might be canceled because the user scrolls the list and the image goes out of the screen before it's available. It's very important to understand how you can manage these use cases when using coroutines.

Usually, an **uncaught exception** would cause the entire program to crash. However, since coroutines have suspending behavior, if an exception occurs, it can also be suspended and managed later.

Much easier is the way you can handle the **cancellation**. You can do it by invoking `cancel()` on the related `Job`. The system is then smart enough to understand the dependencies between Jobs. If you cancel a Job, you automatically cancel all its children. If it has a parent, the parent is canceled. A parent of a Job is also canceled if one of its children fails.

> **Note**: It's possible to use a special parent job, which doesn't require for all the children to complete happily - they can be cancelled or can fail independently. This version of a Job is called the `SupervisorJob`.

As mentioned before, even though you cancel a `Job`, your code might not be co-operative with the cancellation events. You can check this by using its `isActive` property. If your code does computational work, without checking the `isActive` flag, it won't listen to cancellation events. So running `while` loops with the `isActive` flag is safer than with your own conditions. Or you should at least try to depend on `isActive`, on top of your conditions.

Digging deeper into coroutines

So far you've launched a large amount of coroutines, and you've seen how you can create multiple coroutine jobs. But there are other things you can do when launching a coroutine. For example, if you have some work that you have to first delay for a period of time, before running, you can do so with `delay()`. Open up **Main.kt** again, and replace the code with the following snippet:

```
fun main() {
  GlobalScope.launch {
    println("Hello coroutine!")
    delay(500)
    println("Right back at ya!")
  }

  Thread.sleep(1000)
}
```

different from sleep it suspends

If you run the code above, you should see "Hello coroutine," in the console, and, briefly after that, "Right back at ya." `delay()` is really useful because you can effectively wait for the given amount of time and then run work when everything is ready. And most importantly it does not sleep a thread, or block, it just suspends the coroutine.

Dependent Jobs in action

So far, you've learned that, every time you launch a coroutine, you can get a Job reference. You can also create dependencies between different Jobs — but how? Just replace the previous code with this:

```kotlin
fun main() {
    val job1 = GlobalScope.launch(start = CoroutineStart.LAZY) {
        delay(200)
        println("Pong")
        delay(200)
    }

    GlobalScope.launch {
        delay(200)
        println("Ping")
        job1.join()
        println("Ping")
        delay(200)
    }
    Thread.sleep(1000)
}
```

Going through the code above:

- You first launch a coroutine that contains some delays and prints the Pong word, saving the created Job into the `job1` reference.

- Then, you launch a second coroutine that contains a couple of `println`s but also invokes the `join` function on `job1`.

What is the expected output? If you follow the code, you would expect to see Pong and then Ping twice, but this is not the case. As you can see, you used the `CoroutineStart.LAZY` value as `CoroutineStart`, and this means that the related code is going to be executed only when you actually need it.

This happens when the second coroutine invokes the `join` function on `job1`. This is why the result of the previous code is Ping, then Pong and, finally, Ping again.

Managing Job hierarchy

In the previous code, you created a dependency between different `Job` instances, but this is not the kind of relation you can refer to as a parent-child relation. Again, replace the previous code with the following. You can use `with()` in order to avoid the repetition of the `GlobalScope` receiver:

```
fun main() {
  with(GlobalScope) {
    val parentJob = launch {
      delay(200)
      println("I'm the parent")   // this is for parent
      delay(200)
    }
    launch(context = parentJob) {  // child
      delay(200)
      println("I'm a child")
      delay(200)
    }
    if (parentJob.children.iterator().hasNext()) {
      println("The Job has children ${parentJob.children}")
    } else {
      println("The Job has NO children")
    }
    Thread.sleep(1000)
  }
}
```

Going through the above code, in turn:

- Here, you launch a coroutine and assign its `Job` to the `parentJob` reference.
- Then, you launch another coroutine using the previous `Job` as the `CoroutineContext`. This is possible because the `Job` abstraction implements `CoroutineContext`. Under the hood, the `CoroutineContext` you pass here is **merged** with the one from the currently active `CoroutineScope` - `EmptyCoroutineContext`.

If you run the code above, you can see how the `parentJob` has `children`. If you run the same code, removing the context for the second coroutine builder, you can see that the parent-child relationship is not established and the children are not present.

Using standard functions with coroutines

Another thing you can do with coroutines is build retry-logic mechanisms. Using `repeat()` from the standard library, paired up with `delay()` you learned above, you can create code that attempts to run work in delayed periods of time. Once again, replace the **Main.kt** code with the next snippet:

```
fun main() {
  var isDoorOpen = false

  println("Unlocking the door... please wait.\n")
  GlobalScope.launch {
    delay(3000)

    isDoorOpen = true
  }

  GlobalScope.launch {
    repeat(4) {
      println("Trying to open the door...\n")
      delay(800)

      if (isDoorOpen) {
        println("Opened the door!\n")
      } else {
        println("The door is still locked\n")
      }
    }
  }

  Thread.sleep(5000)
}
```

Try running the code. You should see that someone's trying to open the door a few times before ultimately succeeding. So using `delay()`, and `repeat()` from Kotlin's standard library, you managed to build a mechanism that tries to run some code multiple times, before you meet a time or logic condition. You can use the same flow to build networking back-off and retry logic. And once you learn how to return values from coroutines later in this book, you'll see how powerful this can be.

Posting to the UI thread

From what you've seen so far, coroutines are all about simplicity, with a large part of their functionality built into the language itself. Posting to the UI thread isn't complicated; it comes down to starting a new coroutine with a **UI dispatcher** as its threading context.

Since we're talking about applications with a visible user interface, you can post to the main thread in **Android**, **Swing** and **JavaFx** applications. You can do it using `Dispatchers.Main` as the context in the following way:

```
GlobalScope.launch(Dispatchers.Main) { ... }
```

You need to be careful, though, because this is not enough. You need to set one of the following dependencies:

```
implementation 'org.jetbrains.kotlinx:kotlinx-coroutines-android:...'
implementation 'org.jetbrains.kotlinx:kotlinx-coroutines-swing:...'
implementation 'org.jetbrains.kotlinx:kotlinx-coroutines-javafx:...'
```

Otherwise, you'll get an exception like this:

```
Exception in thread "DefaultDispatcher-worker-3"
java.lang.IllegalStateException: Module with the Main dispatcher
is missing. Add dependency providing the Main dispatcher, e.g.
'kotlinx-coroutines-android'
```

You can try this behavior with a simple Swing example. First, you need to add this dependency to the `build.gradle`:

```
"implementation 'org.jetbrains.kotlinx:kotlinx-coroutines-swing:$kotlin_coroutines_version"
```

Then, you can replace `main()` with this:

```
fun main() {
  GlobalScope.launch {
    val bgThreadName = Thread.currentThread().name
    println("I'm Job 1 in thread $bgThreadName")
    delay(200)
    GlobalScope.launch(Dispatchers.Main) {
      val uiThreadName = Thread.currentThread().name
      println("I'm Job 2 in thread $uiThreadName")
```

```
    }
  }
  Thread.sleep(1000)
}
```

The external coroutine prints the name of the thread it's executed in. After a short delay, you launch another coroutine using `Dispatchers.Main` as `CoroutineContext`. This is the one that allows you to interact with the main thread.

If you run the code, you'll get something like:

```
I'm Job 1 in thread DefaultDispatcher-worker-1
I'm Job 2 in thread AWT-EventQueue-0
```

The first `Job` has been executed in the background by a **worker thread**. The second is the main thread in Swing. Pretty simple, right?

To check out the examples from this chapter, import this chapter's final project, using IntelliJ, and selecting **Import Project**, and navigating to the **getting-started-with-coroutines/projects/final** folder, selecting the **getting_started_with_coroutines** project.

Key points

- You can build coroutines using **coroutine builders**.
- The main coroutine builder is the **launch** function.
- Whenever you launch a coroutine, you get a `Job` object back.
- **Jobs** can be canceled or combined together using the `join` function.
- You can nest jobs and cancel them all at once.
- Try to make your code **cooperative** — check for the state of the job when doing computational work.
- Coroutines need a **scope** they'll run in.
- Posting to the UI thread in advanced applications is as easy as passing in the `Dispatchers.Main` instance as the context.
- Coroutines can be postponed, using the `delay` function.

Where to go from here?

You're ready to launch as many coroutine jobs as you want! But this is only a small piece of the Kotlin coroutine API. So far, you've only launched Jobs, pieces of work that you need to finish. The real power of suspending code is being able to return values asynchronously, without any callbacks or additional mechanisms.

In the next chapter, you'll learn a bit more about the fundamentals of coroutines and how code is suspended in programs. You'll learn about the execution of programs, how the computer passes directions to functions and how the program knows where to go back once a suspended function returns.

So let's not leave you in suspense!

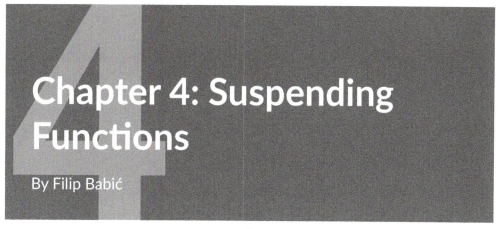

Chapter 4: Suspending Functions

By Filip Babić

suspending code is the way to pause its xecution

So far, you've learned a lot about coroutines. You've seen how to launch coroutines and deliver asynchronous work without any overhead from thread allocations or memory leaks. However, the base foundation of coroutines is the ability to suspend code, control its flow at will, and return values from synchronous and asynchronous operations with the same kind of syntax and sequential code structure.

In this chapter, you'll learn more about how suspendable functions work from within. You will see how you can convert existing code, which relies on callbacks, to suspendable functions, which are called in the same way as regular, blocking, functions. Throughout it all, you will learn what the most important piece of the coroutines puzzle is.

Suspending vs. non-suspending

Up until now, you've learned that coroutines rely on the concept of **suspending code** and **suspending functions**. Suspended code is based on the same concepts as regular code, except the system has the ability to *pause* its execution and continue it later on. But when you're using two functions, a suspendable and a regular one, the calls seem pretty much the same.

If you go a step further and duplicate a function you use, but add the `suspend` modifier keyword at the start, you could call both of the functions with the same parameters. You'd have to wrap the suspendable function in a `launch` block, because the Kotlin coroutines API is built like that, but the actual function call doesn't change.

The system differentiates these two functions by the `suspend` modifier at compile time, but where and how do these functions work differently, and how do both functions work with respect to the suspension mechanism in Kotlin coroutines? The answer can be found by analyzing the bytecode each of the functions generate, and by explaining how the call-stack works in both of the cases. You'll start by analyzing the non-suspendable, regular, variant first.

Analyzing a regular function

To follow the code in this chapter, import this chapter's starter project, using IntelliJ, and selecting **Import Project**, and navigating to the **suspending-functions/projects/starter** folder, selecting the **suspending_functions** project.

If you open up **Main.kt**, in the starter project, you'll notice a small `main` function. It's calling a simple, regular, non-suspendable function, which doesn't rely on callbacks or coroutines. There will be four different variants of this function. This variant is the most rudimentary, so let's analyze it first:

```kotlin
fun getUserStandard(userId: String): User {
  Thread.sleep(1000)

  return User(userId, "Filip")
}
```

The function takes in one parameter: the `userId`. It puts the current thread to sleep for a second, to mimic a long running operation. After that, it returns a `User`. In reality, the function is simple, and there are no hidden mechanisms at work here. Analyze the bytecode generated by pressing **Tools ▶ Kotlin ▶ Show Kotlin Bytecode**. After that you should see the **Kotlin Bytecode** window opened, and by pressing the **Decompile** button, you can see the generated code, which should look something like this

```java
@NotNull
public static final User getUserStandard(@NotNull String userId)
{
  Intrinsics.checkParameterIsNotNull(userId, "userId");
  Thread.sleep(1000L);
  return new User(userId, "Filip");
}
```

After inspecting it, you can see that it doesn't differentiate much from the actual code. It's completely straightforward and does what the code says it does.

The only addition to the code is the nullchecks and annotations the compiler adds, to make sure non-null type system is followed. Once the program starts this function, it will check that the parameters are not null, and return a user after one second.

This function is clean and simple, but the problem here lies in the Thread.sleep(1000) call. If you call the function on the **main thread**, you'll effectively freeze your UI for a second. It's much better if you implement this using a callback, and by creating a new thread for the long-running operation. That is actually the second example; see how you'd implement this using a callback.

Implementing the function with callbacks

A better solution to this problem would be having a function, which takes in a callback as a parameter. This callback would serve as a means of notifying the program about the user value being ready for use. Furthermore, it would create a separate thread of execution, to offload the main thread.

To do this, replace the getUserStandard() with the following code:

```kotlin
fun getUserFromNetworkCallback(
    userId: String,
    onUserReady: (User) -> Unit) {
  thread {
    Thread.sleep(1000)

    val user = User(userId, "Filip")
    onUserReady(user)
  }
  println("end")
}
```

Update the main function to the following:

```kotlin
fun main() {
  getUserFromNetworkCallback("101") { user ->
    println(user)
  }
  println("main end")
}
```

Run the bytecode analyzer again, and you should see the following output:

```java
public static final void getUserFromNetworkCallback(
@NotNull final String userId,
@NotNull final Function1 onUserReady) {
```

```
    Intrinsics.checkParameterIsNotNull(userId, "userId");
    Intrinsics.checkParameterIsNotNull(onUserReady,
 "onUserReady");
    ThreadsKt.thread$default(
      false,
      false,
      (ClassLoader)null,
      (String)null,
      0,
      (Function0)(new Function0 () {
        // $FF: synthetic method
        // $FF: bridge method
        public Object invoke() {
           this.invoke();
           return Unit.INSTANCE;
        }

        public final void invoke () {
           Thread.sleep(1000L);
           User user = new User(userId, "Filip");
           onUserReady.invoke(user);
        }
    }), 31, (Object)null);

    String var2 = "end";
    System.out.println(var2);
}
```

→ new thread

It's quite a big change compared to the previously generated piece of code. Again the system does a series of nullchecks to enforce the type system. After that, it creates a new thread, and within `public final void invoke()` of the thread, it calls the wrapped code. The code itself doesn't change much from the last example, but now it relies on a thread and a callback.

Once the system runs `getUserFromNetworkCallback()`, it creates a thread. Once the thread is fully set up, it runs the block of code, and propagates the result back using the callback. If you run the code above, you'll get the following result:

```
end
main end
User(id=101, name=Filip)
```

This means the `main` function can indeed finish before the `getUserFromNetworkCallback` does. The thread it starts lives on after the main thread, and so can the code. This function is a bit better than the last example, since it offloads the work from the main thread, using the callback to finally consume the data. But the problem here is that the code you use to build up a value can throw an exception. This means that you'd have to wrap it in a `try/catch` block. But it would be best if the `try/catch` block was at the actual place of creating a value. However, if you catch an exception there, how do you propagate it back to the main code?

This is usually done by using a slightly different signature of the callback passed to the function you wish to run, allowing it to pass either a value or an exception. See how to handle both of those paths in which the function can end.

Handling happy and unhappy paths

When programming, you usually have something called a **happy path**. It's the course of action your program takes, when everything goes smoothly. Opposite of that, you have an **unhappy path**, which is when things go wrong. In the example above, if things went wrong, you wouldn't have any way of handling that case from within the callback. You'd either have to wrap the entire function call in a `try/catch` block, or catch exceptions from within the `thread` function. The former is a bit ugly, as you'd really want to have all possible paths handled at the same place. The latter isn't much better either, as all you can pass to the callback is a value, so you'd have to either pass a nullable value, or an empty object, and go from that.

To make this functionality available and a bit more clean, programmers define the callback as a two-parameter lambda, with the first being the value, if there is any, and the second being the error, if it occurred. The signature of the function, and its callback, would be next, so replace the code in **Main.kt**:

```kotlin
fun getUserFromNetworkCallback(
    userId: String,
    onUserResponse: (User?, Throwable?) -> Unit) {
  thread {

    try {
      Thread.sleep(1000)
      val user = User(userId, "Filip")

      onUserResponse(user, null)
    } catch (error: Throwable) {
      onUserResponse(null, error)
    }
  }
}
```

The callback can now accept either a value or an error. Whichever parameter or path is taken, it should be valid, and non-null, while the remaining parameter will be null, showing you that the path it governs hasn't happened. When looking at the bytecode by pressing the **Decompile** button, in the bytecode decompiler window, you should see the following:

```
public static final void getUserFromNetworkCallback(
@NotNull final String userId,
@NotNull final Function2 onUserResponse) {
  Intrinsics.checkParameterIsNotNull(userId, "userId");
  Intrinsics.checkParameterIsNotNull(onUserResponse,
"onUserResponse");
  ThreadsKt.thread$default(
    false,
    false,
    (ClassLoader)null,
    (String)null,
    0,
    (Function0)(new Function0 () {
      // $FF: synthetic method
      // $FF: bridge method
      public Object invoke() {
        this.invoke();
        return Unit.INSTANCE;
      }

      public final void invoke () {
        try {
          Thread.sleep(1000L);
          User user = new User(userId, "Filip");
          onUserResponse.invoke(user, (Object)null);
        } catch (Throwable var2) {
          onUserResponse.invoke((Object)null, var2);
        }

      }
    }), 31, (Object)null);
```

(handwritten annotation: - callback hell / - thread creation)

The code hasn't changed that much, it's just wrapping everything in a try/catch, and passing either the pair of (value, null) or (null, error), back to the user. Head back to main(), and change the code to the following:

```
fun main() {
  getUserFromNetworkCallback("101") { user, error ->
    user?.run(::println)

    error?.printStackTrace()
  }
}
```

If there is a non-null user value, you can print it out or do something else with it.

On the other hand, if there is an error, you can print its stack trace or check the error type and so on. This approach is much better than the previous ones, but there's still one problem with it. It relies on callbacks, so if you needed three or four different requests and values, you'd have to build that dreaded "Callback Hell" staircase. Additionally, there's the overhead of allocating a new Thread, every time you call a function like this.

Analyzing a suspendable function

The caveats found in the examples with callbacks are things which can be remedied with the use of coroutines. Revise the changes you need to make to the example above, to improve it even further:

- Remove the callback and implement the example with coroutines.
- Provide efficient error handling.
- Remove the new Thread allocation overhead.

To surpass all these obstacles, you'll learn another function from the Coroutines API — suspendCoroutine(). This function allows you to manually create a coroutine and handle its control state and flow. Unlike the launch block, which just defined a way in which a coroutine was built, but took care of everything behind the scenes.

But, before we venture into suspendCoroutine(), analyze what happens when you just add the suspend modifier to any existing function. Add another function to the **Main.kt** file, with the following signature:

```
suspend fun getUserSuspend(userId: String): User {
  delay(1000)

  return User(userId, "Filip")
}
```

This function is very similar to the first example, except you added the suspend modifier, and you don't sleep the thread but call delay() - a suspendable function which suspends coroutines for a given amount of time. Given these changes, you're probably thinking the difference in bytecode cannot be that big, right?

Well, the bytecode, which you can get using the **Decompile** button in the kotlin bytecode decompiler is the following:

```java
@Nullable
public static final Object getUserSuspend(
@NotNull String userId,
@NotNull Continuation var1) {
   Object $continuation;
   label28: {
     if (var1 instanceof <undefinedtype>) {
       $continuation = (<undefinedtype>)var1;
       if (((((<undefinedtype>)$continuation).label &
Integer.MIN_VALUE) != 0) {
          ((<undefinedtype>)$continuation).label -=
Integer.MIN_VALUE;
          break label28;
       }
     }

     $continuation = new ContinuationImpl(var1) {
     // $FF: synthetic field
     Object result;
     int label;
     Object L $0;

     @Nullable
     public final Object invokeSuspend (@NotNull Object result) {
       this.result = result;
       this.label | = Integer.MIN_VALUE;
       return MainKt.getUserSuspend((String)null, this);
     }
   };
   }

   Object var2 =((<undefinedtype>)$continuation).result;
   Object var4 = IntrinsicsKt . getCOROUTINE_SUSPENDED ();
   switch(((<undefinedtype>)$continuation).label) {
     case 0:
     if (var2 instanceof Failure) {
       throw ((Failure) var2).exception;
     }

     ((<undefinedtype>)$continuation).L$0 = userId;
     ((<undefinedtype>)$continuation).label = 1;
     if (DelayKt.delay(1000L, (Continuation)$continuation) ==
var4) {
       return var4;
     }
     break;
     case 1:
     userId = (String)((<undefinedtype>)$continuation).L$0;
     if (var2 instanceof Failure) {
```

[Handwritten note: continuation allows functions to work in suspendable mode. they are like callbacks]

```
      throw ((Failure) var2).exception;
   }
   break;
   default:
      throw new IllegalStateException ("call to 'resume' before
'invoke' with coroutine");
   }

   return new User (userId, "Filip");
}
```

This *massive* block of code is a huge difference than from the previous examples, and it's a behemoth compared to the very first example you've seen. Going over the bits one step at a time, to get a sense of what's happening, here:

- One of the first things you'll notice is the extra parameter to the function — the `Continuation`. It forms the entire foundation of coroutines, and it is the most important thing by which suspendable functions are different from regular ones. Continuations allow functions to work in the suspended mode. They allow the system to go back to the originating call site of a function, after it has suspended them. You could say that `Continuations` are just callbacks for the system or the program currently running, and that by using continuations, the system knows how to navigate the execution of functions and the call stack.

- That being said, all functions actually have a hidden, internal, `Continuation` they are tied to. The system uses it to navigate around the call stack and the code in general. However, suspendable functions have an additional instance which they use, so that they can be suspended, and that the program can continue with execution, finally using the second `Continuation`, to navigate back to the suspendable function call site or receive its result.

- The rest of the code first checks which continuation we're in. Since each suspendable function can create multiple `Continuation` objects. Each continuation would describe one flow the function can take. For example, if you call `delay(1000)` on a suspendable function, you're actually creating another instance of execution, which finishes in one second, and returns back to the originating point — the line at which `delay` was called.

- The code wraps the continuation arguments, and calls the function from within. Once that is finished, it checks on the label for the currently active continuation. If the label has reached zero, it means it's at the end of the latest execution — the `delay()`. In that case it just returns the result from that execution, which is in turn the rest of the function call. In the end, it also increases the label, to one, to notify that it's past `delay()`, and should continue on with the code.

- Finally, if the label is one, which is the largest index in the continuation-stack, so to speak, it means the function has resumed after delay(), and that it's ready to serve you the value — the User. If anything went wrong up until that point, the system throws an exception.

There's another, default, case, which just throws an exception if the system tries to resume() with a continuation or execution flow, but hasn't actually invoked the function call. This can sometimes happen when a child Job finishes after its parent. It's a default, fallback mechanism, for cases which are extremely rare. If you use your coroutines carefully and the way they are supposed to be used, parent Jobs should always wait for their children, and this shouldn't happen.

Briefly, the system uses continuations for small **state-machines**, and internal callbacks, so that it knows how to navigate through the code, and which execution flows exist, and at which points it should suspend, and resume later on. The state is described using the label, and it can have as many states as there are suspension points in the function.

To call the newly created function, you can use the next snippet of code:

```
fun main() {
  GlobalScope.launch {
    val user = getUserSuspend("101")

    println(user)
  }

  Thread.sleep(1500)
}
```

The function call is just like the first example. The difference is it's suspendable, so you can push it in a coroutine, offloading the main thread. You also rely on the internal threads from the Coroutine API, so there's no additional overhead. The code is **sequential**, even though it could be **asynchronous**. And you can use try/catch blocks, at the call site, even though the value could be produced asynchronously. All points from the previous example have been addressed!

Changing code to suspendable

Another question is when should you migrate existing code to suspendable functions and coroutines? This is a relatively biased question, but there are still some objective guidelines you can follow, to determine if you're better off with coroutines or standard mechanisms.

Handwritten notes at top:
1) complex Threads 2) do not have ability to create T. Pools 3) Performance 4) lots of callback abuse.

Generally speaking, if your code is filled with **complex threading**, and often allocates new threads to do the work you need, but you don't have the ability to use a fixed pool of threads, instead of creating new threads as you go, you should migrate to coroutines. The performance benefits are visible immediately, as the Coroutines API already has predefined threading mechanisms which make it easy for you to switch between threads and distribute multiple pieces of work between threads.

This often coincides with the first reason to switch, but if you're building new threads, due to asynchronous or long-running operations, you're often **abusing callbacks** heavily, because the easiest way to communicate between threads is through callbacks. And if you're using callbacks, you probably have problems with **code styling**, **readability** and the cognitive load needed to understand the business logic behind the functions. In that case, you should try to migrate your code to coroutines, as well.

The problem comes when there's some API which isn't yours to change. In those cases you cannot change the source code. Let's say you have the following code, but it's coming from an external library:

```
fun readFile(path: String, onReady: (File) -> Unit) {
  Thread.sleep(1000)
  // some heavy operation

  onReady(File(path))
}
```

This function forces you to use a callback, even though you might have a better way to handle the long-running or asynchronous operation. But you could easily wrap this function to work with suspendCoroutine():

```
suspend fun readFileSuspend(path: String): File =
    suspendCoroutine {
      readFile(path) { file ->
        it.resume(file)
      }
    }
```

This code is perfectly fine, because if it manages to read a file, it will pass it to the coroutine as a result. If something is wrong, it will throw an exception, and you can catch it at the call site. Having the ability to completely wrap possibly asynchronous operations with coroutines is extremely powerful. But if your functions rely on callbacks to constantly produce values - like subscribing to sockets, then coroutines such as these don't really make sense. It's better off to implement such mechanisms with the **Channel** or **Flow** APIs, which you'll learn more in "Chapter 11: Channels" and _"Chapter 14: Beginning with Coroutines Flow"_.

Elaborating continuations

Having **first-class** continuations is the key concept which differentiates a standard function, from a suspendable one. But *what* is a continuation after all? Every time a program calls a function, it is added on to the program's **call-stack**. This is a stack of all the functions, in the order they were called, which are currently held in memory, and haven't finished yet. Continuations manipulate this execution flow, and in turn help handle the call-stack.

You've already learned that a `Continuation` is in fact a callback, but implemented at a very low system level. A more precise explanation would be that it's an abstract wrapper around the program's **control state**. It holds means to control how and when the program will execute further, and what its result will be — an exception or a value.

Once a function finishes, the program takes it off the stack, and proceeds with the next function. The trick is how the system knows where to return, after each of the functions are executed. This information is held within the aforementioned `Continuation`. Each continuation holds a little information about the **context** in which the function was called. Like the local variables, the parameters the function got passed, the thread it was called in, and so on. By using that information, the system can simply rely on the continuation, to tell it where it needs to be, when a function ends.

Try and see what the lifecycle of functions, and a `Continuation` is, from the function call, to a finish.

Living in the stack

When a program first starts, its call-stack has only one entry — the initial function, usually called `main()`. This is because within it, no other functions have been called yet. The initial function is important, because when the program reaches its end, it calls back to the continuation of `main()`, which completes the program, and notifies the system to release it from memory.

As the program lives, it calls other functions, adding them to the stack.

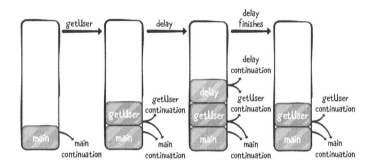

Call stack with Continuation

So if you had this code `fun main() {}`, the lifecycle of the program-level continuation is contained within the brackets of the `main` function. But when another function is called, the first thing the system does is create a new `Continuation` for the new function. It adds some information to the new continuation, like what is the parent function and its `Continuation` object — in this case `main()`. It additionally passes the information about which line of code the function was called at, and with which arguments, and what its return type should be.

Examine what happens with the following code snippet:

```
fun main() {
    val numbers = listOf(1, 2, 5)
}
```

- The system creates a continuation, which will live within `listOf()`.

- Initially, it knows that it's been called at the first line of `main()`, so it can return at the appropriate position in code when finished.

continuation is like checkpoints

- Next, it knows that its parent is main(). This allows listOf() a way to finish the entire program, propagating calls all the way up to the initial Continuation. For example, this can happen when an exception occurs. Finally, it knows that the parameter passed to listOf() is a variable-argument array, with the values 1, 2, 5 and that at the end of the function, we should receive back a List<Int>.

- With all of this information, it navigates the function execution and lifecycle, from the calling point, to the return statement.

When looking at a deeper level, it's just like having a local variable declared, calling an initializer function with a pointer to that variable, so you can set the value elsewhere — in listOf(), and then using a goto statement, to return to a line after the initializer call, having prepared the variable for usage.

Another analogy which could be used to explain continuations is video games. In most video games, you have things which are called **checkpoints**. When you go on an adventure, pursuing a quest or some other task at hand, which would in computing be like calling a function, you have to pass some distance and complete a smaller set of tasks. When you're done, you can go back to your checkpoint, and finish your quest. On the other hand, if something bad happened — you failed the mission in the game, which would be similar to throwing an exception in computing, you always have the ability to reload the game and restart from the checkpoint. You can achieve similar behavior if you wrap a function in a try/catch block, as you can effectively return back to the checkpoint and start over.

Handling the continuation

In the last version of getUser(), you used suspendCoroutine() from the Coroutines API. It's a top level function which allows you to create coroutines, just like launch(), but specifically for returning values, rather than launching work. Another distinct thing about suspendCoroutine() is that it takes in a lambda as an argument, which is of the type block: (Continuation<T>) -> Unit. What this means is, that you can handle a Continuation as a first-class citizen, calling functions on the object as you please. This allows for manual **control-state** and **control-flow** manipulation.

The functions available on Continuations are resume(), resumeWith() and resumeWithException(). You also have access to the CoroutineContext, by calling the continuation.context, but you'll learn about contexts later on in "Chapter 6: Coroutine Context."

Analyzing the Continuation more, resume() passes down a successful value of type T, whichever type you're trying to return from a coroutine. You use this when you deem the conditions in the coroutine valid, and want to go back to the rest of the code. resumeWithException() takes in a Throwable, in case of something going awry. This allows you to finish the coroutine with an error, which you can later on catch and handle.

Having this presents amazing ability to return values from functions, which might be asynchronous, without knowing what's behind. Just like an API should be. You're probably thinking: But what if the function doesn't end?

In that case, once again, you'll be waiting for a value, which isn't coming, resulting yet again in another halting problem, where your code is suspended infinitely.

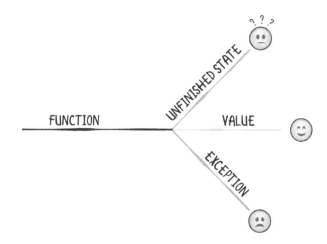

To remedy this, it's best to be *aggressive* with continuations. No matter what, try to always produce a result back, even if it's only an exception. At least in that case your function will end, and you will have something to handle. Conveniently enough, the Continuation has a function to do just that. It's called resumeWith(), and it takes in the aforementioned Result monad. The Result can only be one of the two states at a certain time. Either a Success, holding the value you need, or a Failure, holding the exception.

It also holds some utility functions, like the runCatching(), which receives a lambda it tries to run to get the Success case, with some value. In case something goes wrong, by the help of a try/catch block, it catches the exception and returns a Failure result in the end. After the continuation receives the Result, it unwraps it, and you get the value or the exception, so that you can handle it yourself.

Whenever you're using `suspendCoroutine()`, or any other way of resuming values with continuations, it's strongly recommended to enforce this approach, so you don't end up with coroutines that never finish.

Creating your own suspendable API

One of the things we mentioned Jetbrains had in mind for the Coroutines API was extensibility. You've seen how you can turn your own functions into suspendable ones, but another thing you can do is create an API-like set of utilities which hide the thread and context switching ceremony.

We've prepared some examples for you in **Api.kt**. Open it up, and you should see a few functions ready, but let's go over them one by one.

The first one is a convenience method, which uses `suspendCoroutine()`, and the `Result`'s `runCatching()` to try and process a value for you.

```kotlin
suspend fun <T : Any> getValue(provider: () -> T): T =
    suspendCoroutine { continuation ->
        continuation.resumeWith(Result.runCatching { provider() })
    }
```

If you were to call this function somewhere in your code, it would look something like this:

```kotlin
GlobalScope.launch {
    val user = getValue { getUserFromNetwork("101") }

    println(user)
}
```

This allows you to abstract away all of the functions which try to fetch some data, through the network, file-reading or database lookups and push them to the background thread, allowing the main thread to only worry about rendering the data, and the rest of the code about fetching it.

The next two examples are extremely simple, and are useful for thread-switching:

```
fun executeBackground(action: suspend () -> Unit) {
  GlobalScope.launch { action() }
}

fun executeMain(action: suspend () -> Unit) {
  GlobalScope.launch(context = Dispatchers.Main) { action() }
}
```

The first one takes in an `action` lambda block, and runs it in the background, using the default `launch` context. The second one also takes in the `action` block, but runs it using the `Dispatchers.Main` context, so you can easily switch to the main thread, without knowing the details of the implementation.

Using them, you'd have code similar to this:

```
executeBackground {
  val user = getValue { getUserFromNetwork("101") }

  executeMain { println(user) }
}
```

The naming could be a bit better, but you get the idea behind this. Now you have the same behavior as with `GlobalScope.launch` blocks, but you don't rely upon knowing which scope, and which functions are used behind the scenes.

This is great when you're building the base business logic layer, as you could provide both the main and background contexts, and scopes in which you'd run the functions. And in the concrete implementations, or subclasses of the base presenter, view model or controller, you'd simply call these functions, and let the core part of the layer worry about threading.

Play around with these more, and build even more utility functions on top of them, according to your needs.

If you want to check out these examples, import this chapter's final project, using IntelliJ, and selecting **Import Project**, and navigating to the **suspending-functions/projects/final** folder, selecting the **suspending_functions** project.

Key points

- Having **callbacks** as a means of notifying result values can be pretty ugly and **cognitive-heavy**.
- Coroutines and **suspendable functions** remove the need for callbacks and excessive **thread allocation**.
- What separates a regular function from a suspendable one is the **first-class continuation** support, which the Coroutine API uses internally.
- Continuations are already present in the system, and are used to handle **function lifecycle** — returning the values, jumping to statements in code, and updating the call-stack.
- You can think of continuations as **low-level callbacks**, which the system calls to when it needs to navigate through the call-stack.
- Continuations always persist a batch of information about the **context** in which the function is called — the parameters passed, call site and the return type.
- There are three main ways in which the continuation can *resolve* - in a happy path, **returning a value** the function is expected to return, **throwing an exception** in case something goes bad, and **blocking infinitely** because of flawed business logic.
- Utilizing the `suspend` modifier, and functions like `launch()` and `suspendCoroutine()`, you can create your own API, which abstracts away the threading used for executing code.

Where to go from here?

In this chapter you've learned *a lot* about the foundation of coroutines. Through an extensive overview of differences between suspendable and non-suspendable functions you've seen how suspendable functions utilize `Continuations` to navigate around and return values as results.

The next chapter, Chapter 5, "Async/Await," relies heavily on the usage of functions which leverage continuations and suspendable functions to their favor, to return values from code which may or may not be asynchronous and long-running. So read on to learn more about how you can process values from functions which used to require a ton of callbacks!

Chapter 5: Async/Await

By Filip Babić

- Build a wrapper
- call a function
- Pass it to wrapper

So far you've seen how coroutines and suspendable functions can be used to bridge threads and execute asynchronous work that doesn't add much overhead to your program. You also saw how you can migrate from callback-based APIs to ones that are coroutine-based, which has the signature of a regular function returning the value you need when called. These functions were actually blocking but could have been asynchronous.

In this chapter, you'll see how you can build similar mechanisms which aren't blocking and can work asynchronously and in parallel. They can also return values, as if you're calling a standard function. Sounds too good to be true? Well you'll see how all of this functionality is actually an old concept, so let's get going!

The async/await pattern

One of the biggest problems in computing is being able to return values from asynchronous functions. Even more so, if you're calling a function that creates a different thread to run in, you *can't* return a value to the outer function. This is a program restriction because the system doesn't know when to return, and has a hard time bridging between threads. But there is a way to achieve this behavior with the **async/await** pattern.

It's a very simple idea: Build a **wrapper around the value** you need, then call a function that provides the value and passes it to the wrapper. Once it's ready, you can request it. This goes all the way back to **queues**, as the wrapper may as well be a simple class that holds a queue of the capacity of one item. Once you request the value, you suspend the function you requested it in, until the data shows up. This type of mechanism works, and has been tried and tested through time. A very similar implementation exists even in the Java API — in the form of **futures**. However, if you're coming from a Javascript background, you're probably familiar with **promises** which take a similar approach but execute them differently.

Learning from the past

Sometimes, it's best to take a long, hard look at the past to see what you can learn and maybe use to achieve your goals. When coroutines were designed, the team writing the API did just that. That isn't surprising, given that the concept of coroutines is decades old. More specifically, they looked to the **future** and **promise** patterns. Each of the patterns has a specific syntax and way of dealing with asynchronously provided values. Let's see what they're really about.

Promising values

A **promise** construct is just what the names states — a promise of a value, which might or might not be there at all. The value is promised to surface at some point in time for you to consume it but, in reality, sometimes things break. This is why the promise also allows you to handle any errors that happen along the way.

Promises work by taking a function call and storing it in a construct. That alone doesn't do much, but the key to a promise is that you can chain them indefinitely. Once you create your first one, you can chain the next promise call, which will take the input from the previous one. So, if your first promise returns a String, you can use that value in the next call — to turn it into an Int, for example. Then, in the third call, you'd get an Int, and so on.

Promises rely on two function calls: **then** and **catch**. then() takes in the currently promised value, and allows you to either map it to something else, or just consume it. catch() is the fallback function, catching any errors that happen along the way, and allowing you to act upon it. However, there has to be at least one catch() clause. A standard promise chain would look like this:

```
database
  .findOne({ email: request.email })
  .then(user => {
    if (!user) {
      // the user doesn't exist
      return service.registerUser(request.data)
    } else {
      return null
```

> Promise do not work since you rely on single threaded

```
    }
  })
  .then(registerStatus => {
    // do something after registration
  })
  .catch(error => {
    // handle error
  })
```

This code would try to register a user, if the user doesn't exist in the database already. In the case that it does exist already, you'd return null, or undefined, and then handle it further. If anything bad happens, you can catch it in the catch clause of the promise chain.

Promises look really clean and straightforward, and they are easy to use and learn, but there are caveats. You can't really return a value from a promise; you can only return a promise, since the value might not be there. And, as such, you have to rely on the **call-chain structure**. This makes you rely on promises entirely, which makes sense for web applications, which might not rely on multiple threads. But, for Android applications or similar, which rely on multithreading, this is a limitation. Since you usually want to do some **background processing** in modern applications, but need to consume these values on the **main thread**, promises won't work since they are bound to a single thread.

Additionally, if you have multiple function flows, you have to handle them within the original promise. Since you are returning the response to the user in the outermost promise, you have to propagate all the cases to the internal promise somewhere down the line. This tends to be clunky and tends to require a lot of utility classes, just to bury down the excess code. The worst part of promises is that, if you forget to return values from one of the chained calls, the entire lower part of the chain won't be able to continue, since it won't have any values to consume.

A different approach, yet based on the same principles, is the **future pattern**. Let's see how these two are different.

Thinking about the future

Futures sound a lot like promises, and they behave similarly. When you create futures, you're not promising that a value will be there somewhere along the line, since promises are easy to break. You explicitly say that this value *will* exist, or you have to face some consequences. In promises, it's easy to break things: just miss a return call, and your entire chain won't have anything to consume, in turn freezing the entire function call.

In futures, you have to declare a function that has a return statement; otherwise, you get a compile-time error. Additionally, once you create a future, you can check its status at any point in time, using isDone(). If isDone() returns true, you're ready to use your value.

Once you're ready to use the value, all you have to do is call get() to get it. The internal part of futures is really fun to analyze. Futures use something called an **executor** to run their tasks. They handle the threading and execution of the tasks in each of the futures you create, and you can achieve things like parallelism, using **thread pools**. You'll learn more about **executors**, **scheduling** and thread pools in _"Chapter 7: Context Switch & Dispatching"_.

Since Java-based APIs don't have the concept of **suspending**, every call you make on a Future will be blocking. As such, calling get() right away might in turn block off your main thread for a long time. Let's see how futures work and what they look like:

```
private static ExecutorService executor =
        Executors.newSingleThreadExecutor();

public static Future<Integer> parse(String input) {
  return executor.submit(() -> {
    Thread.sleep(1000)
    return Integer.parseInt(input);
  });
}
```

This snippet of code will create an executor, which uses a **new** thread to do its business. If you call parse(), with a String, it will return a future, which, when executed, will wait for a second, and then it will return the Integer value of the String. To call this code you'd have to do the following:

```
public static void main(String...args) {
  Future<Integer> parser = parse("310");

  while(!parser.isDone()) {
    // waiting to parse
```

```
    }
    int parsedValue = parser.get();
}
```

You create a future, and it begins to execute the task in the thread the executor created. Once your call to `isDone()` returns `true`, you know it's ready to use. Finally, by calling `get()`, you receive the value from the `Future`, which is now cached within the object itself, and can be reused.

This is far more flexible than promises, but it also suffers from the problem of having to wait for the value, either by blocking with `get()`, or running a `while` loop until the future is done - which is blocking as well.

Futures are great when you need to process and produce values in different threads. If you want to achieve **parallelism**, you can create multiple threads for your futures to use, and run multiple tasks at the same time. They also allow you to have clean control flow logic, since the values produced can be used in **sequential code**, and don't have to rely on callbacks or chained function calls. But, on the other hand, their values are always received in a **blocking way**, and as such can be expensive to wait for when you have a user interface to render.

Let's see the key differences in these approaches, and which one **async/await** is more similar to.

Differentiating approaches

The key characteristic that distinguishes promises from async/awaits is that promises rely on chains of function calls, sort of like the **builder pattern**, but ultimately promises are a series of callbacks. Using promises is very similar to **reactive extensions**, which operate on streams of values. You could, for example, chain transforming operators or delay the data being processed.

This code will look very structured at first, but, if you need to have multiple flows or logical paths, you'll end up having **staircases** of **nested** promises. For this reason, promises can be tedious and ugly to work with. Newer versions of Javascript allow you to use the `async` and `await` keywords, which work as promises at a lower level, but hide that boilerplate away from you.

Futures and async/await, however, rely on having a single value primed for usage, burying it down underneath various design patterns and constructs. This also allows you to use their results as values so that you can write sequential code that doesn't use callbacks but suspends the code waiting for their values. They are both fantastic mechanisms when you need clean and understandable code without nested functions or callbacks.

However, by eagerly waiting for values, you risk freezing the UI if you don't pay attention to threading, and you even risk creating a **deadlock**, since your function may not return the value at all while you're waiting for the result. The difference between futures and async/await is that futures rely on blocking calls, which will definitely freeze up the thread you are currently in.

Conversely, the async/await pattern relies on suspending functions, like the Kotlin Coroutines API. As such, it alleviates the need to block code, but it does have caveats as well.

Let's see how async and await are implemented in the Coroutines API, how to use them to your advantage, and which mechanisms exist to stop you from breaking your code or your program in case the data just doesn't show up.

Using async/await

To follow the code in this chapter, import this chapter's starter project, using IntelliJ, and selecting **Import Project**, and navigating to the **async-await/projects/starter** folder, selecting the **async_await** project.

Right about now, you're probably wondering how the async/await pattern works in the Kotlin Coroutines API. Very close to the **future pattern**, async in Kotlin returns a `Deferred<T>`. Just like you would have a `Future<T>`, the deferred value just wraps a potential object you can use. Once you're ready to receive the object, you have to await for it, effectively requesting the data, which might or might not be there. If the data is already provided and delivered, the call will turn into a simple `get()`; otherwise, you're code will have to suspend and wait for the data to come to the wrapper.

Quite simply, it's as if you're creating a `BlockingQueue` instance, with the capacity for a single value. And, at any point in time, you can attempt to get the value or suspend the code while waiting for it. The key difference is that you're not actually blocking threads, but are instead suspending code. It's time for you to see how it's all done backstage using coroutines.

The pattern is called **async/await** for a reason — because the full implementation requires two function calls — `async()`, to prepare and wrap the values, and `await()`, to request the value for use. Let's see what's in the signature of both of these functions, before you jump into using this approach.

If you open up the `async()` definition, you can see the following code:

```
public fun <T> CoroutineScope.async(
    context: CoroutineContext = EmptyCoroutineContext,
    start: CoroutineStart = CoroutineStart.DEFAULT,
    block: suspend CoroutineScope.() -> T
): Deferred<T> {
    val newContext = newCoroutineContext(context)
    val coroutine = if (start.isLazy)
        LazyDeferredCoroutine(newContext, block) else
        DeferredCoroutine<T>(newContext, active = true)
    coroutine.start(start, coroutine, block)
    return coroutine
}
```

[handwritten annotation: context to bind to the disp atcher]

When you call async, you can pass it a `CoroutineContext` to bind it to a certain `Job` or a `Dispatcher`. You can also start it in different modes with the `CoroutineStart` parameter. But, most importantly, you have to pass in a lambda `block`, which has access to the `CoroutineScope` that you called the function in, and needs to return a value it will try to store in the `Deferred`. It does so by creating a new `DeferredCoroutine`, which it starts with the `block` lambda, and returns the aforementioned coroutine. You'll learn a bit more about this coroutine in the next section.

This function call basically wraps the value in a coroutine, which implements the `Deferred<T>` interface on which you will call `await()` later on. Once you call `await()`, the coroutine will try to produce the value for you or suspend until it's there. Let's check out the `await()` signature, to see if there's anything interesting there:

```
/**
 * Awaits for completion of this value without blocking a thread
 * and resumes when deferred computation is complete,
 * returning the resulting value or throwing the
 * corresponding exception if the deferred was cancelled.
 *
 * This suspending function is cancellable.
 * If the [Job] of the current coroutine is cancelled
 * or completed while this suspending function is waiting,
 * this function immediately resumes with
 * [CancellationException].
 *
 * This function can be used in [select] invocation
 * with [onAwait] clause.
 * Use [isCompleted] to check for completion of this
 * deferred value without waiting.
 */
public suspend fun await(): T
```

The function itself is extremely simple, but the idea behind it is genius. Instead of actually blocking a thread, you can suspend the entire function or coroutine, and just have it resolve after the value is ready. It's time to use this approach and migrate a currently blocking snippet of code, to async(). If you haven't already, import the **starter** project from this chapter, under the **async-await**, **projects** folder. Next, open up **AsyncAwait.kt**, and you should see the following code:

```
fun main() {
  val userId = 992

  getUserByIdFromNetwork(userId) { user ->
    println(user)
  }
}

private fun getUserByIdFromNetwork(userId: Int, onUserReady:
(User) -> Unit) {
  Thread.sleep(3000)

  onUserReady(User(userId, "Filip", "Babic"))
}

data class User(val id: Int, val name: String, val lastName:
String)
```

This piece of code tries to get a User from a simulated network call, and prints it out. The problem, though, is that it's calling Thread.sleep(), which halts the execution for three seconds. Just as if you had a blocking network call, you have to wait for the data to come back, before you can use it. To pour a little salt on the wound, it's also using a callback to pass the data back to the caller once it's ready. Next, you'll refactor this to use async() and await() from the Coroutines API.

Change the getUserByIdFromNetwork() code to the following:

```
private fun getUserByIdFromNetwork(userId: Int) =
GlobalScope.async {
  Thread.sleep(3000)

  User(userId, "Filip", "Babic")
}
```

First, you've removed the callback from the parameters, and, secondly, you've returned a GlobalScope.async() block as the return value for the function. Now, the function returns a value, and it doesn't rely on the callbacks to consume it.

Finally, you have to update the code in `main()` to use the new version of `getUserByIdFromNetwork()`:

```
fun main() {
  val userId = 992
  val userData = getUserByIdFromNetwork(userId)

  println(userData)
}
```

Now, if you run the code above, you'll see a similar output to this:

```
DeferredCoroutine{Active}@6eee89b3
```

This is because `getUserByIdFromNetwork()` now returns a `Deferred<User>`. In order to get the user, you have to call `await()` on it. But `await()` is a suspendable function, and to call `await()`, you have to be in another suspendable function or coroutine builder, so you have to wrap the code above in a `launch()`:

```
fun main() {
  val userId = 992

  GlobalScope.launch {
    val userData = getUserByIdFromNetwork(userId)

    println(userData.await())
  }

  Thread.sleep(5000)
}
```

The flow is similar to the earlier code, except that you're also calling `await()` to return the `User` in order to print it out. You've successfully migrated callback-based code to the **async/await** pattern!

Walking through all of the changes and what the resulting code does:

- First, you removed the callback from the function, since you'll be returning a value.

- Then, you had to return the result of `async()` and the `User` from within the lambda block.

- Finally, you had to wrap `await()` in a coroutine, since it's a suspendable function.

These three steps are everything you need to do to migrate your code to async/await.

Now, how it works is a another thing. As mentioned before, it creates a coroutine and masks it with the `Deferred<T>` value. Through the interface, you have access to the value, since the interface exposes `await()`.

Once you call `await()`, you're suspending the function call, effectively avoiding blocking the thread. You then wait for the lambda block to execute in order to use the value that is stored internally. When the value is ready, the function stops being suspended, and your code continues normally.

Now, a lot of the work here is determined by the `Deferred` type, so let's see what it actually is.

Deferring values

Every `async()` block returns a `Deferred<T>`. It's the core mechanism that drives that piece of the Coroutines API, and it's very important to understand how it works.

When you call `async()`, the function returns a `Deferred`. It does so by creating a `DeferredCoroutine` or a `LazyDeferredCoroutine`. Such coroutines have a generic inference and also implement the `Continuation<T>` interface, allowing the interception of execution flow, and passing the values all the way up to the call site, just like with `suspendCoroutine()`. This is similar to how the **future pattern** works, which you've seen before.

Once the coroutine is created, unless its `CoroutineStart` is `CoroutineStart.LAZY`, it will launch immediately. The code will start to execute in the thread that you declared with the `context` parameter using `Dispatchers`. Once the code finishes executing and produces a value, it will be stored internally. If, at any point in time, you call `await()`, it will be a suspended call, which will create a new continuation and execution flow, waiting until the value is ready for use. If it isn't ready, the function will have to wait. If the value is already provided, you'll get it *immediately*.

You can also check the status of a deferred value, since it also implements the `Job` interface. You can check flags like `isActive` and `isCompleted` to find out about its current lifecycle state. You also have a few nifty functions, which you can use to receive a value or an exception if the `Job` was canceled. These functions are `getCompleted()`, which returns the value — or an exception if the deferred value was canceled — and the `getCompletionExceptionOrNull()`, which returns the `CancellationException` or null, if the `Job` was not canceled. Using those functions, you can also check the details around the completed state of the deferred value.

combine them together to call functions with multiple params.

So a good way to explain what a Deferred is, is that it's a Job with a result. The job can run in parallel, it may or may not produce a resulting value, and it can be canceled and joined with other jobs. This provides a powerful API you can bend to your will. One of the ways you can utilize deferred values is by combining them together to call functions with multiple parameters.

Combining multiple deferred values

Being able to create deferred values, which are built in the background but could be accessed on the main thread in one function call, is an amazing thing. But the real power of async is being able to combine two or more deferred values into a single function call. Let's see how to do so.

So far, you've worked with an example that mocked a network request, but it's time to expand on that example. You might have noticed **users.txt** in the project. It's a file containing 13,000 lines of text. Most lines contain the information required to build Users — an id, a name and a last name. Some of the lines are empty, some don't have all three items, and some are just plain gibberish. The idea behind this is to read the entire file, parse and split each line ,and create users out of them. After that, you'll use the list of users and the user you got from the mocked network call to see if that user is stored in the file.

Having this will allow you to see how two deferred values can be primed and used in a single function call. Now, navigate back to **AsyncAwait.kt**. Once there, add the following code to the file:

```
private fun readUsersFromFile(filePath: String) =
    GlobalScope.async {
      println("Reading the file of users")
      delay(1000)

      File(filePath)
          .readLines()
          .asSequence()
          .filter { it.isNotEmpty() }
          .map {
            val data = it.split(" ") // [id, name, lastName]

            if (data.size == 3) data else emptyList()
          }
          .filter {
            it.isNotEmpty()
          }
          .map {
```

```
            val userId = it[0].toInt()
            val name = it[1]
            val lastName = it[2]

            User(userId, name, lastName)
          }
          .toList()
  }
  private fun checkUserExists(user: User, users: List<User>):
  Boolean {
    return user in users
  }
```

This function does everything described above in `async()` and will return a `Deferred` that holds a list of users. Now, you can tweak the `main()` code to look like the following:

```
fun main() {
  val userId = 992

  GlobalScope.launch {
    val userDeferred = getUserByIdFromNetwork(userId)
    val usersFromFileDeferred = readUsersFromFile("users.txt")

    println("Finding user")
    val userStoredInFile = checkUserExists(
        userDeferred.await(), usersFromFileDeferred.await()
    )

    if (userStoredInFile) {
      println("Found user in file!")
    }
  }

  Thread.sleep(5000)
}
```

In the above:

- You create a `userDeferred` by calling `getUserByIdFromNetwork()`. This will set off the block of code, which waits three seconds to return a user.

- You then prime `usersFromFileDeferred` that will return a list of users which are stored in **users.txt**.

- Once both of the values are primed, you can call `checkUserExists()` to see if the user you received from the **network call** matches any user in the list loaded from the file.

- `checkUserExists()` takes in two parameters: a user you need to look up and a list of users in which to look them up.

- You create a `userDeferred` value by calling the `getUserByIdFromNetwork` function. This will set off the block of code, which waits three seconds to return a user.

- You then prime the `usersFromFileDeferred`, holding a list of users which are stored in the **users.txt** file.

The arguments you pass to the function are the `await()` results from both of the deferred values you prepared earlier, and, as such, you have a line of code that suspends the function, waiting for the two values. This is the right way to use multiple deferred values. You're effectively creating a single suspension point in your program, which suspends two functions. Another thing you could do is have `checkUserExists()` suspendable, and then await from within, but it's more convenient to await the values before passing them further to other functions.

If you run this code, you'll see the following output immediately:

```
Finding user
Reading the file of users
Retrieving user from network
```

And after approximately three seconds, you should see `Found user in file!`. This is because the coroutines that were created around the `Deferred` aren't lazy, and they fire off right away — but only when you await for the values do you suspend the code. After calling `await()`, you pass the received values to `checkUserExists()`, and then you receive the output that the user exists in the file.

Using this approach, you can combine any number of deferred values, and, in turn, achieve smart and simple parallelism, which isn't built upon the concept of callbacks of streams of data. With that in mind, the code is extremely easy to understand, since it resembles sequential, synchronous code, even though it might be fully asynchronous behind the curtains. This is the true power of coroutines and the async/await pattern.

However, there is one thing about this code that isn't ideal: the fact that this code isn't that well structured when it comes to cancellation and resource management. Let's see how you can polish that code to perfection by following **Jetbrains'** ideology.

Being cooperative and structured

The above examples of code are pretty well built, and they serve the purpose of explaining how you can prime multiple values in parallel and pass them to functions once they are ready. On the other hand, the problem is if something goes wrong or the async block isn't built properly, you're going to block a thread and potentially freeze the entire system. For example, if your async block contains a while loop, and the condition doesn't have a **break strategy**, your function will never return the value. Moreover, if you build functions that do heavy operations and take a lot of time to finish, you should be able to cancel them at any point in their execution. Otherwise, you risk canceling their parent Job, but not the job itself. Then you'll end up with code that is still running and using up resources, even though its Job has been canceled.

This is why your code should always be **cooperative**.

Some time after releasing coroutines, **Jetbrains** began to see various kinds of usage and libraries being built around them. **Jetbrains** then released an article clarifying some details, explaining how the initial examples and ideas people had about coroutines weren't 100% correct. Take an expanded example of the function you used above:

```
private suspend fun getUserByIdFromNetwork(userId: Int) =
GlobalScope.async {
  println("Retrieving user from network")
  delay(3000)
  println("Still in the coroutine")

  User(userId, "Filip", "Babic") // we simulate the network call
}
```

If you call this function, this simple snippet will return a User after three seconds. Since it's a suspend function, you need to wrap it in a coroutine builder, like so:

```
fun main() {
  GlobalScope.launch {
    val deferredUser = getUserByIdFromNetwork(130)

    println(deferredUser.await())
  }
}
```

But what happens if you cancel the Job from the launch() after its block starts executing? The getUserByIdFromNetwork() would still run for three seconds and return a value, even though the parent job is canceled. This causes a waste of time and resources in computing, which would be better spent elsewhere. Or at least it did with the initial release.

This is why Jetbrains came up with the idea of **structured concurrency** and **cooperative code**. The idea is to write code that reflects upon the state of its caller and to build coroutines that rely on their parent's state. In simple terms, if the parent job is canceled, so should be its children. By default, this behavior does exist in the Coroutines API, as you've seen.

But you could still write code that doesn't enforce this behavior. If you tweak the snippet above to the following, for example:

```
fun main() {
  val launch = GlobalScope.launch {
    val dataDeferred = getUserByIdFromNetwork(1312)
    println("Not cancelled")
    // do something with the data

    val data = dataDeferred.await()
    println(data)
  }

  Thread.sleep(50)
  launch.cancel()

  while (true) { // stops the program from finishing
  }
}
```

You'll see that getUserByIdFromNetwork() executes completely, no matter that you've canceled the coroutine it was called in. This is because the snippet above isn't cooperative, and doesn't allow the code to suspend and cancel if needed. It doesn't care about the place of origin or the scope and context of its parent. The right way to build this function is the following:

```
private suspend fun getUserByIdFromNetwork(
    userId: Int,
    parentScope: CoroutineScope) =
  parentScope.async {
    if (!isActive)          → chck if parent
      return@async User(0, "", "")         is actwi
    }
    println("Retrieving user from network")
    delay(3000)
```

```
        println("Still in the coroutine")

        User(userId, "Filip", "Babic") // we simulate the network call
    }
```

The function now takes in the parent `CoroutineScope` instance as a parameter and launches an async block from there. Furthermore, it checks `isActive` from the parent job so that it doesn't necessarily proceed with execution if the parent turns out to be canceled. If you launch `main()` from above again, passing in the parent scope, the code will only print out `Retrieving user from network` and `Not Cancelled`, after which it won't proceed to wait three seconds to return a value to a coroutine that has been terminated.

Finally, the code for combining two values could be improved as well. If you examine the example from before:

```
GlobalScope.launch {
  val userDeferred = getUserByIdFromNetwork(userId)
  val usersFromFileDeferred = readUsersFromFile("users.txt")

  println("Finding user")
  val userStoredInFile = checkUserExists(
      userDeferred.await(), usersFromFileDeferred.await()
  )

  if (userStoredInFile) {
    println("Found user in file!")
  }
}
```

You might see the same problem as before. You're priming two deferred values and using them right below without checking for the current state of the job. Since this is launched at a global scope, unless you store the returning `Job` somewhere, to cancel it later on, you will be effectively creating a fire-and-forget function, which might take up valuable resources. You probably see a pattern here. You should *always* have control of jobs you start and the coroutine scope you start them in. Coroutine scopes bind coroutines to the lifecycle of an object. This is why you shouldn't really use `GlobalScope` extensively, but provide custom scopes instead.

But how do you assure the `CoroutineScope` you're using for starting coroutines is correct? By implementing the interface yourself!

The guide for cooperative code and structure concurrency states that you should confine your coroutines to objects with a well-defined **lifecycle**, like the Activity in an Android application environment. So let's implement the CoroutineScope in a dummy class. Create a new Kotlin class, and name it **CustomScope.kt**. Change the code within it, to the following:

```
class CustomScope : CoroutineScope {

  private var parentJob = Job()

  override val coroutineContext: CoroutineContext
    get() = Dispatchers.Main + parentJob
}
```

Once you implement the interface, you have to provide a CoroutineContext, so that the coroutines have a context to run with. The suggested implementation is a combination of a Dispatcher, for default threading and a Job to bind the coroutine lifecycle. This is a decent default implementation, but it could be better. Add the following functions to the class:

```
fun onStart() {
  parentJob = Job()
}

fun onStop() {
  parentJob.cancel()
  // You can also cancel the whole scope
  // with `cancel(cause: CancellationException)`
}
```

By adding this functionality, you can stop and cancel all the coroutines started with this scope, and by starting it, you can create a new job the coroutines will depend on for their lifecycle and possible isActive checks. Once you call onStop(), all of the coroutines will be cancelled, and if you've implemented them to be *cooperative*, they shouldn't take up any resources. Now, if you want to start coroutines with the new scope, all you have to do is the following:

```
fun main() {
  val scope = CustomScope()

  scope.launch {
    println("Launching in custom scope")
  }

  scope.onStop() //cancels all the coroutines
}
```

Pretty useful and rather clean!

The second problem you want to solve is producing `async()` blocks that might never return a value. Say you have the following code:

```
fun <T> produceValue(scope: CoroutineScope): Deferred<T> =
    scope.async {
      var data: T? = null

      requestData<T> { value ->
        data = value
      }

      while (data == null) {
          // dummy loop to keep the function alive
      }

      data!!
    }
```

This is a function that allows you to provide any type of value through `async()` by wrapping an existing function that uses callbacks. The implementation of `requestData()` is not important, just think of it as a go-to function to fetch any type of data, and pass it to you, using a callback.

The code will work as expected if nothing goes wrong. But if the callback is never triggered, and you're calling the function this way:

```
fun main() {
  GlobalScope.launch(context = Dispatchers.Main) {
    val data = produceValue<Int>(this)

    data.await()
  }
}
```

It could ultimately suspend the launch block **indefinitely**; halting the function. Even if you cancel the Job returned from launch(), if await() has been called with the Unconfined or Main dispatcher, you could freeze the system and the user interface. This is why you should again integrate the parent Job's isActive flag as the key condition breaker. If you change the code to the following:

```
fun <T> produceValue(scope: CoroutineScope): Deferred<T> =
    scope.async {
      var data: T? = null

      requestData<T> { value ->
        data = value
      }

      while (data == null && scope.isActive) {
        // loop for data, while the scope is active
      }

      data!!
    }
```

You rely not only on your internal-function condition, but also scope.isActive, allowing you to cancel the outer-most coroutine and, in turn, the async block as well. Note that the Jetbrains team has added better cancellation with coroutines, so the freezing of the UI shouldn't happen, but better to be safe than sorry. However, the cancellation sometimes cannot be propagated. If your code doesn't create a suspension point in which it can be cancelled, then you're just calling regular, blocking code and you can still block the thread the coroutine is in. So, be cooperative with your code!

If you want to check out all the examples from this chapter, import this chapter's final project, using IntelliJ, and selecting **Import Project**, and navigating to the **async-await/projects/final** folder, selecting the **async_await** project.

Key points

- The **async/await** pattern is founded upon the idea of **futures** and **promises**, with a slight twist in the execution of the pattern.

- **Promises** rely on callbacks and chained function calls to consume the value in a stream-like syntax, which tends to be clunky and unreadable when you have a lot of business logic.

- **Futures** are built with **tasks**, which provide the value to the user, wrapped in a container class. Once you want to receive the value, you have to block the thread and wait for it or simply postpone getting the value until it is *ready*.

- Using **async/await** relies on **suspending functions**, instead of blocking threads, which provides clean code, without the risk of blocking the user interface.

- The **async/await** pattern is built on two functions: `async()` to wrap the function call and the resulting value in a coroutine, and `await()`, which **suspends code** until the value is ready to be served.

- In order to migrate to the **async/await** pattern, you have to return the `async()` result from your code, and call `await()` on the `Deferred`, from within another coroutine. By doing so, you can **remove callbacks** you used to use, to consume asynchronously provided values.

- Deferred objects are decorated by the `DeferredCoroutine`. The coroutine also implements the `Continuation` interface, allowing it to intercept the execution flow and **pass down values** to the caller.

- Once a deferred coroutine is started, it will attempt to run the block of code you passed, **storing its result internally**.

- The `Deferred` interface also implements the `Job` interface, allowing you to cancel it and check its state — the `isActive` and the `isCompleted` flags.

- You can also **handle errors** a deferred value might produce, by calling `getCompletionExceptionOrNull()`, checking if the coroutine ended with an exception along the way.

- By returning `Deferred`s from function calls, you're able to prime multiple deferred values, and await them all in *one function call*, effectively **combining multiple requests**.

- Always try to create as few suspension points in your code as possible, making the code easier to understand.

- Writing sequential, synchronous-looking code is easy using the **async/await** pattern. It makes your codebase clean and requires less cognitive load to understand the business logic.

- You can write coroutine-powered code in a bad way. Doing so, you might **waste resources** or block the entire program. This is why your code should follow the idea of **structured concurrency**.

- Being structured means your code is connected to other `CoroutineContexts` and `CoroutineScopes`, and carefully deals with threading and resource management.
- Always try to rely on safe `CoroutineScopes`, and the best way is by implementing them yourself.
- When you implement `CoroutineScope`, you have to provide a `CoroutineContext`, which will be used to start every coroutine.
- It's useful to tie the custom `CoroutineScope` to a **well-established lifecycle**, like the Android `Activity`.
- It's important to write **cooperative code** as well, which checks the `isActive` state of the parent job or scope to finish early, release resources, and avoid the potential of a blocking thread.

Where to go from here?

Since this is the last chapter in the first section, you should be pretty proud of yourself! You've learned a huge chunk of the Coroutines API. At this point, you're ready to migrate from callback-based code to coroutine-powered functions. You should be able to write code that runs multiple functions in parallel, ultimately combining their result in one function call.

There's still a few hidden gems within the core Coroutines API, which we haven't covered, but you should be able to look it up yourself and understand what's going on as a result of things you've learned so far. You can look up the `withContext` function, which is very similar to `async` and `await`, but serves to immediately suspend the code and await for the value from a coroutine-powered lambda call. It's very useful if you don't want to call `async` and `await` all the time, but want to do it in a cleaner way.

In the next sections of the book, you'll dive deeper into the rest of the Coroutines API. More specifically, coroutine-powered **sequences**, stream-like mechanisms called **channels** and the comparison of coroutines and **RxKotlin**. You'll also see how coroutines can be leveraged in Android, to offload the main thread from heavy, long-running work, and to bridge the background threads with the main thread easily. So keep reading on!

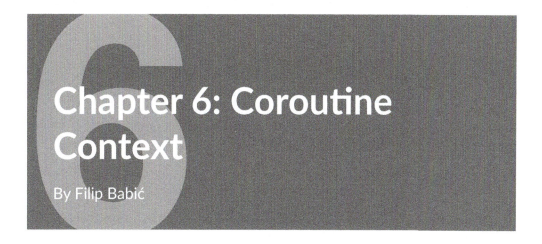

Chapter 6: Coroutine Context

By Filip Babić

You're getting pretty handy with coroutines, aren't ya? In the first section of this book you've seen how you can start coroutines, bridge between threads in coroutines to return values, create your own APIs and much more. In the second section, you'll focus on the internal coroutine concepts. And the most important is the CoroutineContext. Even though it's at the core of every coroutine, you'll see that it's fairly simple after you take a look at its implementation and usage.

Contextualizing coroutines

Each coroutine is tied to a CoroutineContext. The context is a wrapper around a set of CoroutineContext.Elements, each of which describes a vital part that builds up and forms a coroutine: like the way exceptions are propagated, the execution flow is navigated, or just the general lifecycle.

These elements are:

- **Job**: A cancellable piece of work, which has a defined lifecycle.

- **ContinuationInterceptor**: A mechanism which listens to the continuation within a coroutine and intercepts its resumption.

- **CoroutineExceptionHandler**: A construct which handles exceptions in coroutines.

So, when you run `launch()`, you can pass it a context of your own choice. The context defines which elements will fit into the puzzle. If you pass in another `Job`, which also implements `CoroutineContext.Element`, you'll define what the new coroutine's parent is. As such, if the parent job finishes, it will notify all of its children, including the newly created coroutine.

If, however, you pass in an exception handler, another `CoroutineContext.Element`, you give the coroutine a way to process errors if something bad happens.

And the last thing you can pass in is a `ContinuationInterceptor`. These constructs control the flow of each coroutine-powered function, by determining which thread it should operate on and how it should distribute work.

The problem is, you wouldn't want to provide a full implementation that manually handles continuations. If you want something else to do that part for you, while also being a `CoroutineContext.Element`, you have to provide a **coroutine dispatcher**.

You've used some of them before — like `Dispatchers.Default`. So the key to understanding `ContinuationInterceptor` usage is by learning what a dispatcher really is, which you'll do in "Chapter 7: Context Switch and Dispatching". For now, you'll focus on combining and providing `CoroutineContexts`.

Using CoroutineContext

To follow the code in this chapter, import this chapter's starter project using IntelliJ by selecting **Import Project**. Then navigate to the **coroutine-context/projects/starter** folder, selecting the **coroutine-context** project.

Even though you haven't gone too deep into it, you've already used `CoroutineContext` extensively. Every time you've created a coroutine, from a `CoroutineScope`, you've passed in the scope's `CoroutineContext` to the builders. Take the following snippet for an example:

```
GlobalScope.launch {
  println("In a coroutine")
}
```

You don't see it, but there's work done around the `CoroutineContext` for this simple snippet of code. Once again, if you look at the definiton of the `launch`, this is what you can see:

```
public fun CoroutineScope.launch(
    context: CoroutineContext = EmptyCoroutineContext,
    start: CoroutineStart = CoroutineStart.DEFAULT,
    block: suspend CoroutineScope.() -> Unit
): Job
```

You can see that the default context is the `EmptyCoroutineContext`. This basically means it's going to use the most default behavior - no special lifecycle, no exception handling from within the coroutine, and most importantly - no custom threading. Futher along, `launch()` calls `newCoroutineContext(context)`, to build up a full context for the coroutine. The code underneath is a bit complex, but in essence if the context is fully empty, it adds the `Dispatchers.Default` to it, adding default background worker threading.

So even though you don't see it, the API itself uses contexts to achieve at least the default behavior. But you should always strive to explicitly and clearly provide what you want to happen.

Combining contexts can lead to very powerful mechanisms, so let's see what it's about.

Combining different contexts

Another interesting aspect to coroutine contexts is the ability to compose them and combine their functionality. Using the `+`/`plus` operator, you can create a new `CoroutineContext` from the combination of the two. Since you know each coroutine is composed of several objects, like the continuation interceptor for the flow, exception handler for errors and a job for lifecycle, there has to be a way to create a new coroutine with all these pieces of the puzzle. And this is where summing contexts comes in handy. You can do it as simply as this:

```
fun main() {
  val defaultDispatcher = Dispatchers.Default

  val coroutineErrorHandler = CoroutineExceptionHandler
{ context, error ->
    println("Problems with Coroutine: ${error}") // we just print the error here
  }

  val emptyParentJob = Job()
```

```
  val combinedContext = defaultDispatcher +
coroutineErrorHandler + emptyParentJob

  GlobalScope.launch(context = combinedContext) {
    println(Thread.currentThread().name)
  }

  Thread.sleep(50)
}
```

The code above is an example of how to create a context from both the `Dispatchers.Default` and the error handler. As such, you can add more functionality to a context all at once, effectively building up all of the features your coroutine should use — error handling, threading and lifecycle. So, if you've built a complex `CoroutineContext` for error handling, it would be cool to be able to use it in every coroutine you create. The same goes for the lifecycle of coroutines and their threading mechanisms.

By summing `CoroutineContexts`, you combine all of their `CoroutineContext.Elements`, creating a union of their functionality. However, there are some things which don't make sense, like combining two different `Dispatchers`. This would mean the second dispatcher's threading will override the first one's. If you try to do that, the compiler will even give you a message saying it doesn't make sense.

Providing contexts

When it comes to software, you usually want to build it in a way that abstracts away the communication between layers. With threading, it's useful to abstract the way you switch between different threads. You can abstract this by attaching a **thread provider**, providing both main and background threads. It's no different with coroutines! Since the threading mechanism is abstracted with `CoroutineContext` objects, and their respective `CoroutineDispatcher` instances, you can build a provider that you'd use to delegate which context should be used every time you build coroutines. Usually, these providers have a declared interface, which gives you the **main** and **background** threads or schedulers, since that's what's important in applications with user interfaces.

Let's see how you'd build such a provider.

Building the ContextProvider

You've already learned which `CoroutineContext` objects exist and what their behavior is. To build the provider, you first have to define an interface, which provides a generic context, which you'll run the expensive operations on. Note that this Provider interface is not part of Coroutines but will help us abstract out the main and background contexts. The interface would look like this:

```
interface CoroutineContextProvider {

  fun context(): CoroutineContext
}
```

This way, you can build many different `CoroutineContextProviders`, each for a specific use case you may have in mind. In the implementation, you can pass in the required `CoroutineContext` to the constructor, abstracting away the information in a factory function, or your dependency injection graph.

```
class CoroutineContextProviderImpl(
    private val context: CoroutineContext
) : CoroutineContextProvider {

  override fun context(): CoroutineContext = context
}
```

This way, whenever you're building coroutines, you can use the context provider:

```
GlobalScope.launch(context = provider.context()) {
}
```

Because of this you're able to depend on the abstract provider of contexts, rather than manually writing all of the contexts you use. Additionally, when you build the provider, you could pass in any context you want, effectively switching out the pools of threads that let the event of work swim in. To create such a provider, you can do the following:

```
val backgroundContextProvider =
  CoroutineContextProviderImpl(Dispatchers.Default)
```

You could go another step forward, and make the context provider provide not only thread-based contexts, but also error handling contexts and a lifecycle-related context. Or virtually any combination of those coroutine context elements.

This is extremely useful if you want to abstract away the contexts you're using often. Additionally, it can help you with testing, which you'll see in the "Chapter 16: Testing coroutines".

You can check out these examples by importing this chapter's final project, using IntelliJ, and selecting **Import Project**, and navigating to the **coroutine-context/projects/final** folder, selecting the **coroutine-context** project.

Key points

- All the information for coroutines is contained in a `CoroutineContext` and its `CoroutineContext.Elements`.
- There are three main coroutine context elements: the `Job`, which defines the lifecycle and can be cancelled, a `CoroutineExceptionHandler`, which takes care of errors, and the `ContinuationInterceptor`, which handles function execution flow and threading.
- Each of the coroutine context elements implements `CoroutineContext`.
- `ContinuationInterceptors`, which take care of the input/output of threading. The main and background threads are provided through the `Dispatchers`.
- You can combine different `CoroutineContexts` and their `Elements` by using the +/plus operator, effectively summing their elements.
- A good practice is to build a `CoroutineContext` provider, so you don't depend on explicit contexts.
- With the `CoroutineContextProvider` you can abstract away complex contexts, like custom error handling, coroutine lifecycles or threading mechanisms.

Chapter 7: Coroutine Contexts & Dispatchers

By Filip Babić

Right about now, you've amassed a good amount of knowledge about coroutines, suspendable functions and the Kotlin's Coroutines API. But you haven't learned much about how you can deal with threading, and which threading solutions exist within the API itself. However, you did learn what the `CoroutineContext` is, and what it's used for. Having the ability to combine multiple `CoroutineContexts`, and different context types, to produce powerful coroutine mechanisms makes coroutines really extensible and versatile.

In fact, the `CoroutineContext` is a fundamental part of something called **context switching**, and the process of **dispatching**, which in turn revolves around threading.

Work scheduling

Organizing work at a system level is the bread and butter of all things related to multi-threading and parallel computing. Back in the day, when systems had a single core processor and could only utilize a single thread, it was extremely important to write optimized organizing algorithms so that the system didn't freeze up and so that actions didn't take forever to complete.

The process of figuring out the order, severity and resource usage for units of work the system needs to complete is called **scheduling**. Just like with a regular schedule, which holds all your meetings and chores, it serves to best organize which event should happen before others. It also deals with where the work lives in memory and when it starts or ends — the lifecycle and how it behaves when things break.

So when the system receives, let's say, five events it needs to process, it first looks at the computational power it has available. If it's already under 70% load, then it cannot take on a task which would require 40% of the total load. It then tries to fill in the available computational power by dividing the resources between other tasks which won't overload the system. But there's a caveat here, if you keep trying to fill in the workload with smaller tasks, you may never get to free up enough computational power to finally process the bigger unit of work.

In an operating system, all of these responsibilities belong to a construct called a **scheduler**. Schedulers decide when and how they should assign the computer's resources to which tasks. They also take care of the lifecycle of the work you give them, since the events won't start until a scheduler gives the system a **green light**, nor will they finish until they are completely processed. If any of the events breaks, an exception occurs, the scheduler is notified, and the system kills the process.

In terms of coroutines and modern-day systems, scheduling usually comes down to the distribution and organization of work between threads in **thread pools**. They allow the system to abstract away all of the responsibilities in one seemingly simple object.

Swimming in a pool of threads

A **thread pool** is a number of threads **pooled** together and distributed between work events that the system receives in its queue. Today's hardware supports doing multiple things at the same time and effectively handling quite a few times the amount of work than before due to multiple cores. Combining that with the fact that coroutines can be completed one piece at a time, instead of running the entire operation, it can make coroutines extremely performant. This allows you to run several coroutines at once and schedule threads in such a way that each of the threads does a bit of work on each of the coroutines until all of the work is done, while all of the threads are constantly being reassigned.

Internally, this is where thread pools kick in. You can tell a thread pool to complete five coroutines, like the example above. The thread pool will then assign threads to each of the coroutines, effectively switching them out if needed and suspending coroutines if some work that's higher priority comes up — like an important system call that is triggered from outside of your application. Once the thread is free again, it returns to the thread pool, and the system once again decides if there's work to be done or if it should hold on and wait for more work events.

It's also important to know how the system handles the state of each of the threads.

Context switching

In the Coroutines API, you don't have to worry about creating your own threads or thread pools, or about scheduling how multiple coroutines are executed, and their lifecycle. The Coroutines API has a specific way of communicating all of this information — via **ContinuationInterceptor**s, which you provide through **Dispatchers**, which you'll learn about later in this chapter.

To fully understand how these `Dispatchers` work, it's important to understand the underlying pattern of communication of the process and thread state, which the system prepares for you. This pattern is called **context switching**. However, the definition varies from single to multi-tasking systems. But we'll focus on multi-tasking in this chapter.

Essentially, when the system switches the context, it means that it's moving from one task to another, saving the state of the previous task, so it can be resumed later on. This sounds familiar? It's very similar to what the `Continuation` does, internally, when it comes to suspension points in a suspendable function. Well, this is also why all the dispatchers actually implement `ContinuationInterceptor`, because through the process of intercepting `Continuations`, and their execution flow, can the system suspend and resume - *switch the context*, of the current task, or function, at hand.

But pausing and resuming tasks is not everything, the system should also be able to switch between the threads in a single task. When you think about it, these two concepts stand toe-to-toe in Kotlin Coroutines.

If you need to do something in the background, and then switch to the main thread, posting a value or some result of an operation, you ultimately create another coroutine, push it to the main thread, and then switch to that coroutine from within. This is basically **context switching**, with the addition that it switched between threads. So it's no coincidence that the most important part of every coroutine is called the `CoroutineContext`.

Now that you understand a bit how the system can handle coroutines' context switching, it's time to move onto **dispatching**! :]

Explaining ContinuationInterceptors

Even though this chapter mentions `ContinuationInterceptors`, it may still be a bit unclear on how they work. If you remember from the diagram of what happens with functions in the call stack and when suspendable functions are called:

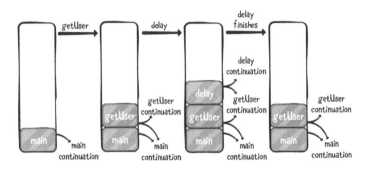

Call stack with Continuation

When you had multiple functions in the stack, and multiple continuations, you learned that you can return all the way down to the main `Continuation`, by propagating the value, or an exception, back down the stack.

`ContinuationInterceptors` work with that function execution and threading. Every time you launch a coroutine, or call a suspend function with a `Dispatcher`, you give the interceptor the ability to pause and resume the continuation of the coroutine - the execution flow. It can intercept value propagation at one point, and redirect it to another coroutine or task.

Because of that, if you create one coroutine using `Dispatchers.Default` to get some value, and then within it, you launch a new coroutine with `Dispatchers.Main` to push it on the main thread, you'll effectively intercept the first coroutine's execution, *continue* on with the second coroutine passing in the context and values so you can do some work on the main thread, and then you finish both coroutines when you're done. If anything goes wrong in the second coroutine, the interceptor will propagate the exception all the way up, to the parent coroutine, cancelling both coroutines.

This type of behavior is achieved through the process of **wrapping continuations**. Every time you switch the context with a `ContinuationInterceptor`, it creates a new `Continuation`, by wrapping the previous one, using `interceptContinuation()`. The signature of the function is the following:

```
abstract fun <T> interceptContinuation(
    continuation: Continuation<T>
): Continuation<T>
```

It is very simple, but also very powerful. Any time the system signals a function's `Continuation`, with a new value or an exception, the `ContinuationInterceptor` can take that `Continuation`, do some work with it, and finally resume execution. In case of `Dispatchers` the work `ContinuationInterceptors` do is generally context switching, by shifting from one `Thread` pool to another.

Coroutine dispatcher types

Kotlin provides a concise way of communicating threading options in coroutines using **Dispatchers**. They are a `CoroutineContext.Element` implementation, forming one part of the puzzle that handles how coroutines behave when executed. In general computing, a dispatcher is a module that gives control of the CPU to whichever process the scheduling mechanism selected for execution. So a scheduler decides which **process** is next in line for a bit of CPU power, but it passes the process down to a dispatcher to allow the process to use up the actual resources. Together, these two modules or mechanisms control processes in an operating system.

A similar thing happens with `CoroutineDispatchers`. They decide how coroutines use up available resources by delegating threads or thread pools to them. Once you attach a certain dispatcher to a coroutine, it is assigned to a thread or thread pool the dispatcher knows about.

Since they deal with threads, dispatchers in coroutines can be **confined** and **unconfined**. Confined dispatchers always rely on predefined system contexts — like the `Dispatchers.Main`. No matter how many times you use the `Main` dispatcher, it will always make the coroutine work on the main thread. Unconfined dispatchers, on the other hand, don't have a specific context they operate in, nor do they follow any strict rules. They either create new threads to run coroutines in or push the work to the thread in which the code was called, making them **unpredictable**.

There's only a finite number of pre-defined dispatchers, and these are:

- `Dispatchers.Default`: The default threading strategy for starting coroutines, confined to the parent's context, usually a thread pool of workers.
- `Dispatchers.IO`: Similar to `Default`, it's based on the JVM, and is backed by a thread pool to offload IO-related tasks.
- `Dispatchers.Main`: The **main thread** dispatcher, connected to the thread, which operates with UI objects.
- `Dispatchers.Unconfined`: The name states it, it's unconfined, and it will run on whichever thread is currently using it.

Let's go over each of them individually and see what you can use them for.

Default dispatcher

The default dispatcher's name pretty much gives it away. It's used in the foundation of coroutines and is used whenever you don't specify a dispatcher. It's convenient to use because it's backed by a worker thread pool, and the number of tasks the `Default` dispatcher can process is always equal to the number of cores the system has, and is at least two. Because the entire threading mechanism and the thread pool is pre-built, you can rely on it for your day-to-day work related to coroutines and operations you want to off-load from the main thread.

IO dispatcher

Again, the name says a lot. Whenever you're trying to process something with input and output, like uploading or decrypting/encrypting files, you can use this dispatcher to make things easier for you. That being said, it's bound to the JVM, so if you're using Kotlin/JavaScript or Kotlin/Native projects, you won't be able to use it.

Main dispatcher

This dispatcher is tied to systems that have some form of **user interface**, such as Android or visual Java applications. And as mentioned, it dispatches work to the thread that handles UI objects. You cannot use this without a UI, and if you try to call `Dispatchers.Main` in a project that doesn't use **Swing**, **JavaFX** or isn't an Android app, your code will crash.

It's best used within another coroutine after you fetch the data you need, and then handle all the logic before displaying it. You simply post the data back to the main thread, and have it render. Or better yet, you can run the coroutine on the main thread, bridging to the background, using `withContext` or `async/await`, ultimately pulling the result back to the main thread for rendering.

Using dispatchers

Now that you know which dispatchers are out there, it's time to learn how to utilize them. Import this chapter's starter project, using IntelliJ, and selecting **Import Project**, and navigating to the **context-switch-and-dispatching/projects/starter** folder, selecting the **context-switch-and-dispatching** project. Let's say you had the following code:

```
GlobalScope.launch {
  println("This is a coroutine")
}
```

You can't tell anything about the threading or scheduling, which happens behind the scenes. Let's review the `launch` function's signature:

```
public fun CoroutineScope.launch(
  context: CoroutineContext = EmptyCoroutineContext,
  start: CoroutineStart = CoroutineStart.DEFAULT,
  block: suspend CoroutineScope.() -> Unit
): Job
```

The first part is important, here. It uses `EmptyCoroutineContext` by default, unless you specify a different one. You've learned that the **context** defines how the coroutine is started and where, how it handles errors, and what its lifecycle is. An `EmptyCoroutineContext` doesn't have any error-handling defined, it has no parent context, it uses the default lifecycle management, and it doesn't have a `CoroutineInterceptor`, so it uses `Dispatchers.Default`.

From what you've learned about the dispatchers, this means the coroutine will use a predefined pool of threads to do its work. If you want to use any other dispatcher, simply pass it in to replace the `EmptyCoroutineContext` default argument. Once you do that, the dispatcher will be used as the context of the coroutine, and it will dictate **all-things-threading**.

Next, change the example a little. Instead of printing some dummy text, make the coroutine print the thread it's located in, using the following snippet of code:

```
fun main() {
  GlobalScope.launch { println(Thread.currentThread().name) }

  Thread.sleep(50)
}
```

If you run this, it will print out something similar to this:

```
DefaultDispatcher-worker-1
```

This supports what you know about the default dispatcher. You get the same result with the following:

```
fun main() {
  GlobalScope.launch(context = Dispatchers.Default) {
    println(Thread.currentThread().name)
  }

  Thread.sleep(50)
}
```

If you were to pass in a different dispatcher, you'd get different results. An example would be the `Dispatchers.Unconfined` instance. So if you had the following code:

```
fun main() {
  GlobalScope.launch(context = Dispatchers.Unconfined) {
    println(Thread.currentThread().name)
  }

  Thread.sleep(50)
}
```

It will print out `main` as it's thread. This is because the unconfined dispatcher just takes in whichever thread the code is run in, and attaches the coroutine to that thread. But what if you don't want to **confine** your code to a certain set of constrains, which the Coroutines API provides for you? What if you need tasks which require a separate thread?

Creating a work stealing Executor

With the standard Coroutines API, you also have the ability to create new threads or thread pools for coroutines. This is done by creating a new **Executor**. Executors are objects that execute given tasks. They are usually tied with **Runnable**s, since they wrap the task in a runnable, which needs executing. Creating a work-stealing executors for example means that it will use all available resources at its disposal, in order to achieve a certain level of parallelism, which you can define. To use the work-stealing-executor, you have to do the following:

```kotlin
fun main() {
  val executorDispatcher = Executors
      .newWorkStealingPool()
      .asCoroutineDispatcher()

  GlobalScope.launch(context = executorDispatcher) {
    println(Thread.currentThread().name)
  }

  Thread.sleep(50)
}
```

If you run this code, it will print out something similar to this:

```
ForkJoinPool-1-worker-9
```

The executor uses all available resources here, like the `ForkJoinPool` thread pool, to finish your task. Once it's done with the task, it can re-allocate the taken resources to the rest of the application. If you were to pass that executor the parallelism level of **four**, and you used the executor in many coroutines, it would distribute resources to achieve four parallel executions as long as there's work to be distributed.

If you want to check out this final example in the final project, import this chapter's final project, using IntelliJ, and selecting **Import Project**, and navigating to the **context-switch-and-dispatching/projects/final** folder, selecting the **context-switch-and-dispatching** project.

Key points

- One of the most important concepts in computing, when using execution algorithms, is **scheduling** and **context switching**.
- Scheduling takes care of resource management by coordinating **threading** and the **lifecycle** of processes.
- To communicate thread and process states in computing and task execution, the system uses **context switching** and **dispatching**.
- Context switching helps the system store thread and process state, so that it can **switch between tasks** which need execution.
- Dispatching handles which tasks get resources at which point in time.
- `ContinuationInterceptors`, which take care of the input/output of threading, and the main and background threads are provided through the `Dispatchers` class.
- Dispatchers can be **confined** and **unconfined**, where being confined or not relates to using a fixed threading system.
- There are four main dispatchers: `Default`, `IO`, `Main` and `Unconfined`.
- Using the `Executors` class you can create new thread pools to use for your coroutine work.

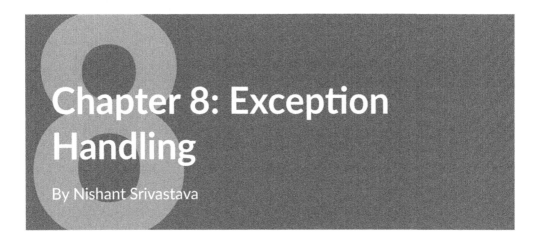

Chapter 8: Exception Handling

By Nishant Srivastava

Exception and error handling is an integral part of asynchronous programming. Imagine that you initiate an asynchronous operation, it runs through without any error and finishes with the result. That's an ideal case. What if an error occurred during the execution? As with any unhandled exception, the application would normally crash. You may set yourself up for failure if you assume that any asynchronous operation is going to run through successfully without any error.

Before you can understand error and exception handling during coroutine execution, it is important that you have an understanding of how these errors and exceptions are propagated through the process.

Exception propagation

You can build a coroutine in multiple ways. The kind of coroutine builder you use dictates how exceptions will propagate and how you can handle them.

- When using **launch** and **actor** coroutine builders, exceptions are propagated automatically and are treated as unhandled, similar to Java's `Thread.uncaughExceptionHandler`.

- When using **async** and **produce** coroutine builders, exceptions are exposed to the users to be consumed finally at the end of the coroutine execution via **await** or **receive**.

Understanding how exceptions are propagated helps to figure out the right strategy for handling them.

Handling exceptions

Exception handling is pretty straightforward in coroutines. If the code throws an exception, the environment will automatically propagate it and you don't have to do anything. Coroutines make asynchronous code look synchronous, similar to the expected way of handling synchronous code — i.e., try-catch applies to coroutines, too.

Here is a simple example that creates new coroutines in GlobalScope and throws exceptions from different coroutine builders:

```
fun main() = runBlocking {
  val asyncJob = GlobalScope.launch {
    println("1. Exception created via launch coroutine")

    // Will be printed to the console by
    // Thread.defaultUncaughtExceptionHandler
    throw IndexOutOfBoundsException()
  }

  asyncJob.join()
  println("2. Joined failed job")

  val deferred = GlobalScope.async {
    println("3. Exception created via async coroutine")

    // Nothing is printed, relying on user to call await
    throw ArithmeticException()
  }

  try {
    deferred.await()
    println("4. Unreachable, this statement is never executed")
  } catch (e: Exception) {
    println("5. Caught ${e.javaClass.simpleName}")
  }
}
```

Output:

```
1. Exception created via launch coroutine
Exception in thread "DefaultDispatcher-worker-1"
java.lang.IndexOutOfBoundsException
    - - -
2. Joined failed job
3. Exception created via async coroutine
5. Caught ArithmeticException
```

> **Note**: You can find the executable version of the above snippet of code in the starter project in the file called **CoroutineExceptionHandlingExample.kt**.

In the previous code, you launch a coroutine using the `GlobalScope.launch` coroutine builder and you throw an `IndexOutOfBoundsException` in its body. This is an example of the normal exception propagation which is handled by the default `Thread.uncaughExceptionHandler` implementation. This is the object responsible for managing the unhandled exceptions thrown in the application. It just propagates the exceptions to the caller's thread handler, if any, or prints their message on the standard output. In this case, you're into the `main` function so the error message is part of the output.

As you know, the `GlobalScope.launch` creates a `Job` instance and you invoke the `join` function on it. The first job, because of the exception, completes so the `println()` methond that prints `2. Joined failed job` is also part of the output. In the second coroutine, you use the `GlobalScope.async` coroutine builder which throws an `ArithmeticException` into its body. In this case, the exception is not handled by the `Thread.uncaughExceptionHandler` the moment it's been created, but can be thrown by the `await` function invoked on the `Deferred` object that the `GlobalScope.async` returns. In this case, also the possible exception is deferred in time.

CoroutineExceptionHandler

Similar to using Java's **Thread.defaultUncaughtExceptionHandler**, which returns a handler for uncaught thread exceptions, coroutines offer an optional and generic **catch** block to handle uncaught exceptions called **CoroutineExceptionHandler**.

> **Note**: On Android, **uncaughtExceptionPreHandler** is the global coroutine exception handler.

Normally, uncaught exceptions can only result from coroutines created using `launch` coroutine builder. A coroutine that was created using `async` **always** catches all its exceptions and represents them in the resulting **Deferred** object.

When using the **launch** builder, the exception will be stored in a **Job** object. To retrieve it, you can use the **invokeOnCompletion** helper function:

```kotlin
fun main() {
  runBlocking {
    val job = GlobalScope.launch {
      println("1. Exception created via launch coroutine")

      // Will NOT be handled by
      // Thread.defaultUncaughtExceptionHandler
      // since it is being handled later by `invokeOnCompletion`
      throw IndexOutOfBoundsException()
    }

    // Handle the exception thrown from `launch` coroutine builder
    job.invokeOnCompletion { exception ->
      println("2. Caught $exception")
    }

    // This suspends coroutine until this job is complete.
    job.join()
  }
}
```

Output:

```
1. Exception created via launch coroutine
Exception in thread "main" java.lang.IndexOutOfBoundsException
....
2. Caught java.lang.IndexOutOfBoundsException
```

> **Note**: You can find the executable version of the above snippet of code in the starter project in the file called **ExceptionHandlingForLaunch.kt**.

By default, when you don't set a handler, the system handles uncaught exceptions in the following order:

1. If the exception is `CancellationException` then the system ignores it because that is the mechanism to cancel the running coroutine.

2. Otherwise, if there is a `Job` in the context, then `Job.cancel` is invoked.

3. Otherwise, all instances of `CoroutineExceptionHandler` found via ServiceLoader and current thread's `Thread.uncaughtExceptionHandler` are invoked.

> **Note**: **CoroutineExceptionHandler** is invoked only on exceptions which are not expected to be handled by the user, so registering it in **async** coroutine builder and the like of it has no effect.

Here is a simple example to demonstrate the usage of **CoroutineExceptionHandler**:

```kotlin
fun main() {
  runBlocking {
    // 1
    val exceptionHandler = CoroutineExceptionHandler { _, exception ->
       println("Caught $exception")
    }
    // 2
    val job = GlobalScope.launch(exceptionHandler) {
      throw AssertionError("My Custom Assertion Error!")
    }
    // 3
    val deferred = GlobalScope.async(exceptionHandler) {
      // Nothing will be printed,
      // relying on user to call deferred.await()
      throw ArithmeticException()
    }
    // 4
    // This suspends current coroutine until all given jobs are complete.
    joinAll(job, deferred)
  }
}
```

Output:

```
Caught java.lang.AssertionError: My Custom Assertion Error!
```

> **Note**: You can find the executable version of the above snippet of code in the starter project in the file called **GlobalExceptionHandler.kt**

Here is the explanation of the code block:

1. Implementing a global exception handler; i.e. `CoroutineExceptionHandler`. This is where you define how to handle the exception when one is thrown from an unhandled coroutine.
2. Creating a simple coroutine using `launch` coroutine builder, that throws a custom message `AssertionError`
3. Creating a simple coroutine using `async` coroutine builder, that throws an `ArithmeticException`
4. `joinAll` is used to suspend the current coroutine until all given jobs are complete.

CoroutineExceptionHandler is useful when you want to have a global exception handler shared between coroutines, but if you want to handle exceptions for a specific coroutine in a different manner, you are required to provide the specific implementation. Let us take a look at how.

Try-Catch to the rescue

When it comes to handling exceptions for a specific coroutine, you can use a **try-catch** block to catch exceptions and handle them like you would do in normal synchronous programming with Kotlin.

There is the catch though. Coroutines created with **async** coroutine builder can typically "swallow" exceptions if you're not careful. If an exception is thrown during an async block, the exception is not actually thrown immediately. Instead, it will be thrown at the time you call **await** on the **Deferred** object that is returned. This behavior, if not taken into account, can lead to situations where no exceptions are ever tracked, but deferring exception handling until a later time can also be a desired behavior depending on the use case at hand.

Here is an example to demonstrate the same:

```
fun main() {
  runBlocking {
    // Set this to 'true' to call await on the deferred variable
    val callAwaitOnDeferred = true

    val deferred = GlobalScope.async {
      // This statement will be printed with or without
      // a call to await()
      println("Throwing exception from async")
      throw ArithmeticException("Something Crashed")
```

```
      // Nothing is printed, relying on a call to await()
    }
    if (callAwaitOnDeferred) {
      try {
        deferred.await()
      } catch (e: ArithmeticException) {
        println("Caught ArithmeticException")
      }
    }
  }
}
```

Note: You can find the executable version of the above snippet of code in the starter project in the file called **TryCatch.kt**.

Output for the case in which `callAwaitOnDeferred` is set to `false` — i.e., no call to `await` is made:

```
1. Throwing exception from async
```

Output for the case in which `callAwaitOnDeferred` is set to `false` — i.e., no call to `await` is made:

```
1. Throwing exception from async
2. Caught ArithmeticException
```

Handling multiple child coroutine exceptions

Having just a single coroutine is an ideal use case. In practice, you may have multiple coroutines with other child coroutines running under them. What happens if those child coroutines throw exceptions? This is where all this might become tricky. In this case, the general rule is "the first exception wins." If you set a **CoroutineExceptionHandler**, it will manage only the first exception suppressing all the others.

Here is an example to demonstrate this:

```
fun main() = runBlocking {

  // Global Exception Handler
  val handler = CoroutineExceptionHandler { _, exception ->
    println("Caught $exception with suppressed " +
```

```kotlin
        // Get the suppressed exception
        "${exception.suppressed?.contentToString()}")
}

// Parent Job
val parentJob = GlobalScope.launch(handler) {
  // Child Job 1
  launch {
    try {
      delay(Long.MAX_VALUE)
    } catch (e: Exception) {
      println("${e.javaClass.simpleName} in Child Job 1")
    } finally {
      throw ArithmeticException()
    }
  }

  // Child Job 2
  launch {
    delay(100)
    throw IllegalStateException()
  }

  // Delaying the parentJob
  delay(Long.MAX_VALUE)
}
// Wait until parentJob completes
parentJob.join()
```

> **Note**: You can find the executable version of the above snippet of code in the starter project in the file called **ExceptionHandlingForChild.kt**.

Output:

```
JobCancellationException in Child Job 1
Caught java.lang.IllegalStateException with suppressed
[java.lang.ArithmeticException]
```

In the previous example:s

- You define a **CoroutineExceptionHandler** to print the name of the first exception caught along with the suppressed ones that it obtains from the **suppressed** property.
- After this, you start a parent coroutine using the `launch` coroutine builder with the exception handler as the parameter. The parent coroutine contains a couple of child coroutines that you launch using again the `launch` function. The first coroutine contains a **try-catch-finally** block.
- In the **try** block, you invoke the `delay` function with a huge parameter value in order to wait for a long time.
- In the **catch**, you print a message about the caught exception.
- With **finally**, you throw an **ArithmeticException**.
- In the second coroutine, you `delay` just some milliseconds and then throw an **IllegalStateException**.
- You then complete the parent coroutine, invoking the `delay` function for another long period of time.
- The last instruction of the `main` function allows the program to wait for the completion of the parent job.

When you run this code, the parent coroutine starts and so do its children. The first child waits and the second throws an **IllegalStateException**, which is the first exception that the handler will manage as you can see in the output. Because of this, the system forces the `delay` of the first coroutine to be canceled and this is the reason for the **JobCancellationException** message. This also makes the parent Job fail and, so, the handler will be invoked and its output displayed.

It's important to note that the **CoroutineExceptionHandler** is part of the parent coroutine and so it manages exceptions related to it.

Callback wrapping

Handling asynchronous code execution usually involves implementing some sort of callback mechanism. For example, with an asynchronous network call, you probably want to have **onSuccess** and **onFailure** callbacks so that you can handle the two cases appropriately.

Such code can often become quite complex and hard to read. Luckily, coroutines provide a way to wrap callbacks to hide the complexity of the asynchronous code handling away from the caller via a **suspendCoroutine** suspending function, which is included in the coroutine library. It captures the current continuation instance and suspends the currently running coroutine.

The **Continuation** object provides two functions with which you can resume the coroutine execution. Invoking the **resume** function resumes the coroutine execution and returns a value, while **resumeWithException** re-throws the exception right after the last suspension point.

Resuming is done by scheduling calling to **Continuation** method in the future inside a suspending function.

Look at an example of a simple long-running job with a callback for handling the result. You're going to wrap the callback in a coroutine and simplify the job significantly:

```kotlin
fun main() {
  runBlocking {
    try {
      val data = getDataAsync()
      println("Data received: $data")
    } catch (e: Exception) {
      println("Caught ${e.javaClass.simpleName}")
    }
  }
}

// Callback Wrapping using Coroutine
suspend fun getDataAsync(): String {
  return suspendCoroutine { cont ->
    getData(object : AsyncCallback {
      override fun onSuccess(result: String) {
        cont.resumeWith(Result.success(result))
      }

      override fun onError(e: Exception) {
        cont.resumeWith(Result.failure(e))
      }

    })

  }
}

// Method to simulate a long running task
fun getData(asyncCallback: AsyncCallback) {
  // Flag used to trigger an exception
```

```kotlin
    val triggerError = false

    try {
      // Delaying the thread for 3 seconds
      Thread.sleep(3000)

      if (triggerError) {
        throw IOException()
      } else {
        // Send success
        asyncCallback.onSuccess("[Beep.Boop.Beep]")
      }
    } catch (e: Exception) {
      // send error
      asyncCallback.onError(e)
    }
  }

// Callback
interface AsyncCallback {
  fun onSuccess(result: String)
  fun onError(e: Exception)
}
```

> **Note:** You can find the executable version of the above snippet of code in the starter project in the file called **CallbackWrapping.kt**.

Output:

- When `triggerError` field is set to `false` in `getData()` method:

  ```
  Data received: [Beep.Boop.Beep]
  ```

- When `triggerError` field is set to `true` in `getData()` method:

  ```
  Caught IOException
  ```

Key points

- If an exception is thrown during an asynchronous block, it is not actually thrown immediately. Instead, it will be thrown at the time you call await on the **Deferred** object that is returned.
- To ignore any exceptions, launch the parent coroutine with the **async** function; however, if required to handle, the exception uses a **try-catch** block on the **await()** call on the **Deferred** object returned from **async** coroutine builder.
- When using **launch** builder the exception will be stored in a **Job** object. To retrieve it, you can use the **invokeOnCompletion** helper function.
- Add a **CoroutineExceptionHandler** to the parent coroutine context to catch unhandled exceptions and handle them.
- **CoroutineExceptionHandler** is invoked only on exceptions that are not expected to be handled by the user; registering it in an **async** coroutine builder or the like has no effect.
- When multiple children of a coroutine throw an exception, the general rule is **the first exception wins**.
- Coroutines provide a way to wrap callbacks to hide the complexity of the asynchronous code handling away from the caller via a **suspendCoroutine** suspending function, which is included in the coroutine library.

Where to go from here?

Exception handling is a crucial step in working with asynchronous programming. If the basics are not clear, it makes the process of programming and dealing with various asynchronous tasks pretty complex. Thankfully, when it comes to coroutines, you are now well versed with the concepts and implementations.

Next up, you will explore cancelling coroutines, so as to be able to stop them from executing when required.

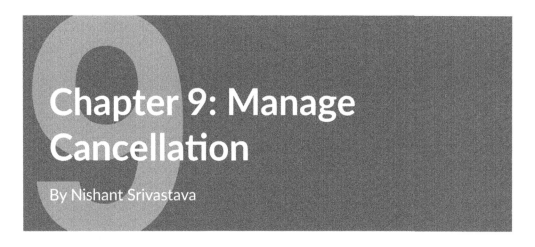

Chapter 9: Manage Cancellation

By Nishant Srivastava

When you initiate multiple asynchronous operations that are dependent on each other, the possibilities of one failing, then leading to others also failing, increases. This means that the result is not going to end as you expected. Coroutines address this problem and provide mechanisms to handle this and many other cases.

This chapter will dive deeper into the concepts and mechanics of cancellation in coroutines.

Cancelling a coroutine

As with any multi-threading concept, the lifecycle of a coroutine can become a problem. You need to stop any potentially long-running background tasks when it is in an inconsistent state in order to prevent memory leaks or crashes. To resolve this, coroutines provide a simple cancelling mechanism.

Job object

As you've seen in Chapter 3: "Getting Started with Coroutines," when you launch a new routine using the **launch** coroutine builder, you get a **Job** object as the return value. This **Job** object represents the running coroutine, which you can cancel at any point by calling the **cancel** function.

This is interesting because with Kotlin coroutines, you have the ability to specify a parent job as a context for multiple coroutines, and calling **cancel** on the parent coroutine will result in all coroutines being canceled.

> **Note**: When you cancel the parent coroutine, all of its children are recursively cancelled, too.

The **launch** coroutine builder is used as a **fire-and-forget** way of starting a coroutine. It is similar to starting a new thread. If the code inside the coroutine that was started from launch terminates with an exception, the system treats it like an uncaught exception in a thread — usually printed to stderr in backend JVM applications — and the Android applications crash. You use **join** to wait for the completion of the launched coroutine but it does not propagate its exception. However, a crashed child coroutine cancels its parent with the corresponding exception, too.

Cancel

In a long-running application, you might need fine-grained control on your background coroutines. For example, a task that launched a coroutine might have finished, and now its result is no longer needed; consequently, its operation can be canceled. This is where the **cancel** method comes in.

In order to cancel a coroutine, you simply need to call the **cancel** method on the Job object that was returned from the coroutine builder. Calling the **cancel** function on a **Job**, or on a **Deferred** instance, will stop the inner computation on a coroutine if the handling of the **isActive** flag is properly implemented.

Coroutine cancelation is **cooperative**. This means that the suspending function has to cooperate in order to support cancelling. In practice, the suspending function has to periodically test the **isActive** property, which is set to `false` when the coroutine is canceled. This applies to your suspending functions, too. All suspending functions provided by the Kotlin coroutine library support cancelation already.

> **Note: isActive** is checked between child coroutine suspension points by the standard library, so you only have to check **isActive** in your own long-running computations.

In the code snippet below, the launch function returns a Job that can be used to cancel the running coroutine:

```kotlin
fun main() = runBlocking {
  val job = launch {
    repeat(1000) { i ->
      println("$i. Crunching numbers [Beep.Boop.Beep]...")
      delay(500L)
    }
  }
  delay(1300L) // delay a bit
  println("main: I am tired of waiting!")
  job.cancel() // cancels the job
  job.join() // waits for job's completion
  println("main: Now I can quit.")
}
```

> **Note**: You can find the executable version of the above snippet of code in the starter project in the file called **CancelCoroutine.kt**.

Crunching numbers via coroutine

Output:

```
0. Crunching numbers [Beep.Boop.Beep]...
1. Crunching numbers [Beep.Boop.Beep]...
2. Crunching numbers [Beep.Boop.Beep]...
main: I am tired of waiting!
main: Now I can quit.
```

CancellationException

Coroutines internally use **CancellationException** instances for cancellation, which are then ignored by all handlers. They are typically thrown by cancellable suspending functions if the Job of the coroutine is canceled while it is suspending. It indicates normal cancellation of a coroutine.

> **Note**: **CancellationException** is not printed to the console/log by the default uncaught exception handler.

When you cancel a coroutine using the **cancel** function on its **Job** object without a cause, it terminates but it does not cancel its parent. Cancelling without cause is a mechanism for a parent to cancel its children without canceling itself.

The following piece of code shows an example of **CancellationException** handling when child jobs are canceled, which is pretty straightforward:

```kotlin
fun main() = runBlocking {
  val handler = CoroutineExceptionHandler { _, exception ->
    println("Caught original $exception")
  }
  val parentJob = GlobalScope.launch(handler) {
    val childJob = launch {
      // Sub-child job
      launch {
        // Sub-child job
        launch {
          throw IOException()
        }
      }
    }

    try {
      childJob.join()
    } catch (e: CancellationException) {
      println("Rethrowing CancellationException" +
          " with original cause")
      throw e
    }
  }
  parentJob.join()
}
```

> **Note**: You can find the executable version of the above snippet of code in the starter project in the file called **CancellationExceptionExample.kt**.

Output:

```
Rethrowing CancellationException with original cause
Caught original java.io.IOException
```

Join, CancelAndJoin and CancelChildren

The Kotlin standard library provides a couple of convenience functions for handling coroutine completion and cancellation.

1. When using coroutines, you will most likely be interested in the result of a completed job. To know about the completion of the coroutine, the **join** function is available, which suspends the coroutine execution until the canceled job is complete:

```kotlin
fun main() = runBlocking {
  val job = launch {
    println("Crunching numbers [Beep.Boop.Beep]...")
    delay(500L)
  }

  // waits for job's completion
  job.join()
  println("main: Now I can quit.")
}
```

> **Note**: You can find the executable version of the above snippet of code in the starter project in the file called **JoinCoroutineExample.kt**.

Output:

```
Crunching numbers [Beep.Boop.Beep]...
main: Now I can quit.
```

2. If you would like to wait for the completion of more than one coroutine, then you should use the **joinAll** function:

```kotlin
fun main() = runBlocking {
  val jobOne = launch {
    println("Job 1: Crunching numbers [Beep.Boop.Beep]...")
    delay(500L)
  }

  val jobTwo = launch {
    println("Job 2: Crunching numbers [Beep.Boop.Beep]...")
    delay(500L)
  }

  // waits for both the jobs to complete
  joinAll(jobOne, jobTwo)
  println("main: Now I can quit.")
}
```

> **Note:** You can find the executable version of the above snippet of code in the starter project in the file called **JoinAllCoroutineExample.kt**.

Output:

```
Job 1: Crunching numbers [Beep.Boop.Beep]...
Job 2: Crunching numbers [Beep.Boop.Beep]...
main: Now I can quit.
```

3. If you would like to cancel and then wait for the completion of a coroutine, then a **cancelAndJoin** function that combines the two is also provided:

```kotlin
fun main() = runBlocking {
  val job = launch {
    repeat(1000) { i ->
      println("$i. Crunching numbers [Beep.Boop.Beep]...")
      delay(500L)
    }
  }
  delay(1300L) // delay a bit
  println("main: I am tired of waiting!")
  // cancels the job and waits for job's completion
  job.cancelAndJoin()
  println("main: Now I can quit.")
}
```

> **Note**: You can find the executable version of the above snippet of code in the starter project in the file called **CancelAndJoinCoroutineExample.kt**

Output:

```
0. Crunching numbers [Beep.Boop.Beep]...
1. Crunching numbers [Beep.Boop.Beep]...
2. Crunching numbers [Beep.Boop.Beep]...
main: I am tired of waiting!
main: Now I can quit.
```

4. If your coroutine has multiple child coroutines and you would like to cancel all of them, then you should use the **cancelChildren** method:

```
fun main() = runBlocking {
  val parentJob = launch {
    val childOne = launch {
      repeat(1000) { i ->
        println("Child Coroutine 1: " +
            "$i. Crunching numbers [Beep.Boop.Beep]...")
        delay(500L)
      }
    }

    // Handle the exception thrown from `launch`
    // coroutine builder
    childOne.invokeOnCompletion { exception ->
      println("Child One: ${exception?.message}")
    }

    val childTwo = launch {
      repeat(1000) { i ->
        println("Child Coroutine 2: " +
            "$i. Crunching numbers [Beep.Boop.Beep]...")
        delay(500L)
      }
    }

    // Handle the exception thrown from `launch`
    // coroutine builder
    childTwo.invokeOnCompletion { exception ->
      println("Child Two: ${exception?.message}")
    }

  }
  delay(1200L)

  println("Calling cancelChildren() on the parentJob")
  parentJob.cancelChildren()
```

```
        println("parentJob isActive: ${parentJob.isActive}")
    }
```

> **Note**: You can find the executable version of the above snippet of code in the starter project in the file called **CancelChildren.kt**.

Output:

```
Child Coroutine 1: 0. Crunching numbers [Beep.Boop.Beep]...
Child Coroutine 2: 0. Crunching numbers [Beep.Boop.Beep]...
Child Coroutine 1: 1. Crunching numbers [Beep.Boop.Beep]...
Child Coroutine 2: 1. Crunching numbers [Beep.Boop.Beep]...
Child Coroutine 1: 2. Crunching numbers [Beep.Boop.Beep]...
Child Coroutine 2: 2. Crunching numbers [Beep.Boop.Beep]...
Calling cancelChildren() on the parentJob
parentJob isActive: true
Child One: Job was canceled
Child Two: Job was canceled
```

This is all nice, but how do you cancel a coroutine after a set time? The next section covers that specific scenario.

Timeout

Long-running coroutines are sometimes required to terminate after a set time has passed. While you can manually track the reference to the corresponding **Job** and launch a separate coroutine to **cancel** the tracked one after a delay, the coroutines library provides a convenience function called **withTimeout**.

Take a look at the following example:

```
fun main() = runBlocking {
  withTimeout(1500L) {
    repeat(1000) { i ->
      println("$i. Crunching numbers [Beep.Boop.Beep]...")
      delay(500L)
    }
  }
}
```

> **Note**: You can find the executable version of the above snippet of code in the starter project in the file called **WithTimeoutExample.kt**.

Output:

```
0. Crunching numbers [Beep.Boop.Beep]...
1. Crunching numbers [Beep.Boop.Beep]...
2. Crunching numbers [Beep.Boop.Beep]...
Exception in thread "main"
kotlinx.coroutines.TimeoutCancellationException: Timed out
waiting for 1500 MILLISECONDS
...
```

The **TimeoutCancellationException** that **withTimeout** throws is a subclass of **CancellationException**. You haven't seen its stack trace printed on the console before. That is because, inside a canceled coroutine, **CancellationException** is considered to be a normal reason for coroutine completion. However, in this example, you have used **withTimeout** right inside the **main** function.

Because cancellation is just an exception, you close all the resources in the usual way. You can wrap the code with a timeout in a **try {...} catch (e: TimeoutCancellationException) {...}** block if you need to do some additional action, specifically on any kind of timeout or use the **withTimeoutOrNull** function:

```kotlin
fun main() = runBlocking {
  try {
    withTimeout(1500L) {
      repeat(1000) { i ->
        println("$i. Crunching numbers [Beep.Boop.Beep]...")
        delay(500L)
      }
    }
  } catch (e: TimeoutCancellationException) {
    println("Caught ${e.javaClass.simpleName}")
  }
}
```

> **Note**: You can find the executable version of the above snippet of code in the starter project in the file called **TimeoutCancellationExceptionHandling.kt**.

Output:

```
0. Crunching numbers [Beep.Boop.Beep]...
1. Crunching numbers [Beep.Boop.Beep]...
2. Crunching numbers [Beep.Boop.Beep]...
Caught TimeoutCancellationException
```

If you want to set a timeout for a coroutine **Job**, wrap the suspended code with the **withTimeoutOrNull** function, which will return null in case of timeout:

```kotlin
fun main() = runBlocking {
  val result = withTimeoutOrNull(1300L) {
    repeat(1000) { i ->
      println("$i. Crunching numbers [Beep.Boop.Beep]...")
      delay(500L)
    }
    "Done" // will get canceled before it produces this result
  }
  // Result will be `null`
  println("Result is $result")
}
```

> **Note:** You can find the executable version of the above snippet of code in the starter project in the file called **WithTimeoutOrNullExample.kt**.

Output:

```
0. Crunching numbers [Beep.Boop.Beep]...
1. Crunching numbers [Beep.Boop.Beep]...
2. Crunching numbers [Beep.Boop.Beep]...
Result is null
```

Key points

- When the parent coroutine is canceled, all of its children are recursively canceled, too.

- **CancellationException** is not printed to the console/log by the default uncaught exception handler.

- Using the **withTimeout** function, you can terminate a long-running coroutine after a set time has elapsed.

Where to go from here?

Being able to cancel an ongoing task is almost always required. The cycle of starting a coroutine and canceling it when an exception is thrown or when the business logic demands it is part of some of the common patterns in programming. Coroutines in Kotlin were built keeping that in mind since the very beginning.

Next up, you will explore how to efficiently process collections involving more than one processing step using coroutines.

Section II: Channels & Flows

Coroutines provide you a set of suspending functions and coroutine builders for the most common use cases. In order to use them, you need to know some more details on how they work under the hood. In this section, you'll explore channels, Coroutine Flow and testing your coroutines.

- **Chapter 10: Building Sequences & Iterators with Yield**: Sequences are one of the most interesting features of Kotlin because they allow generating values lazily. When you implement a sequence you use the yield function which is a suspending function. In this chapter, you'll learn how to create sequences and how the yield function can be used to optimize performance.

- **Chapter 11: Channels**: Although experimental, channels are a very important API you can use with coroutines. In this chapter, you'll create examples to understand what a channel is and how to act as a producer or consumer for it synchronously and asynchronously. You'll understand how to use multiple channels in the case of multiple senders and receivers. You'll finally compare channels with Java's BlockingQueue.

- **Chapter 12: Broadcast Channels**: In this chapter, you'll write many examples to experiment with using channels with multiple receivers and emitted items need to be shared by all of them.

- **Chapter 13: Producer & Actors**: In this chapter, you'll learn how coroutines can help implement a producer/consumer pattern using different types of producers and consumers. Another approach to running tasks in the background is to use the actors model. In the second part of this chapter, you'll learn what an Actor is and how you can use it with coroutines.

- **Chapter 14: Beginning with Coroutine Flow**: In this chapter, you'll learn what Coroutine Flow is and how to use them in your project.

- **Chapter 15: Testing Coroutines**: Testing is a fundamental part of the development process and coroutines are not different. In this chapter, you'll learn how to test coroutines using the main testing frameworks.

Chapter 10: Building Sequences & Iterators with Yield

By Nishant Srivastava

Functional programming is one of the coolest concepts you can use in Kotlin. In this chapter, you'll see how you can use coroutines with sequences and iterators in order to manage theoretically infinite collections of data.

Getting started with sequences

Kotlin provides many ways to manage collections of data with a well-defined **Collections** API together with many functional operators at your disposal.

However, Collections themselves are not the most efficient. There are many cases in which they lead to lower performance and can cause bottlenecks when executing multiple operations on multiple items. That is mostly because all the functional operators on a Collection are eagerly evaluated; i.e., all items are operated upon completely before passing the result to the next operator.

To provide more insight, take a look at the signature of Collection interface:

```
public interface Collection<out E> : Iterable<E>
```

As you can see, the Collection interface inherits from **Iterable** interface. Now Iterable<E> is non-lazy by default or eager-evaluated. Thus, all Collections are eager-evaluated.

To demonstrate the eager-evaluation nature of **Iterable**, check out the below code snippet:

```
fun main() {
  // 1
  val list = listOf(1, 2, 3)

  // 2
  list.filter {
    // 3
    print("filter, ")
    // 4
    it > 0
  // 5
  }.map {
    // 6
    print("map, ")
  // 7
  }.forEach {
    // 8
    print("forEach, ")
  }
}
```

Here's what's going on:

1. Creating a collection — in this case, a list of integers 1,2 and 3.

2. Executing a `filter` operator on the list.

3. Printing a message `"filter, "` to standard output.

4. Defining the filter condition — here, any item that is greater than zero.

5. Executing a `map` operator on the list.

6. Printing a message `"map, "` to standard output.

7. Executing a `forEach` operator on the list.

8. Printing a message `"forEach, "` to standard output.

The output for this is will be as follows:

```
filter, filter, filter, map, map, map, forEach, forEach,
forEach,
```

> **Note**: You can find the executable version of the above snippet of code in the starter project in the file called **IteratorExample.kt**.

Here, notice how each functional operator on the list:

- Iterates over the whole list.
- Processes the result.
- Then passes it to the next functional operator.

For example, `filter`:

- Runs on the whole list of three items three times.
- Evaluates all the items that are greater than zero.
- Returns a list back that is then passed on to the next functional operator map.

Then, `map`:

- Runs through the whole resulting list (here it is the same list since all the integers in the list are greater than zero) three times.
- Passes it on to the next functional operator `forEach`.
- Since nothing was done inside the `map` operator block except printing a log statement, the resulting list again has three items.

Next, `forEach` runs three times on the three items in the resulting list.

To understand how the process ended up to be like above, take a look at the source code of one of the functional operator `filter`:

```
/**
 * Returns a list containing only elements matching the given
[predicate].
 */
public inline fun <T> Iterable<T>.filter(predicate: (T) ->
Boolean): List<T> {
    return filterTo(ArrayList<T>(), predicate)
}
```

`filter` is an extension function that returns a `filterTo` function. Drilling down more into the source code of `filterTo` function:

```
/**
 * Appends all elements matching the given [predicate] to the
given [destination].
 */
public inline fun <T, C : MutableCollection<in T>>
Iterable<T>.filterTo(destination: C, predicate: (T) -> Boolean):
C {
    for (element in this) if (predicate(element))
destination.add(element)
    return destination
}
```

As is evident from source code, the `filter` operator eventually executes a simple for loop over all elements, effectively checking against the condition in an if block to append elements to the new ArrayList. When done iterating over all the items and appending elements to the new ArrayList, the resulting ArrayList is returned back to the `filter` operator. This kind of behavior is similar in other operators, wherein their implementation returns a complete collection back by the time they finish executing.

If you were to add more operators to the pipeline, the performance will start to degrade as the number of elements in the collection increase. That is because each operator will first need to run through all the elements in the collection and then return a new collection (of the same kind) as a result to be passed on to the next functional operator, which will do the same. This is taxing in two ways:

1. Memory: New collections are returned at every step.

2. Performance: Complete collections are processed at every step.

This situation effectively makes it impossible to use the Collections API for an infinite collection of elements. The Kotlin language creators noticed this bottleneck issue and came up with a solution.

Enter: Sequence

To overcome such performance bottleneck issues, Kotlin came up with another data structure called **Sequence**, which handles the collection of items in a lazy evaluated manner. The items processed in a sequence are not evaluated until you access them. They are great at representing collection wherein the size isn't known in advance, like reading lines from a file.

Sequence is based on a basic rule: It allows you to do multiple intermediate operations on a collection of elements but enforces the requirement of having a terminal operation to actually get the result from the sequence. As a result, it is possible for a Sequence to process collections of infinite size elements.

Notice that Sequence is similar to **Iterable** from Java (covered earlier), except it performs lazily whenever possible. The key difference lies in the semantics and the implementation of the Standard Library extension functions for **Iterable** and **Sequence**, which both have a method called `iterator()`.

To demonstrate the lazy-evaluation of a Sequence, check out the below code snippet:

```
fun main() {
  val list = listOf(1, 2, 3)
  // 1
  list.asSequence().filter {
    print("filter, ")
    it > 0
  }.map {
    print("map, ")
  }.forEach {
    print("forEach, ")
  }
}
```

Here, the code snippet is exactly as it was for Iterable earlier, except:

1. Here, `asSequence()` is used to convert the list to a sequence.

The output for this is as follows:

```
filter, map, forEach, filter, map, forEach, filter, map, forEach,
```

> **Note**: You can find the executable version of the above snippet of code in the starter project in the file called **SequenceExample.kt**.

Here, first, notice the call to `asSequence()` function on the list. Sequences can be created in various ways. The most common use case is to create a sequence from a collection of elements by calling the method **asSequence()** on an **Iterable** type (such as a list, set or map).

The method **asSequence()** is actually an extension function on the **Iterable** defined as:

```
public fun <T> Iterable<T>.asSequence(): Sequence<T> {
    return Sequence { this.iterator() }
}
```

Next, notice how each functional operator on the sequence iterates over the whole pipeline on every pass, processes the result at each step and then passes it to the next functional operator.

For example, `filter`:

- Runs on the first item in the sequence.
- Prints "filter, ".
- Evaluates if the item is greater than zero and returns the result back.

This resulting item is then passed on to the next functional operator map. Here, under the map operator code block, a print statement is executed which prints "map, " to standard output. Since nothing is processed the item is passed to the next operator in the pipeline, `forEach`.

Now, under `forEach` code block, a print statement is executed which prints "forEach, " to standard output and the iteration completes. The next iteration of the sequence is processed next over the whole pipeline and so on, until all iterations are executed, thereby resulting in the right output.

It is quite evident that using Sequence helps to avoid unnecessary temporary allocations overhead and may significantly improve the performance of complex processing pipelines because the whole collection of items is not required to be evaluated when processing. At the same time, the Sequence structure enables you to easily operate upon collections of elements by chaining pure function calls with a rich and fluent API.

However, laziness also introduces some overhead, which is undesirable for common simple transformations of smaller collections and makes them less performant. It is recommended to use simple Iterables in most of the cases. The benefit of using a Sequence is only when there is a huge/infinite collection of elements with multiple operations.

> **Note**: Java 8 and Scala both have the concept of streams, which is the same as a Sequence. Kotlin chose to use Sequence as a new class to avoid naming conflicts when running on a Java 8 JVM and also be able to backport it older JVM targets.

Knowing about how to process an infinite collection of items in Kotlin, opens up the door to many more possibilities of working with infinite items. One of those possibilities is of building **Generator** functions.

Generators and Sequences

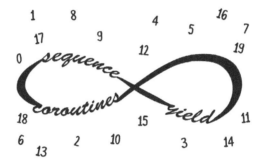

Sequence & Yield

Using Coroutines with Sequence, it is possible to implement **Generators**. Generators are a special kind of function that can return values and then can be resumed when they're called again. Think about lazy, infinite streams of values, like the Fibonacci sequence.

> **Note**: You can also find Generator functions in other languages such as Python and Javascript where they exist with the yield keyword.

Owing to the lazy-evaluated behavior of Sequence and the suspend-resume from using Coroutines, creating a Generator function is quite easy.

To understand how that can be achieved, take a look at the below code snippet about generating an infinite sequence of Fibonacci numbers:

```
fun main() {
  // 1
  val sequence = generatorFib().take(8)

  // 2
  sequence.forEach {
    println("$it")
  }
}

// 3
fun generatorFib() = sequence {
  // 4
  print("Suspending...")

  // 5
  yield(0)
  var cur = 0
  var next = 1
  while (true) {
    // 6
    print("Suspending...")
    // 7
    yield(next)
    val tmp = cur + next
    cur = next
    next = tmp
  }
}
```

Here, you are:

1. Creating a sequence using the method `generatorFib()`, but limiting it to eight items only using the `take()` method.

2. Iterating over the sequence and printing each item.

3. Definition of `generatorFib()` function using the `sequence` DSL.

4. Printing a message `"Suspending..."` to standard output.

5. Generating the item `0` and suspending via the `yield()` function.

6. Printing a message `"Suspending..."` to standard output.

7. Generating infinitely the next item in the Fibonacci numbers sequence and suspending via the `yield()` function.

Output of the above code snippet on execution will be:

```
Suspending...0
Suspending...1
Suspending...1
Suspending...2
Suspending...3
Suspending...5
Suspending...8
Suspending...13
```

Note: You can find the executable version of the above snippet of code in the starter project in the file called **GeneratorFunctionExample.kt**.

Here, notice the use of sequence function inside the generatorFib() function body, which is used to builds a **Sequence** lazily generating values one by one.

This will suspend when values are not needed, and it will end appropriately when the sequence is no longer being used or is exhausted.

Take note of the yield() function. This function is a suspending function as is visible from its signature from the source code:

```
override suspend fun yield(value: T)
```

This means that whenever execution point will reach yield() function it will suspend. This can be validated from the output of the code snippet, too. Right before the call to yield() function, "Suspending..." is printed to the standard output. Next, when yield() function is encountered, the function suspends and returns the value passed to the yield() function. This value is thus generated in the sequence and, while running through, the forEach is printed on the standard output. The function is then resumed back until the next Fibonacci number is generated and the yield() function is called.

Typically, the code is jumping into the middle of the generatorFib() function and executing a part of it. It works because not only the result is returned in this case but the remaining part of the code also and moving it as it is with the instance of a **Continuation**; i.e., result of the function along with the context of where the code returned.

However, the more important question here is from where did this yield() function come from? Move onto the next section to find out.

SequenceScope is here to stay

When working with Coroutines, you need to define a scope within which the coroutines or suspension functions will work. **SequenceScope** is defined for the same reason, for yielding values of a Sequence or an Iterator using suspending functions or coroutines.

Taking a peek at the source code provides more insight:

```kotlin
public abstract class SequenceScope<in T> internal constructor()
{
    public abstract suspend fun yield(value: T)

    public abstract suspend fun yieldAll(iterator: Iterator<T>)

    public suspend fun yieldAll(elements: Iterable<T>) {
        if (elements is Collection && elements.isEmpty()) return
        return yieldAll(elements.iterator())
    }

    public suspend fun yieldAll(sequence: Sequence<T>) =
yieldAll(sequence.iterator())
}
```

Thus **SequenceScope** provides `yield()` and `yieldAll()` suspension functions.

The next question is how does this all tie up in the sequence?

Well, turns out that the `sequence{}` DSL that was used earlier, passes **SequenceScope** as the only argument to it.

```kotlin
public fun <T> sequence(@BuilderInference block: suspend
SequenceScope<T>.() -> Unit): Sequence<T> = Sequence
{ iterator(block) }
```

Since Kotlin allows to convert functions with a single argument to be replaced by a lambda expression in place of the single argument, what you have is a `sequence{}` DSL that provides a **SequenceScope**.

Thus, when using the `sequence{}` DSL, body of the DSL is ready to handle suspension function, enabling the usage of `yield()` and `yieldAll()` suspension functions.

Yield and YieldAll at your service

Using the `yield()` function, there are various ways by which a generator function can be written to handle infinite collections of data.

When considering a Sequence that generates a single value, simply using the `yield()` function suffices the use case. It suspends the sequence when encountered and resumes back for the next iteration and so on.

Here is a working example to demonstrate the functionality:

```
fun main() {
  // 1
  val sequence = singleValueExample()

  // 2
  sequence.forEach {
    println(it)
  }
}

// 3
fun singleValueExample() = sequence {
  // 4
  println("Printing first value")
  // 5
  yield("Apple")

  // 6
  println("Printing second value")
  // 7
  yield("Orange")

  // 8
  println("Printing third value")
  // 9
  yield("Banana")
}
```

Here, in the code snippet, you are:

1. Creating a sequence using the method `singleValueExample()`.
2. Iterating over the sequence and printing each item.
3. Defining a `singleValueExample()` function using the `sequence` DSL.
4. Printing a message "Printing first value" to standard output.
5. Generating the item "Apple" and suspending via the `yield()` function.

6. Printing a message "Printing second value" to standard output.
7. Generating the item "Orange" and suspending via the yield() function.
8. Printing a message "Printing third value" to standard output.
9. Generating the item "Banana" and suspending via the yield() function.

When you execute this code snippet, the output is:

```
Printing first value
Apple
Printing second value
Orange
Printing third value
Banana
```

Note: You can find the executable version of the above snippet of code in the starter project in the file called **SequenceYieldExample.kt**.

The code snippet here is printing one value at a time, suspending, and then resuming back until encountering the next yield() function. It is quite a simple process in which the items are being generated one by one, and yield() is making sure that the items are processed one at a time. Effectively, one can keep on *yielding* more values via the yield() function.

However, this leads to the question like how would this work when a sequence is generated over a range? You probably wouldn't want to call the yield() function every time a new value is generated in a sequence within a range of items. This is where the function yieldAll(elements: Iterable<T>) comes into use. The signature of this function is as follows:

```
public suspend fun yieldAll(elements: Iterable<T>)
```

To demonstrate the behavior, here is a functional example code snippet:

```
fun main() {
  // 1
  val sequence = iterableExample()

  // 2
  sequence.forEach {
    print("$it ")
  }
}
```

```
// 3
fun iterableExample() = sequence {
  // 4
  yieldAll(1..5)
}
```

Here, you are:

1. Creating a sequence using the method `iterableExample()`.

2. Iterating over the sequence and printing each item.

3. Defining the `iterableExample()` function using the `sequence` DSL.

4. Generating the integers over a range of 1 to 5 via the `yieldAll()` function and suspending every time an integer is generated.

On executing this code snippet, the output is:

```
1 2 3 4 5
```

Note: You can find the executable version of the above snippet of code in the starter project in the file called **IteratorYieldAllExample.kt**.

Here, the sequence generation executes over a range of 1 to 5, using the `yieldAll()` function the code block suspends and resumes every time a new value is yielded.

In case the sequence becomes infinite, the Kotlin Standard Library provides another helper method, which is basically an overloaded function named `yieldAll(sequence: Sequence<T>)`; i.e., it takes in a sequence as an argument instead of an iterator.

Here is the declaration of the function from the source code:

```
public suspend fun yieldAll(sequence: Sequence<T>) =
  yieldAll(sequence.iterator())
```

To demonstrate the usage, checkout the below example:

```
fun main() {
  // 1
  val sequence = sequenceExample().take(10)

  // 2
  sequence.forEach {
```

```
      print("$it ")
    }
}

// 3
fun sequenceExample() = sequence {
  // 4
  yieldAll(generateSequence(2) { it * 2 })
}
```

Here, you are:

1. Creating a sequence using the method `sequenceExample()`, but limiting it to 10 items only using the `take()` method.

2. Iterating over the sequence and printing each item.

3. Defining the `sequenceExample()` function using the sequence DSL.

4. Generating infinite integers using the `generateSequence()` function and passing each generated integer to the `yieldAll()` function.

On executing the code snippet, the output is:

```
2 4 8 16 32 64 128 256 512 1024
```

> **Note:** You can find the executable version of the above snippet of code in the starter project in the file called **SequenceYieldAllExample.kt**.

Here, the function `sequenceExample()` generates an infinite sequence, but to keep the program usable the sequence was limited to first 10 items in the sequence by passing the limit via the method call `take(10)` on the `sequenceExample()` function, which generates the infinite sequence.

The code block under `sequenceExample()` function suspends every time an integer is generated, prints the item using the `forEach` in the `main()` function, and resumes back when a new item is generated by the `generateSequence()` function.

Key points

1. **Collection** are eagerly evaluated; i.e., all items are operated upon completely before passing the result to the next operator.

2. **Sequence** handles the collection of items in a lazy-evaluated manner; i.e., the items in it are not evaluated until you access them.

3. **Sequences** are great at representing collection where the size isn't known in advance, like reading lines from a file.

4. `asSequence()` can be used to convert a list to a sequence.

5. It is recommended to use simple **Iterables** in most of the cases, the benefit of using a **sequence** is only when there is a huge/infinite collection of elements with multiple operations.

6. **Generators** is a special kind of function that can return values and then can be resumed when they're called again.

7. Using Coroutines with Sequence it is possible to implement **Generators**.

8. **SequenceScope** is defined for yielding values of a **Sequence** or an **Iterator** using suspending functions or Coroutines.

9. **SequenceScope** provides **yield()** and **yieldAll()** suspending functions to enable Generator function behavior.

Where to go from here?

Working with an infinite collection of items is pretty cool, but what is even more interesting is understanding how Coroutines work with Context and Dispatcher. You will be learning about those in the next chapter.

Chapter 11: Channels

By Nishant Srivastava

From the previous chapters, you already learned how to deal with sending a request for receiving a single value. This approach works perfectly when you just need to get a value once and show it to the user, e.g., fetching a user profile or downloading an image. In this chapter, you will learn how to send and receive **streams** of values.

Streams are convenient when you need to continuously get updates of data or handle a potentially infinite sequence of items. Kotlin isn't the first one to offer a solution to these problems. Observable from *ReactiveX* and Queue from *Java* solve them as well. How Channels compare with Observable and Queue, as well as their benefits and disadvantages, will be covered further in this book.

> **Note**: A stream is a source or repository of data that can be read or written only sequentially while a thread is a unit of execution, lighter in weight than a process, generally expected to share memory and other resources with other threads executed concurrently.

Getting started with channels

Channels are conceptually similar to reactive streams. It is a simple abstraction that you can use to transfer a stream of values between coroutines. Consider a source that sends content to a destination that receives it; i.e., elements are sent into the channel by producer coroutines and are received by consumer coroutines. Essentially, channels are like blocking queues that send and operate on data asynchronously.

Channel

A fundamental property — and an important concept to understand — of a channel is its **capacity**, which defines the maximum number of elements that a channel can contain in a buffer. Suppose you have a channel with capacity **N**. A producer can send values into the channel but, when the channel reaches its N capacity, the producer suspends until a consumer starts to read data from the same channel. You can think of the capacity like the size of the buffer for a specific channel; it's a way to optimize performances in the case producing and consuming are operations, which take different amounts of time.

You can change the default capacity of a channel by passing it as an argument to its factory method. Take a look at the following method signature:

```
public fun <E> Channel(capacity: Int = RENDEZVOUS): Channel<E>
```

You will notice that the default capacity is set to **RENDEZVOUS**, which corresponds to **0** as per the source code:

```
public const val RENDEZVOUS = 0
```

What does it mean in practice? It means that the producer channel won't produce anything until there is a consumer channel that needs data; essentially, there is no buffer.

An element is transferred from producer to consumer only when the producer's `send` and consumer's `receive` invocations meet in time (rendezvous). Because of this, the send function suspends until another coroutine invokes `receive` and `receive` suspends until another coroutine invokes `send`. This is the reason for the RENDEZVOUS name.

> **Note**: The same happens in Java with the **SynchronousQueue** class.

Creating a channel is pretty straightforward. Write the following:

```
val kotlinChannel = Channel<Int>()
```

Consuming its values can be done via the usual `for` loop:

```
for (x in kotlinChannel){
   println(x)
}
```

Channels implement the `SendChannel` and `ReceiveChannel` interfaces.

```
public interface SendChannel<in E> {
    @ExperimentalCoroutinesApi
    public val isClosedForSend: Boolean

    public suspend fun send(element: E)
    public fun offer(element: E)
    public fun close(cause: Throwable? = null): Boolean
    ...
}

public interface ReceiveChannel<out E> {
    @ExperimentalCoroutinesApi
    public val isClosedForReceive: Boolean

    public suspend fun receive(): E
    public fun cancel(): Unit
    ...
}
```

Notice that **SendChannel** exposes the operation **close**, which is used — surprise — for closing the channel. As soon as the sender calls `close()` on the channel, the value of `isClosedForSend` becomes `true`.

> **Note**: `close()` is an idempotent operation; repeated invocations of this function have no effect and return `false`.

You can't send any message into a closed channel. Closing a channel conceptually works by sending a special **close token** over it. You close a channel when you have a finite sequence of elements to be processed by consumers. You must then signal to the consumers that this sequence is over. The iteration stops as soon as this close token is received, so there is a guarantee that all previously sent elements before the close are received. You don't have to close a channel otherwise.

On the other hand, **ReceiveChannel** exposes the **cancel** operation, which cancels the reception of remaining elements from the channel. Once finished, this function closes the channel and removes all messages in the buffer, if any. After `cancel()` completes, `isClosedForReceive` starts returning `true`. If the producer has already closed the channel invoking the **close()** function, then `isClosedForReceive` returns true only after all previously sent elements are received.

The **isClosedForReceive** property can be used along with `channel.receive()` to iterate and get items from a channel one at a time:

```
while (!kotlinChannel.isClosedForReceive) {
    val value = kotlinChannel.receive()
    println(value)
}
```

Channels are not tied to any native resource and they don't have to be closed to release their memory; hence, simply dropping all the references to a channel is fine. When the garbage collector runs, it will clean out those references.

Other important methods are **send** and **receive**. You can send items to the channel with the method `send(element: E)` and receive from it with `receive():E`.

This is typical usage for a channel:

```
fun main() {

  // 1
  val fruitArray = arrayOf("Apple", "Banana", "Pear", "Grapes",
      "Strawberry")
```

```
// 2
val kotlinChannel = Channel<String>()

runBlocking {

  // 3
  GlobalScope.launch {
    for (fruit in fruitArray) {
      // 4
      kotlinChannel.send(fruit)

      // 5
      if (fruit == "Pear") {
        // 6
        kotlinChannel.close()
      }
    }
  }

  // 7
  for (fruit in kotlinChannel) {
    println(fruit)
  }

  // 8
  println("Done!")
}
```

Output:

```
Apple
Banana
Pear
Done!
```

Breaking down each part of the above code snippet, which you can find the executable version of the above snippet of code in the starter project in the file called **ChannelsIntro.kt**:

1. An array of string items.

2. Create a channel with default — i.e., 0 capacity.

3. Set up the producer.

4. Send data in the channel.

5. Conditional check, if the current item is equal to value `Pear`.

6. Signal the closure of the channel via calling `close()` on the channel.

7. Set up the consumer that is printing the received values using `for` loop (until the channel is closed).

8. Print the final `Done` status.

In the previous example, you create a `Channel` of `String` objects. Then, into the body of the `launch` coroutine builder, you iterate over an `Array<String>` and put each element into the channel using the `send` function. While iterating, you check if the current value equals to `Pear`, in which case you close the channel invoking the **close** method. This is an example of a condition for the closing of the channel.

On the receiving side, you use a normal iteration with a **for** cycle in order to consume all the elements available in the channel. The `for` cycle is smart enough to understand when the channel is closed because it uses the underlying `Iterator`.

The `for` loop solution is excellent because it allows you to use channels in the normal pattern that you'd use for iterating over a normal collection. If you want more control over what you're doing, you can consume the channel using code like this:

```
while (!kotlinChannel.isClosedForReceive) {
    val value = kotlinChannel.receive()
    println(value)
}
```

However, there is yet another way to iterate over the channel values, via using `repeat()` Kotlin construct:

```
// Another way to iterate over the channel values
// You use channel.receive() to
// get the messages one by one
repeat(3){
  val fruit = kotlinChannel.receive()
  println(fruit)
}
```

Here, you explicitly use the `receive` method but you have to know exactly how many elements you're getting from the channel, which is not always possible. If you try to put 4 instead of 3 as argument of the `repeat` function, you'll have a `ClosedReceiveChannelException` exception like this:

```
Apple
Banana
Pear
Exception in thread "main"
kotlinx.coroutines.channels.ClosedReceiveChannelException:
```

```
Channel was closed
    at
kotlinx.coroutines.channels.Closed.getReceiveException(AbstractC
hannel.kt:1070)
```

It's interesting to note that the exception is not thrown on the receive function but on the **close** one. This happens because the close function is a suspend function, which actually completes only when the receiver consumes all the items in the channel. If the receiver requests more items that the one available, the producer tries to provide some new data. But, in this, case the channel is closed and this is not possible. This is the reason for the **ClosedReceiveChannelException**. In the case that you put a value smaller than the number of available objects, on the other hand, you're going to miss some data.

Understanding closed channels

In order to understand the state of the channel, you can use two handy properties: **isClosedForReceive** and **isClosedForSend**.

When you close a channel from the sender, like in the previous example, you implicitly put its isClosedForSend property to true, which means that you can't send new data. It's important to understand that this doesn't imply that isClosedForReceive is also true. This is because there should still be some data in the channel. When the receiver consumes all the data, then the isClosedForReceive is also set to true. Because of this, you can consume the data using the following code:

```
while (!kotlinChannel.isClosedForReceive) {
  val fruit = kotlinChannel.receive()
  println(fruit)
}
```

Here, you're receiving data until the isClosedForReceive property is true. Sadly, if you run this example, you might still get an exception on the close function. Why? Unfortunately, channel APIs are unstable and, in this case, there's a race condition on the update of the isClosedForReceive property. In order to fix this, you could add a simple delay, which gives time to the channel for the update, but this is not deterministic and sometimes it won't work:

```
while (!kotlinChannel.isClosedForReceive) {
  val fruit = kotlinChannel.receive()
  delay(10)
  println(fruit)
}
```

A more reliable way to produce the same results is to use the **produce** coroutine builder on the producer side and an extension function **consumeEach**, that replaces a for loop on the consumer side. Basically, it makes everything run smoothly, bringing order and a clean approach to consuming items in the channel:

```kotlin
@ObsoleteCoroutinesApi
@ExperimentalCoroutinesApi
fun main() {

  val fruitArray = arrayOf("Apple", "Banana", "Pear", "Grapes", "Strawberry")

  fun produceFruits() = GlobalScope.produce<String> {
    for (fruit in fruitArray) {
      send(fruit)

      // Conditional close
      if (fruit == "Pear") {
        // Signal that closure of channel
        close()
      }
    }
  }

  runBlocking {
    val fruits = produceFruits()
    fruits.consumeEach { println(it) }
    println("Done!")
  }
}
```

The end result is the same, but the approach to producing and consuming is much cleaner. By way of reminder, you can find the executable version of the above snippet of code in the starter project in the file called **ChannelIntroWithProduce.kt**.

> **Note**: Channels are still under development and considered experimental. You will need to annotate the main method with **@ExperimentalCoroutinesApi** annotation. Behavior of producers may change in the future. You will also notice that we added another annotation, **@ObsoleteCoroutinesApi** because **consumeEach** API will become obsolete in future updates with the introduction of lazy asynchronous streams. See issue #254 here: https://github.com/Kotlin/kotlinx.coroutines/issues/254.

Pipelines

With channels, you always have a producer and a consumer. Sometimes, a consumer receives the data from a channel, applies some transformations and becomes the producer of a new channel. When a consumer of a channel becomes the producer of another channel, you create a **Pipelines**. The source channel might be infinite and the pipeline might contain different steps.

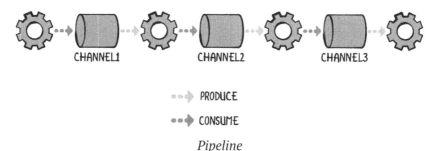

Pipeline

Check out an example in which you generate a list of items that are red fruits. You will make use of multiple channels connected as a pipeline to get the final result:

```kotlin
data class Fruit(override val name: String, override val color: String) : Item
data class Vegetable(override val name: String, override val color: String) : Item

@ExperimentalCoroutinesApi
fun main() {

  // -------------- Helper Methods --------------
  fun isFruit(item: Item): Boolean = item is Fruit

  fun isRed(item: Item): Boolean = (item.color == "Red")

  // -------------- Pipeline --------------
  // 1
  fun produceItems() = GlobalScope.produce {
    val itemsArray = ArrayList<Item>()
    itemsArray.add(Fruit("Apple", "Red"))
    itemsArray.add(Vegetable("Zucchini", "Green"))
    itemsArray.add(Fruit("Grapes", "Green"))
    itemsArray.add(Vegetable("Radishes", "Red"))
    itemsArray.add(Fruit("Banana", "Yellow"))
    itemsArray.add(Fruit("Cherries", "Red"))
    itemsArray.add(Vegetable("Broccoli ", "Green"))
    itemsArray.add(Fruit("Strawberry", "Red"))
```

```kotlin
      // Send each item in the channel
      itemsArray.forEach {
        send(it)
      }
    }

    // 2
    fun isFruit(items: ReceiveChannel<Item>) = GlobalScope.produce {
      for (item in items) {
        // Send each item in the channel only if it is a fruit
        if (isFruit(item)) {
          send(item)
        }
      }
    }

    // 3
    fun isRed(items: ReceiveChannel<Item>) = GlobalScope.produce {
      for (item in items) {
        // Send each item in the channel only if it is red in
color
        if (isRed(item)) {
          send(item)
        }
      }
    }

    runBlocking {
      // 4
      val itemsChannel = produceItems()
      // 5
      val fruitsChannel = isFruit(itemsChannel)
      // 6
      val redChannel = isRed(fruitsChannel)

      // 7
      for (item in redChannel) {
        print("${item.name}, ")
      }

      // 8
      redChannel.cancel()
      fruitsChannel.cancel()
      itemsChannel.cancel()

      // 9
      println("Done!")
    }
  }
```

Take note of the Item interface being used, which you can find in the starter project in Items.kt file with the below definition:

```
interface Item {
  val name: String
  val color: String
}
```

Now, run the above example:

Output:

```
Apple, Cherries, Strawberry, Done!
```

Breaking down the above code snippet:

1. Channel 1: Produces a finite number of items that are either a fruit or vegetable on the internal channel for the produce coroutine builder.

2. Channel 2: Produces only the items that are fruit on the internal channel for the produce coroutine builder.

3. Channel 3: Produces only the items that red in color on the internal channel for the produce coroutine builder.

4. Wire up and set up the pipeline by initializing the **itemsChannel** via the produceItems() method, which produces a stream of items.

5. **itemsChannel** is then passed to the **fruitsChannel** via the isFruit(itemsChannel) method, which feeds the stream of items into the **fruitsChannel**. This channel then checks if the item is a fruit or not. If it is, then it sends the item in its own channel.

6. **fruitsChannel** is then passed to the **redChannel** via the isRed(fruitsChannel) method, which feeds the stream of fruit items into the **redChannel**. This channel then checks if the fruit item is red colored or not. If it is, then it sends the item in its own channel.

7. Using a for loop, print all the items that are fruits and of red color from the **redChannel**.

8. It is recommended to cancel all the coroutines for good measure.

9. Finally, print the final "Done" status to the console.

You can find the executable version of the above snippet of code in the starter project in the file called **PipelineExample.kt**.

As you would have noticed, there are three channels being utilized here, which are connected one after the other to get the final result, representing a **Pipeline**:

- The **produceItems** function creates a channel with objects that are either a fruit or a vegetable.

- The `isFruit` function iterates over the `ReceiveChannel` passed as a parameter, creating a new channel that only produces fruit. It's important to note that this function consumes all the items in the input channel while ignoring the ones that are not a fruit, which is basically lost.

- The `isRed` function does something similar with a different predicate, creating a channel, which produces the only items in input that are red.

- The `main()` function creates the pipeline setting `itemsChannel` as the input for the `isFruit` function and the output of this as the input for the `isRed` function.

Notice also that you do not close the channels, but only directly canceled the coroutines. That is because you are signaling the end of transmission as a whole.

Fan out

In the previous example, you created a pipeline as a sequence of channels, each one with a single producer and a single consumer. Coroutines were consuming the data from a channel and testing if that data satisfied certain conditions. In the case of success, the items were put into the new channel; otherwise, they were discarded.

Sometimes, the scenario is a little bit more complicated and you'd like to send each item to a different coroutine depending on a specific condition. You need some kind of **demultiplexer**, which, in the context of channels, is a use case called **Fan-out**.

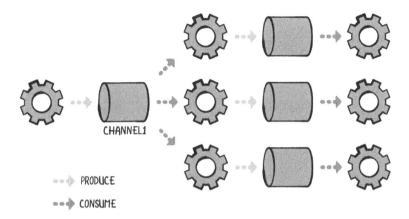

Fan-out

The challenge here is that you can't test the item if you don't consume it first. A possible solution would be to consume the item, test it and put it again into the original channel if it's not compliant with your coroutine. Unfortunately, this is not a doable approach because of the laziness of the channel.

In this case, a better solution consists in the creation of a coroutine with **demultiplexer** feature, which sends an item to a channel or another given a predicate. In the following example, we use an approach inspired by the **Chain of Responsibility** design pattern.

You can find the code for this example in the starter project in the file called **FanOut.kt**.

In this case, you need some initial abstractions:

```
typealias Predicate<E> = (E) -> Boolean

typealias Rule<E> = Pair<Channel<E>, Predicate<E>>
```

A **Predicate** is any function with a parameter of generic type E which can return either **true** or **false**. A **Rule** is a name for a **Pair** of a Channel and a Predicate. The idea is to allow a coroutine to send a value to a specific channel only if its predicate returns true if evaluated for the value itself.

You can encapsulate the demultiplexing logic into a class like below:

```kotlin
class Demultiplexer<E>(vararg val rules: Rule<E>) {

  suspend fun consume(recv: ReceiveChannel<E>) {
    for (item in recv) {
      // 1
      for (rule in rules) {
        // 2
        if (rule.second(item)) {
          // 3
          rule.first.send(item)
        }
      }
    }
    // 4
    closeAll()
  }

  // Closes all the demultiplexed channels
  private fun closeAll() {
    rules.forEach { it.first.close() }
  }
}
```

1. You iterate over all the values of the channel to consume.

2. Iterate over the possible destination channels into the rules passed as varargs parameters.

3. If the predicate for the current value evaluates to `true`, you invoke the `send` function on the corresponding channel. If the predicate is `false`, the value is skipped.

4. When you exit the `for` loop it means that the source channel is closed, and so you close all the destination channels. A cancelation like the one in the previous example could be another option.

Finally, you can refer to the following example, which generates a list of items that are either a fruit or a vegetable, and it dispatches them to two different channels depending on their type:

```kotlin
@ExperimentalCoroutinesApi
fun main() {

  data class Fruit(override val name: String, override val color: String) : Item
  data class Vegetable(override val name: String, override val color: String) : Item

  // ------------- Helper Methods -------------
  fun isFruit(item: Item) = item is Fruit

  fun isVegetable(item: Item) = item is Vegetable

  // 1
  fun produceItems(): ArrayList<Item> {
    val itemsArray = ArrayList<Item>()
    itemsArray.add(Fruit("Apple", "Red"))
    itemsArray.add(Vegetable("Zucchini", "Green"))
    itemsArray.add(Fruit("Grapes", "Green"))
    itemsArray.add(Vegetable("Radishes", "Red"))
    itemsArray.add(Fruit("Banana", "Yellow"))
    itemsArray.add(Fruit("Cherries", "Red"))
    itemsArray.add(Vegetable("Broccoli", "Green"))
    itemsArray.add(Fruit("Strawberry", "Red"))
    itemsArray.add(Vegetable("Red bell pepper", "Red"))
    return itemsArray
  }

  runBlocking {

    // 2
    val kotlinChannel = Channel<Item>()

    // 3
    val fruitsChannel = Channel<Item>()
    val vegetablesChannel = Channel<Item>()

    // 4
    launch {
      produceItems().forEach {
        kotlinChannel.send(it)
      }
      // 5
      kotlinChannel.close()
    }

    // 6
    val typeDemultiplexer = Demultiplexer(
```

```kotlin
            fruitsChannel to { item: Item -> isFruit(item) },
            vegetablesChannel to { item: Item -> isVegetable(item) }
    )
    // 7
    launch {
        typeDemultiplexer.consume(kotlinChannel)
    }

    // 8
    launch {
        for (item in fruitsChannel) {
            // Consume fruitsChannel
            println("${item.name} is a fruit")
        }
    }

    // 9
    launch {
        for (item in vegetablesChannel) {
            // Consume vegetablesChannel
            println("${item.name} is a vegetable")
        }
    }
  }
}
```

Here, in the above code snippet, you:

1. Create a `produceItems` function for producing a finite number of items, which are either a fruit or vegetable.

2. Create a channel for `Item`.

3. Create the `fruitsChannel` channel for items that are fruits and a `vegetablesChannel` channel for items that are vegetables.

4. Launch a coroutine for sending all items generated by the **produceItems** function.

5. When completed, close the channel.

6. Create a **Demultiplexer** instance, which maps items that are fruit to the `fruitsChannel` and items that are vegetables to the `vegetablesChannel`.

7. The `Demultiplexer` has a `consume` method, which is suspending, and it needs a coroutine that you launch.

8. You consume the `fruitsChannel` channel, printing its values.

9. You consume the `vegetablesChannel` channel, printing its values.

As you can see, the output will be:

```
Apple is a fruit
Zucchini  is a vegetable
Grapes is a fruit
Radishes  is a vegetable
Banana is a fruit
Cherries is a fruit
```

```
Broccoli  is a vegetable
Strawberry is a fruit
Red bell pepper  is a vegetable
```

The order of the item type evaluation is now different. This is obvious because now each channel can be consumed independently.

Fan in

In the previous example, you created a coroutine that was able to demultiplex the items into different channels based on certain criteria. That was a way to simulate the case in which you have one producer and many consumers.

A different case happens when you have multiple producers and one consumer: This is called **Fan-in**, and it's a simpler situation compared to the previous.

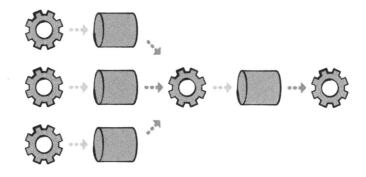

Fan-in

As an example, you can implement the following code:

```kotlin
@ExperimentalCoroutinesApi
fun main() {

  data class Fruit(override val name: String, override val color: String) : Item
  data class Vegetable(override val name: String, override val color: String) : Item

  // ------------- Helper Methods --------------
  fun isFruit(item: Item) = item is Fruit

  fun isVegetable(item: Item) = item is Vegetable

  // 1
  fun produceItems(): ArrayList<Item> {
    val itemsArray = ArrayList<Item>()
    itemsArray.add(Fruit("Apple", "Red"))
    itemsArray.add(Vegetable("Zucchini", "Green"))
    itemsArray.add(Fruit("Grapes", "Green"))
    itemsArray.add(Vegetable("Radishes", "Red"))
    itemsArray.add(Fruit("Banana", "Yellow"))
    itemsArray.add(Fruit("Cherries", "Red"))
    itemsArray.add(Vegetable("Broccoli", "Green"))
    itemsArray.add(Fruit("Strawberry", "Red"))
    itemsArray.add(Vegetable("Red bell pepper", "Red"))
    return itemsArray
  }


  runBlocking {

    // 2
    val destinationChannel = Channel<Item>()

    // 3
    val fruitsChannel = Channel<Item>()
    val vegetablesChannel = Channel<Item>()

    // 4
    launch {
      produceItems().forEach {
        if (isFruit(it)) {
          fruitsChannel.send(it)
        }
      }
    }

    // 5
    launch {
      produceItems().forEach {
```

```kotlin
      if (isVegetable(it)) {
        vegetablesChannel.send(it)
      }
    }
  }

  // 6
  launch {
    for (item in fruitsChannel) {
      destinationChannel.send(item)
    }
  }

  // 7
  launch {
    for (item in vegetablesChannel) {
      destinationChannel.send(item)
    }
  }

  // 8
  destinationChannel.consumeEach {
    if (isFruit(it)) {
      println("${it.name} is a fruit")
    } else if (isVegetable(it)) {
      println("${it.name} is a vegetable")
    }
  }

  // 9
  coroutineContext.cancelChildren()
  }
}
```

You can find the code for this example in the starter project in the file called **FanIn.kt**.

In the above:

1. Create a **produceItems** function for producing a finite number of items, which are either a fruit or vegetable.

2. Initialize the destination channel.

3. Create the `fruitsChannel` channel for items that are fruits and `vegetablesChannel` channel for items that are vegetables.

4. Launch the coroutine that inserts the items that are fruits into the `fruitsChannel` channel.

5. Launch the coroutine that inserts the items that are vegetables into the `vegetablesChannel` channel.

6. Here is where the multiplexing is happening for items that are fruits that are sent into the destination channel.

7. Here is where the multiplexing is happening for items that are vegetables that are sent into the destination channel.

8. You consume the destination channel and print a label depending on the type of item.

9. You cancel all the coroutines when there's nothing more to consume.

Now, the output will be something like this:

```
Apple is a fruit
Zucchini is a vegetable
Grapes is a fruit
Banana is a fruit
Radishes is a vegetable
Cherries is a fruit
Broccoli is a vegetable
Strawberry is a fruit
Red bell pepper is a vegetable
```

Buffered channel

As you might have noticed above, the channel examples demonstrated previously used a default value for the capacity, called RENDEZVOUS. These kinds of channels are called **unbuffered channels** because the producer produces only if there's a consumer ready to consume.

However, this behavior can be overcome easily by specifying the buffer capacity of the channel as a parameter in the factory method. In this way, your channel won't suspend on a send operation when there is a free space in the buffer. You can create buffered channels that will allow senders to send multiple elements before suspending:

```
// Channel of capacity 2
val kotlinBufferedChannel = Channel<String>(2)
```

Check out a working example:

```kotlin
fun main() {

  val fruitArray = arrayOf("Apple", "Banana", "Pear", "Grapes", "Strawberry")

  val kotlinBufferedChannel = Channel<String>(2)

  runBlocking {
    launch {
      for (fruit in fruitArray) {
        kotlinBufferedChannel.send(fruit)
        println("Produced: $fruit")
      }
      kotlinBufferedChannel.close()
    }

    launch {
      for (fruit in kotlinBufferedChannel) {
        println("Consumed: $fruit")
        delay(1000)
      }
    }
  }
}
```

Output:

```
Produced: Apple
Produced: Banana
Consumed: Apple
Produced: Pear
Consumed: Banana
Produced: Grapes
Consumed: Pear
Produced: Strawberry
Consumed: Grapes
Consumed: Strawberry
```

You can find the executable version of the above snippet of code in the starter project in the file called **BufferedChannelExample.kt**.

The output is a perfect description of what is happening: You create a channel with capacity two and then you start a producer.

In the output, you can see that the producer sends two items and fills the channel. At this point, the producer suspends waiting for a consumer to consume the item and this is what is happening with the Apple. Then, a new place is available and the producer sends a Pear. The consumer consumes the Banana and frees another place in the buffer and so on. In the end, the producer stops and the consumer can consume all the remaining items in the channel.

As mentioned earlier, the capacity of a channel depends on the performance requirement of your app. A typical example is when you have a pipeline that dispatches items from a channel into multiple channels. If the throughput of the producer and consumer is different, using a buffered channel is usually a good solution.

Comparing send and offer

In the previous examples, you sent values into a channel using the send function. Depending on the channel's capacity, send is a function that can suspend. This is happening when the channel's buffer is full or, in case of RENDEZVOUS, when there's not receiver ready to consume.

In the case in which you don't want to suspend, the Channel abstraction provides the offer(element: E) function whose signature is:

```
abstract fun offer(element: E): Boolean
```

Since this method is not a suspending function, it doesn't need to be XXX into a coroutine. If there's enough capacity, the item goes into the channel and it returns true. If there's not enough capacity, the function does nothing and returns false. In both cases, it doesn't suspend.

You can try it with the following code:

```
fun main() {
  val fruitArray = arrayOf("Apple", "Banana", "Pear", "Grapes", "Strawberry")

  val kotlinChannel = Channel<String>()

  runBlocking {
    launch {
      for (fruit in fruitArray) {
        val wasSent = kotlinChannel.offer(fruit)
        if (wasSent) {
          println("Sent: $fruit")
        } else {
          println("$fruit wasn't sent")
        }
      }
    }
```

```
        kotlinChannel.close()
      }

      for (fruit in kotlinChannel) {
        println("Received: $fruit")
      }
      println("Done!")
    }
  }
```

Output:

```
Sent: Apple
Banana wasn't sent
Pear wasn't sent
Grapes wasn't sent
Strawberry wasn't sent
Received: Apple
```

Here, you will notice a few things:

1. The capacity of the channel is 0 (RENDEZVOUS).

2. Using offer() is similar to send().

3. As soon as the first value("Apple") is sent, the channel is full.

4. Once the channel is full, calls to offer() doesn't send anything. Instead, it returns false, which is denoted by print statements Banana wasn't sent and similar statements.

5. Once all the calls to offer() have been made, only one item was actually added to the channel. Thus, when the consumer receives the values it is just that value.

You can find the executable version of the above snippet of code in the starter project in the file called **OfferExample.kt**

> **Note**: The caveat with the offer() is that it doesn't guarantee that the element will be added to the channel. It won't be added if the channel is full.

Comparing receive and poll

In the previous section, you've seen that a producer can use `offer` as a not suspending version of the `send` function. What about the consumer? In this case, the version of `receive` without suspending is the `poll` function whose signature is:

```
abstract fun poll(): E?
```

Since this method is not a suspending function, there is no need to invoke it inside a coroutine. It retrieves and removes the element from the channel and returns `null` if the channel is empty. If the channel was closed for `receive`, it throws the close cause exception:

```
fun main() {

  val fruitArray = arrayOf("Apple", "Banana", "Pear", "Grapes", "Strawberry")

  val kotlinChannel = Channel<String>()

  runBlocking {

    launch {
      for (fruit in fruitArray) {
        if (fruit == "Pear") {
          break
        }
        kotlinChannel.send(fruit)
        println("Sent: $fruit")
      }
    }

    launch {
      repeat(fruitArray.size) {
        val fruit = kotlinChannel.poll()
        if (fruit != null) {
          println("Received: $fruit")
        } else {
          println("Channel is empty")
        }

        delay(500)
      }

      println("Done!")
    }
  }
}
```

Output:

```
Received: Apple
Sent: Apple
Received: Banana
Sent: Banana
Channel is empty
Channel is empty
Channel is empty
Done!
```

Here, you will notice a few things:

1. The capacity of the channel is 0 (RENDEZVOUS).

2. Using poll() is similar to receive().

3. As soon as the first value("Apple") is sent, the channel is full. The consumer then receives the value, after which time the channel is empty again.

4. Another cycle of the above process runs with the second value "Banana".

5. For the third value, "Pear", because of the if check in the for loop, no more items are sent in the channel, i.e., the channel is empty.

6. Once the channel is empty, calls to poll() returns null, which is denoted by print statements "Channel is empty".

You can find the executable version of the above snippet of code in the starter project in the file called **PollExample.kt**

Error handling

As you have seen in the previous examples, exceptions play an important role in the way you can use a channel. It's crucial to understand what the main exceptions are and what you should do when they happen. You have to consider two main use cases, depending on if you're on the producer side or on the consumer side of the channel.

You've already seen that, when you consume all elements from a closed channel, its isClosedForReceive property returns true. If you consume the channel using a for loop, everything works in a transparent way. If you attempt to consume a new value, you get a **ClosedReceiveChannelException**.

When this happens, the channel is considered a **failed channel**. A failed channel re-throws the original close clause exception on received attempts.

Here's an example:

```kotlin
fun main() {

  val fruitArray = arrayOf("Apple", "Banana", "Pear", "Grapes",
"Strawberry")

  val kotlinChannel = Channel<String>()

  runBlocking {
    launch {
      for (fruit in fruitArray) {
        // Conditional close
        if (fruit == "Grapes") {
          // Signal that closure of channel
          kotlinChannel.close()
        }

        kotlinChannel.send(fruit)
      }
    }

    repeat(fruitArray.size) {
      try {
        val fruit = kotlinChannel.receive()
        println(fruit)
      } catch (e: Exception) {
        println("Exception raised: ${e.javaClass.simpleName}")
      }
    }
    println("Done!")
  }
}
```

Output:

```
Apple
Banana
Pear
Exception raised: ClosedReceiveChannelException
Exception raised: ClosedReceiveChannelException
Done!
```

Here, you will notice a few things:

1. The capacity of the channel is 0 (default).
2. Once `close` is called, all values retrieved after that raise the `ClosedReceiveChannelException`.

> **Note:** You can find the executable version of the above snippet of code in the starter project in the file called **ClosedReceiveChannelExceptionExample.kt**

However, this is what is happening for a receive operation. When you close a channel on the producer side, its `isClosedForSend` property becomes true.

If you attempt to send another value, you'll get a **ClosedSendChannelException**. Also in this case, when this happens, the channel is a failed channel. Any further attempts to send an element to a failed channel throws the original close cause exception.

Here is a functional example:

```kotlin
fun main() {

  val fruitArray = arrayOf("Apple", "Banana", "Pear", "Grapes", "Strawberry")

  val kotlinChannel = Channel<String>()

  runBlocking {
    launch {
      for (fruit in fruitArray) {
        try {
          kotlinChannel.send(fruit)
        } catch (e: Exception) {
          println("Exception raised: ${e.javaClass.simpleName}")
        }
      }

      println("Done!")
    }

    repeat(fruitArray.size - 1) {
      val fruit = kotlinChannel.receive()
      // Conditional close
      if (fruit == "Grapes") {
        // Signal that closure of channel
        kotlinChannel.close()
      }
```

```
            println(fruit)
        }
    }
}
```

Output:

```
Apple
Banana
Pear
Grapes
Exception raised: ClosedSendChannelException
Done!
```

Here you will notice a few things:

1. The capacity of the channel is 0 (default).

2. Once `close` is called, all values sent after that raise the ClosedSendChannelException.

You can find the executable version of the above snippet of code in the starter project in the file called **ClosedSendChannelExceptionExample.kt**.

Comparing Channels to Java Queues

As mentioned, Java offers a similar solution for handling streams, called Queue<E>, which is an interface and has several implementations. Take a look at an implementation of the BlockingQueue<E> interface, as it supports a similar behavior as Channel of waiting until a queue has space before inserting an element.

```
public class BlockingQueueExample {

  public static void main(String[] args) {

    BlockingQueue<String> queue = new LinkedBlockingQueue<>();

    System.out.println("Beginning:");
    try {
      System.out.println("Let's put in basket: Apple");
      queue.put("Apple");
      System.out.println("Let's put in basket: Banana");
      queue.put("Banana");
    } catch (InterruptedException e) {
      e.printStackTrace();
    }
```

```java
        System.out.println("Done!");
    }
}
```

Output:

```
Beginning:
Let's put in basket: Apple
Let's put in basket: Banana
Done!
```

You can find the executable version of the above snippet of code in the starter project in the file called **BlockingQueueExample.java**.

In the code snippet above, you create an instance of `LinkedBlockingQueue<String>` and put a couple of values in the queue. Pay attention to the differences between Java `Queue` and Kotlin `Channel`:

1. If the queue has no space left, the current thread would be **blocked**, until another thread takes an item from the queue, instead of just **suspending** the coroutine, which is not a good option considering the resources necessary for thread handling.

2. BlockingQueue has a blocking put operation, while Channel has a suspending send. Moreover, instead of a suspending receive operation on Channel, it has a blocking take operation.

3. As the current thread potentially could be interrupted, it's necessary to use `try-catch` block to handle the possible exception.

4. There is no way to stop queues from accepting more values, whereas a Channel can be turned off to indicate that no more elements will enter the Channel.

Therefore, the common recommendation for the usage of Java Queues is to use non-blocking method for inserting and retrieving items (`offer(E item)` and `poll()`) to avoid blocking a thread and spending extra resources.

It's possible to use a **BlockingQueue** instead of a **Channel** for a typical producer/consumer scenario like the one in this Kotlin code:

```kotlin
fun main(args: Array<String>) {
    // 1
    val queue = LinkedBlockingQueue<Int>()
    runBlocking {

        // 2
        launch {
```

```
      (1..5).forEach {
        queue.put(it)
        yield()
        println("Produced ${it}")
      }
    }

    // 3
    launch {
      while (true) {
        println("Consumed ${queue.take()}")
        yield()
      }
    }

    println("Done!")
  }
}
```

1. You create a **LinkedBlockingQueue** as an implementation of the `BlockingQueue` interface.

2. You launch a coroutine that inserts 10 numbers into the queue: the producer.

3. This is the consumer that uses the blocking `take` function in order to consume.

In general, the `yield` method for the `Thread` class is a way for asking the system to suspend the current thread in order to allow other threads to proceed. It's important to note that this is not guaranteed and the scheduler could simply ignore it. Anyway, in your case, this is a Kotlin suspending function and the output is proof that it actually works:

```
Consumed 1
Produced 1
Consumed 2
Produced 2
Consumed 3
Produced 3
Consumed 4
Produced 4
Consumed 5
Produced 5
```

As you can see, the `yield` suspending function knows what coroutines are running and can then suspend one in favor of another.

You can find the executable version of the above snippet of code in the starter project in the file called **BlockingQueue.kt**

Key points

1. **Channels** provide the functionality for sending and receiving **streams** of values.

2. `Channel` implements both `SendChannel` and `ReceiveChannel` interfaces; therefore, it could be used for sending and receiving streams of values.

3. A **Channel** can be closed. When that happens, you can't send or receive an element from it.

4. The `send()` method either adds the value to a channel or **suspends** the coroutine until there is space in the channel.

5. The `receive()` method returns a value from a channel if it is available, or it suspends the coroutine until some value is available otherwise.

6. The `offer()` method can be used as an alternative to `send()`. Unlike the `send()` method, `offer()` doesn't suspend the coroutine, it returns `false` instead. It returns `true` in case of a successful operation.

7. `poll()` similarly to `offer()` doesn't suspend the running, but returns `null` if a channel is empty.

8. Java `BlockingQueue` has a similar to Kotlin `Channel` behavior, the main difference is that the current thread gets blocked if the operation of inserting or retrieving is unavailable at the moment.

Chapter 12: Broadcast Channels

By Nishant Srivastava

A channel is all about transferring a stream of values. It is quite common to put a stream of items in the channel and then have receivers consume the items as they are emitted. It works when an item is sent in a basic channel and when emitted it is consumed by a receiver. Other receivers do not get the same item; instead, they wait for another item to consume from the channel.

Often times, you will encounter use cases in which you would like all the receivers to consume the same value. This is where a **broadcast channel** comes into the picture. This and much more related to broadcast channels are covered in this chapter.

Broadcast Channels

Getting started with broadcast channels

With the **channel**, if you have many receivers waiting to receive items from the channel, the emitted item will be consumed by the first receiver and all other receivers will not get the item individually. In fact, in such a scenario wherein there are more than one receivers, there is the possibility of a **race condition**.

Take a look at this code snippet:

```
fun main() {

  // 1
  val fruitArray = arrayOf("Apple", "Banana", "Pear", "Grapes",
      "Strawberry")
  // 2
  val kotlinChannel = Channel<String>()

  // 3
  runBlocking {

    // 4 Producer
    GlobalScope.launch {
      // Send data in channel
      kotlinChannel.send(fruitArray[0])
    }

    // 5 Consumers
    GlobalScope.launch {
      kotlinChannel.consumeEach { value ->
        println("Consumer 1: $value")
      }
    }
    GlobalScope.launch {
      kotlinChannel.consumeEach { value ->
        println("Consumer 2: $value")
      }
    }

    // 6
    println("Press a key to exit...")
    readLine()

    // 7
    kotlinChannel.close()
  }
}
```

Here:

1. A string array of fruit names is created, named `fruitArray`.
2. A basic channel is created named `kotlinChannel`.
3. Next, a **runBlocking** section is defined to run coroutines in our main function.
4. Start producing items and send them in the channel, all inside a launch coroutine builder.
5. Start consuming items from the channel, all inside two different launch coroutine builders.
6. Wait for a keystroke to exit the program. `readLine()` basically waits for standard input, and it is used here to stop the program from exiting before finishing its async operations.
7. Close the channel so that the consumers on it are canceled, too.

The output of this code snippet when run will be:

```
Press a key to exit...
Consumer 1: Apple
```

> **Note**: To finish the program, you need to press the **Enter** key.

Here, you can see that there is one channel to which some values are sent. Then there are two consumers — i.e., two `consumeEach` calls on the channel being executed to consume the values being emitted by the channel. Now, which of these two consumers gets the value is not obvious. In fact, if you run the same program many times you might see the below output, too:

```
Consumer 2: Apple
Press a key to exit...
```

> **Note**: You can find the executable version of the above snippet of code in the starter project in the file called **RaceConditionChannel.kt**.

Thus, as you can see, it is not obvious which consumer will get the value every time the program is executed. Based on which consumer receives the value first, the value is consumed by that consumer and the other consumer does not get the value.

To mitigate this, the Kotlin Standard Library provides another type of channel called the **BroadcastChannel**.

The BroadcastChannel is non-blocking by nature and maintains a stream of values between the sender and the many receivers that subscribe.

> **Note**: This is an experimental API. It may be changed in future updates.

To do this BroadcastChannel uses the **openSubscription** function and subscribes to values being sent into the channel. It is important to understand here that only when the subscription is obtained will the consumer receive the values being sent into the channel. Anything sent before obtaining the subscription is not received by the subscribed consumers of the channel.

You will use a similar code snippet of the channel's race condition when there are many receivers. But this time you will make a slight modification. Take a look:

```
fun main() {

  val fruitArray = arrayOf("Apple", "Banana", "Pear", "Grapes",
      "Strawberry")
  // 1
  val kotlinChannel = BroadcastChannel<String>(3)

  runBlocking {

    // 2
    kotlinChannel.apply {
      send(fruitArray[0])
      send(fruitArray[1])
      send(fruitArray[2])
    }

    //3  Consumers
    GlobalScope.launch {
      // 4
      kotlinChannel.openSubscription().let { channel ->
        // 5
        for (value in channel) {
          println("Consumer 1: $value")
        }
        // 6
      }
    }
    GlobalScope.launch {
      kotlinChannel.openSubscription().let { channel ->
        for (value in channel) {
```

```
          println("Consumer 2: $value")
        }
      }
    }

    // 7
    kotlinChannel.apply {
      send(fruitArray[3])
      send(fruitArray[4])
    }

    // 8
    println("Press a key to exit...")
    readLine()

    // 9
    kotlinChannel.close()
  }
}
```

Here's what's going on above:

1. A `BroadcastChannel` with a capacity of three is created named `kotlinChannel`.

2. Start producing items and send them in the channel, all inside a launch coroutine builder. The first three items from `fruitArray` have already been sent in `kotlinChannel`.

3. Start consuming items from the channel.

4. Here, a subscription is opened on the `kotlinChannel` using the `openSubscription()` function — i.e., start listening to values being sent in the `kotlinChannel`.

5. Iterate over all the values in the channel and print them out.

6. When finished iterating over the values in the channel, the subscription is closed — i.e., stop listening to values being sent in the `kotlinChannel`.

7. Now that the subscription has been obtained on the `kotlinChannel`, send two more values in the `kotlinChannel`.

8. Wait for a keystroke to exit the program.

9. Close the channel so that the consumers on it are canceled, too.

The output of executing this code snippet will be:

```
Press a key to exit...
```

```
Consumer 2: Grapes
Consumer 1: Grapes
Consumer 2: Strawberry
Consumer 1: Strawberry
```

> **Note**: To finish the program, you need to press the **Enter** key.

As you can see, both the consumers that had opened subscription on the `BroadcastChannel` received both the values sent into the channel — i.e., **Grapes** and **Strawberry**. That is how the broadcast channel simplifies the whole process of broadcasting the values in the channel to all receivers.

> **Note**: You can find the executable version of the above snippet of code in the starter project in the file called **BroadcastChannelOpenSubscriptionExample.kt**.

Yet, there is one optimization that you can still do. Similar to how there is a `consumeEach` helper DSL defined for a channel, there is one defined for `BroadcastChannel`, which subscribes and performs the specified operation for each received item.

Take a look at the implementation of the consumeEach method:

```kotlin
public suspend inline fun <E>
BroadcastChannel<E>.consumeEach(action: (E) -> Unit) =
    consume {
        for (element in this) action(element)
    }
```

Diving deeper into the source code:

```kotlin
public inline fun <E, R> BroadcastChannel<E>.consume(block:
ReceiveChannel<E>.() -> R): R {
    val channel = openSubscription()
    try {
        return channel.block()
    } finally {
        channel.cancel()
    }
}
```

You will notice that consumeEach will call the openSubscription() method. That means we can replace openSubscription() calls with just the consumeEach DSL straight up.

In the last code snippet, simply replace the following lines of code:

```
kotlinChannel.openSubscription().let { channel ->
        for (value in channel) {
          println("Consumer 1: $value")
        }
        // subscription will be closed
}
```

With:

```
kotlinChannel.consumeEach { value ->
    println("Consumer 1: $value")
}
```

> **Note:** The replacement code snippet shown is only for Consumer 1, you will need to do the same replacement for Consumer 2

Now run the code snippet again. You will see that the results are the same. This is just a more concise and idiomatic Kotlin way of consuming values on a channel.

> **Note:** You can find the updated executable version of the above snippet of code in the starter project in the file called **BroadcastChannelExample.kt**.

Often times, one of the common use cases is to be able to get, at least, the most recently emitted value on subscription. This is where ConflatedBroadcast channel comes into play and is explained in the next section.

ConflatedBroadcast channel

Like a BroadcastChannel, **ConflatedBroadcastChannel** enables many subscribed receivers to consume items sent in the channel but it differs in one aspect: a ConflatedBroadcastChannel only emits the most recently sent item while the older items are lost. Also, any future subscribers to this channel will receive the item that was most recently emitted.

To understand how it works in practice, take a look at the following code snippet:

```
fun main() {

  val fruitArray = arrayOf("Apple", "Banana", "Pear", "Grapes",
      "Strawberry")

  // 1
  val kotlinChannel = ConflatedBroadcastChannel<String>()

  runBlocking {

    // 2
    kotlinChannel.apply {
      send(fruitArray[0])
      send(fruitArray[1])
      send(fruitArray[2])
    }

    // 3
    GlobalScope.launch {
      kotlinChannel.consumeEach { value ->
        println("Consumer 1: $value")
      }
    }
    GlobalScope.launch {
      kotlinChannel.consumeEach { value ->
        println("Consumer 2: $value")
      }
    }

    // 4
    kotlinChannel.apply {
      send(fruitArray[3])
      send(fruitArray[4])
    }

    // 5
    println("Press a key to exit...")
    readLine()

    // 6
    kotlinChannel.close()
  }
}
```

Going through this step-by-step:

1. A `ConflatedBroadcast` channel is created named `kotlinChannel`.

2. Start producing items and send them in the channel, all inside a launch coroutine builder. The first three items from `fruitArray` are already sent in `kotlinChannel`.

3. Start consuming items from the channel. Here a subscription is opened on the `kotlinChannel` and each emitted value is consumed and acted upon using the `consumeEach` DSL block — i.e., start listening to values being sent in the `kotlinChannel` and act on them as defined inside the DSL block.

4. Now that the subscription has been possibly obtained on the `kotlinChannel`, send two more values in the `kotlinChannel`.

5. Wait for a keystroke to exit the program.

6. Close the channel so that the consumers on it are canceled, too.

The output of executing this code snippet will be:

```
Press a key to exit...
Consumer 2: Strawberry
Consumer 1: Strawberry
```

> **Note**: To finish the program, you need to press the **Enter** key.

From the output, you can see that only the last emitted item in the channel, which is "Strawberry" — i.e., value at `fruitArray[4]`, is only consumed by the receivers. Initially, there were three items sent in the channel, but no subscriptions were made on the channel. Then two receivers subscribed to the channel. Next, two more items were sent in the channel namely "Grapes" and "Strawberry" in order. Since `ConflatedBroadcast` channel only sends the most recently emitted item, "Strawberry" was sent to both the subscribed receivers.

> **Note**: You can find the executable version of the above snippet of code in the starter project in the file called **ConflatedBroadcastChannelExample.kt**.

Notice that this example is exactly the same as the one for BroadcastChannel. The only difference is the kind of channel initialized in both. This was done specifically to show the difference in how BroadcastChannel and ConflatedBroadcastChannel works, as well as their output.

Another thing to note about how ConflatedBroadcastChannel differs from BroadcastChannel is their suspend behavior of the send operation. The send operation on a BroadcastChannel does not suspend if there are no receivers, but the send operation on a ConflatedBroadcastChannel never suspends at all.

ReactiveX vs. BroadcastChannel

Reactive programming uses a similar kind of approach to handle streams of data as the Kotlin coroutine channel. Like channels, reactive programming has **observables** with data sources that emit items and should be observed. Then you also have the **observer**, which is basically a consumer of items emitted by the observables. To track the flow of data, observers subscribe to observables, which emit data items and those are then consumed by observers. There can be many observers observing an observable.

Notice that the data flow here is unidirectional. Observables emit data items and observers consume the emitted data.

> **Note**: Reactive programming is a complete topic in itself on which a book can be written. You will be focusing on the reactive approach as it resembles the behavior of a broadcast channel.

To implement this approach in various languages, there are corresponding libraries. For JVM-based languages, you have RxJava, which simplifies and enables the reactive programming approach when writing code for the Java platform.

To add RxJava to your projects, you simply need to add the dependency in your build.gradle file with:

```
implementation "io.reactivex.rxjava2:rxjava:2.2.6"
```

> **Note**: As of this writing, RxJava is at version 2.2.6.

Once you sync your project, you will have access to RxJava classes.

RxJava consists of a class that enables broadcasting capabilities, called a **subject**. When you create a subject and send an element, all subscribers will get the same object at the same time.

Take a look at the code snippet below:

```
fun main() {
  val fruitArray = arrayOf("Apple", "Banana", "Pear", "Grapes",
      "Strawberry")
  // 1
  val subject = PublishSubject.create<String>()

  // 2
  subject.apply {
    onNext(fruitArray[0])
    onNext(fruitArray[1])
    onNext(fruitArray[2])
  }

  // 3
  subject.subscribe {
    println("Consumer 1: $it")
  }
  subject.subscribe {
    println("Consumer 2: $it")
  }

  // 4
  subject.apply {
    onNext(fruitArray[3])
    onNext(fruitArray[4])
  }

  // 5
  println("Press a key to exit...")
  readLine()

  // 6
  subject.onComplete()
}
```

Here:

1. An instance of type **PublishSubject** is created and called `subject`.

2. Start producing items — i.e., publish them using the `subject.onNext(item)` function. Here, you will see that the first three items from the `fruitArray` are published to the `subject`.

3. Subscribe to items published from the `subject` using `subject.subscribe{}` — i.e., start listening to items `subject` is publishing. When a value is published then they are printed out to the standard console.

4. Next, publish two more values from the `subject`.

5. Wait for a keystroke to exit the program.

6. Signal completion of the subscription.

The output of executing this code snippet will be:

```
Consumer 1: Grapes
Consumer 2: Grapes
Consumer 1: Strawberry
Consumer 2: Strawberry
Press a key to exit...
```

> **Note**: To finish the program, you need to press the **Enter** key.

Here, you will notice three things:

1. This code snippet is very similar to `BroadcastChannel`'s code snippet. The only thing that changed was that the channel was replaced by a subject, and the corresponding methods for sending/consuming were used when it came to using subjects. There are two observers/consumers subscribed to the subject and, when a value is published from the subject, the observers all receive the value.

2. The output is the same, although it is ordered for the subject.

3. Before the subscription is made, values published by the subject are ignored. Once the subscription is made, the two values published by the subject are received by both the observers.

> **Note**: You can find the executable version of the above snippet of code in the starter project in the file called **RxSubjectExample.kt**.

Similarly to how the **Subject** is the dual of the **BroadcastChannel** in behavior, **ConflatedBroadcastChannel** has a dual in RxJava called **BehaviorSubject**.

It means an observer will receive all the elements that the source of information emits after its subscription, but also the last item emitted by the source of information before the observer subscribed to the **BehaviorSubject**.

Take a look at the code snippet below to get an idea of how it works:

```
fun main() {

  val fruitArray = arrayOf("Apple", "Banana", "Pear", "Grapes",
      "Strawberry")
  // 1
  val subject = BehaviorSubject.create<String>()

  // 2
  subject.apply {
    onNext(fruitArray[0])
    onNext(fruitArray[1])
    onNext(fruitArray[2])
  }

  // 3
  subject.subscribe {
    println("Consumer 1: $it")
  }

  subject.subscribe {
    println("Consumer 2: $it")
  }

  // 4
  subject.apply {
    onNext(fruitArray[3])
    onNext(fruitArray[4])
  }

  // 5
  println("Press a key to exit...")
  readLine()

  // 6
  subject.onComplete()
}
```

Taking each part in turn:

1. An instance of type **BehaviorSubject** is created, named as `subject`.

2. Start producing items — i.e., publish them using `subject.onNext(item)` function. Here, you will see the first three items from the `fruitArray` are published to the `subject`.

3. Subscribe to items published from the `subject` using `subject.subscribe{}` — i.e., start listening to items `subject` is publishing. When a value is published then they are printed out to the standard console.

4. Next, publish two more values from the `subject`.

5. Wait for a keystroke to exit the program.

6. Signal completion of the subscription.

The output of executing this code snippet will be:

```
Consumer 1: Pear
Consumer 2: Pear
Consumer 1: Grapes
Consumer 2: Grapes
Consumer 1: Strawberry
Consumer 2: Strawberry
Press a key to exit...
```

> **Note**: To finish the program, you need to press the **Enter** key.

Here, when you execute this code snippet, the output is very interesting. First, the **BehaviorSubject** publishes three values. Now, two observers subscribe to the subject and as soon as the subscription completes the most recent value published, which is `fruitArray[2]` — i.e., "Pear" is received by both the observers. Next, when the subject publishes two more values, both the subscribed observers receive the values and consume it — i.e., print it to the standard console.

> **Note**: You can find the executable version of the above snippet of code in the starter project in the file called **RxBehaviorSubjectExample.kt**.

You will notice it is a bit different in behavior than **ConflatedBroadcastChannel** because it receives the last published value when observers subscribe and then waits until the observers are unsubscribed for the values published by the subject to be received by the observers. But for **ConflatedBroadcastChannel** only the last published value is received.

Key points

- With **channels**, if you have many receivers waiting to receive items from the channel, the emitted item will be consumed by the first receiver and all other receivers will not get the item individually.
- **BroadcastChannel** enables many subscribed receivers to consume all items sent in the channel.
- **ConflatedBroadcastChannel** enables many subscribed receivers to consume the most recently sent item provided the receiver consumes items slower.
- **Subject** from RxJava is the dual of the **BroadcastChannel** in behavior.
- **BehaviorSubject** from RxJava is the dual of **ConflatedBroadcastChannel** in behavior.

Where to go from here?

Kotlin channels introduce a very simplified approach to handling a stream of data with well set-up constructs to enable better and faster development. This is not all the information about channels because there are operators, which enable various operations on the consumption of results. You will read about those in detail in the next chapter.

Chapter 13: Producer & Actors
By Filip Babić

Multi-processing communication is one of the most enticing challenges you can face when developing multi-threaded software. Multi-threading technologies have been around for years and there are a few solutions that are industry standard. In this chapter, you'll be learning about two of those solutions, which can be really useful in your future applications.

Producing and consuming data

The first is the **producer-consumer** problem, which describes a two-process communication standard. One process produces data, places it in a queue, while the other picks items off of the queue, one by one, and consumes it. Hence the name. A problem arises if the consumer tries to pick data off an empty queue, or if the producer tries to overfill the queue. This is familiar to what you've learned so far in the book.

Furthermore, this pattern doesn't have to describe a 1:1 relationship. One approach is for the producer to try and push as many events in the queue, and the system to consume them as fast as possible, using multiple consumers.

If you think about it, you can picture a **thread pool** the same way. You have one producer or **worker**, and **threads**, which are the consumers.

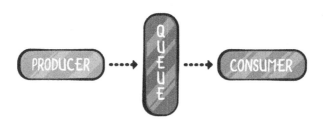

Producer-consumer problem

Just like with pipelines, producers face the same challenge. As previously mentioned, a full or an empty queue could cause loss of information, thread blocking or exceptions. On the other hand, creating producers with coroutines is much easier and avoids these problems. Let's see how you'd create a basic producer using the Coroutines API.

Creating a producer

If you haven't already, open up the starter project for this chapter with the name **produce_actor**. Then, open **Produce.kt** in the **producer** package in the project. Finally, to create a producer, call `produce()`, on a `CoroutineScope`, in `main()`, like so:

```
val producer = GlobalScope.produce<Int>(capacity = 10) {}
```

To understand what the snippet does, let's take a look at the `produce()` signature, and what you can pass to it:

```
public fun <E> CoroutineScope.produce(
  context: CoroutineContext = EmptyCoroutineContext,
  capacity: Int = 0,
  @BuilderInference block: suspend ProducerScope<E>.() -> Unit
): ReceiveChannel<E>
```

You can pass it a context, which by default it receives from the `CoroutineScope` you may have passed in. You can define the `capacity`, which is the maximum number of items it can hold in the queue. And finally, you pass in a lambda from which you can define the behavior of the producer.

You'll also notice something in the lambda, the `BuilderInference`. This annotation allows the compiler to infer the type of the outer generic function, using functions inside the lambda block. So if you use a function that the `ProducerScope` can run with like a `String`, `produce()` will know it's going to create a `Producer<String>`.

Producing values

The producer has to produce some values. Since the return type of `produce()` is a `ReceiveChannel`, you can't use it for sending values. You have to do it within the lambda you pass as parameter. The simplest way would be using a loop. Change the code in `main()`, in **Produce.kt**, to this:

```
val producer = GlobalScope.produce(capacity = 10) {
  while (isActive) {
    if (!isClosedForSend) {
      val number = Random.nextInt(0, 20)
      if (offer(number)) {
        println("$number sent")
      } else {
        println("$number discarded")
      }
    }
  }
}
```

In this simple example, you run a loop that produces numbers from within a coroutine. Since you do it in a coroutine, this is not really a blocking call, as the program can finish, without having to wait for the **infinite** loop to stop.

Here, you're calling `offer()`, which attempts to queue a new element, if there's room for the element, otherwise the element is going to be discarded. This function has a `Boolean` return type, which is `true` in the former case and `false` in the latter.

It's very useful, and you can use it in order to print a different message in the output. Before **offering** the random number, you check in the loop the value of the isClosedForSend, which becomes false as soon as the channel is closed explicitly with close() or because of an exception.

It's very interesting to note that if you run the code now you'll get nothing in the output. This is because produce() is not blocking and the application exits immediately.

In order to see some output you can add a simple Thread.sleep() to the end of the code like this:

```
val producer = GlobalScope.produce(capacity = 10) {
  while (isActive) {
    if (!isClosedForSend) {
      val number = Random.nextInt(0, 20)
      if (offer(number)) {
        println("$number sent")
      } else {
        println("$number discarded")
      }
    }
  }
}
Thread.sleep(30L)
```

You can wait a very short period of time like 30ms in order to have an output like this where the values will obviously be different because they are randomly generated:

```
3 sent
17 sent
2 sent
9 sent
15 sent
11 sent
16 sent
13 sent
10 sent
11 sent
9 discarded
8 discarded
. . .
```

As you can see the previous code generates 10 elements — the capacity of the channel — and then it discards the following because the channel is full and offer() returns false.

This suggests a different option for implementing the same producer. Instead of checking for the return value of the `offer` method you can use `isFull` whose meaning is pretty obvious. Its value is `true` when the channel is full. You can then change the previous code with this:

```
val producer = GlobalScope.produce(capacity = 10) {
  while (isActive) {
    val number = Random.nextInt(0, 20)
    if (!isFull) {
      if (offer(number)) {
        println("$number sent")
      }
    } else {
      println("$number discarded")
    }
  }
}
Thread.sleep(30L)
```

Now, you check `isFull` and you invoke `offer()` only if it's going to be successful because the channel still has a place for the value. The discarded message is now in the `else` block of the test on the `isFull`. You can do better, though. In the previous code you're generating the random value even if you don't offer it to the channel and, if the channel is full, you're basically wasting it. A better approach is the one which uses the `send` method instead of `offer()`. `send()` is actually suspendable and it allows you to write the following code:

```
val producer = GlobalScope.produce(capacity = 10) {
  while (isActive) {
    val number = Random.nextInt(0, 20)
    send(number)
    println("$number sent")
  }
}
Thread.sleep(30L)
```

In this case, you don't waste any values because `send()` is suspendable and it won't continue until the channel has enough space for it. You'll then get an output like this:

```
11 sent
3 sent
16 sent
1 sent
11 sent
17 sent
15 sent
11 sent
```

```
3 sent
11 sent
```

If you run the previous code, you'll only get the first 10 values and nothing will happen until you create a consumer for it. So let's move onto building that!

Consuming the values

The produce function conveniently returns a `ReceiveChannel`. This means you can iterate through the values, transform or filter them, or run an infinite loop, reading the values.

Let's start off with the most basic example: a `while` loop. Add this code to the end of `main` function:

```kotlin
while (!producer.isClosedForReceive) {
  val number = producer.poll()

  if (number != null) {
    println("$number received")
  }
}
```

If you build and run the application, you'll see output like this:

```
12 sent
18 sent
19 sent
12 sent
17 sent
6 sent
9 sent
9 sent
1 sent
5 sent
12 received
3 sent
18 received
. . .
```

In the previous code you're invoking `poll()` on the producer until its `isClosedForReceive` has a `false` value. This is happening if the channel has been closed on the producer side invoking the `close` method and all the values have been consumed. Because you use the `poll` method you have to check for nullability.

This is because poll is not blocking and it returns `null` if the channel is empty and so something else should be produced. If in the producer side you're using `send()`, `null` values should never happen. A better approach uses coroutines.

Replace the `while(true)` loop with the following code:

```
GlobalScope.launch {
  producer.consumeEach { println("$it received") }
}

Thread.sleep(30L)
```

This code does the same thing as the previous loop. Because you're launching a coroutine, you still have to halt the program so it doesn't finish before printing out any numbers, which is why you added the `Thread.sleep()` invocation.

In real systems this will run normally, as long as your application is running. What `consumeEach` does is listen for each of the items, and processes **it**, ultimately removing it from the producer queue.

`poll()` is not blocking, and it's returning `null` if nothing is available. You also have the option of using the `receive` method, which is suspendable. You can then replace the previous code with this:

```
GlobalScope.launch {
  while (isActive) {
    val value = producer.receive()
    println("$value received")
  }
}

Thread.sleep(30L)
```

While the producer is active you can wait for a value and then display it.

If you use a coroutine you also have another very simple way of implementing a consumer. Try to replace the previous consumer code with this:

```
GlobalScope.launch {
  for (value in producer) {
    println("$value received")
  }
}

Thread.sleep(30L)
```

In this case, you can use the classic `for` loop over the producer and print all its value. The `ReceiveChannel` implements the `Iterable` in a proper way so you can use what you normally use for iterating over a collection in the context of a producer/consumer pattern.

As you can see, all of these are easy to implement as opposed to having to write a complex synchronization mechanism yourself. The **producer-consumer** pattern is really useful when you're trying to broadcast events from one place for other people to listen to.

A different paradigm of multi-threaded communication is when you're trying to delegate events to others, such as work that you need to complete. This is called the **actor model**. Let's see what it's about.

Acting upon data

The **actor model** is a bit different from what you've seen so far and it exists as a possible solution for a very common problem: **sharing data in a multithreading environment**. When you create an instance of an object, you know you can interact with it using the operations it exposes: its **interface**. Most of the objects also have some **state**, which can change after interacting with other objects. Everything is simple if all the objects collaborate on the same thread. In a multithreading environment you have to introduce complexity in the code in order to make all the classes **type safe**. When multiple threads access shared data you know you can have problems like data race conditions. Locks, implicit or not, are a possible solution but are usually difficult to manage and test.

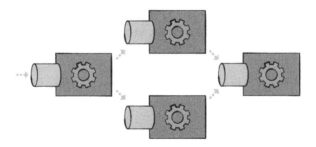

Actors interact using messages

You can solve this problem by allowing the interaction with the object only to a specific component, which is also the only consumer of a queue. If you want to interact with the object in a thread safe way, you just have to send messages to the queue of the encapsulating component. The component then is only responsible to consume the message and, depending on its type, change the state of the object it encapsulates. This component is then called an **actor**.

When you implement a solution using **actors** you're basically defining **local** or **private** states and what are the possible operations on them. Each operation maps to a message type you can send to its queue.

Usually an actor is responsible for a single operation and can delegate some other operations to other actors if needed in order to have a clear separation of concerns.

The usage of actors helps us to focus on the specific operation and ignoring all the multithreading aspects, which can be very difficult to implement.

Handling actors properly

Having many actors at your disposal, being limited only by memory, is both a great thing and a challenge. The true challenge comes when you have to clean up old actors. If you hold a reference to your actor children, in each of the actors, you'd end up with a large reference tree. And you couldn't clean up actors as you go, since they hold references to new, fresh actors, as well.

You could create threads, in which you create new actors, so you don't hold an implicit reference to the parent, but then again, threads are even more expensive.

Kotlin Coroutines have a more efficient way to create actors, which avoids lots of strong references and thread allocations. Let's see how to do so.

Building actors using coroutines

> **Note**: The Jetbrains team is currently working on both the Flow API, and **complex actors**. They haven't yet decided what to do with the current Actor API, and as such it's been marked as obsolete. However, the API still works, so it's worth checking it out.

An **actor** is then a consumer bound to a specific channel that you can create invoking a simple coroutine builder called — drumroll — **actor**. In order to understand how it works it can be useful to have a look at its signature:

```
public fun <E> CoroutineScope.actor(
    context: CoroutineContext = EmptyCoroutineContext,
    capacity: Int = 0,
    start: CoroutineStart = CoroutineStart.DEFAULT,
    onCompletion: CompletionHandler? = null,
    block: suspend ActorScope<E>.() -> Unit
): SendChannel<E>
```

It is very similar to produce(), but it has a few more parameters you can pass. The CoroutineStart parameter you've already learned about, but there's also the CompletionHandler. You can use this handler to listen to actor completions. And, finally, there's the block parameter, which is of the type ActorScope<E>.() -> Unit. This is another CoroutineScope, which also holds a reference to its enclosing channel, so you could poll for new values. It's important to note how the return type is SendChannel. The returned object is the one you're going to use in order to interact with the actor you've just created.

Now, since you know a bit more about actors, open up **Actor.kt**, in the **actor** package, and you should see this snippet of code:

```
// 1
object completionHandler : CompletionHandler {
  override fun invoke(cause: Throwable?) {
    println("Completed!")
  }
}

fun main() {
  // 2
  val actor = GlobalScope.actor<String>(
      onCompletion = completionHandler,
      capacity = 10) {
    // 3
    for (data in channel) {
      println(data)
    }
  }

  // 4
  (1..10).forEach {
    actor.offer(Random.nextInt(0, 20).toString())
  }
  // 5
  actor.close()
  // 6
```

```
    Thread.sleep(500L)
}
```

Here is what each part of the above code snippet is doing:

1. You create a simple implementation of the **CompletionHandler**, which just prints a **Completed!** message when the actor is complete. This is happening when close() is invoked on its SendChannel.

2. Here you create the **actor** passing a capacity of 10 and the reference to the CompletionHandler.

3. In the lambda of the actor you define the consumer logic. Here you're just printing what the actor is receiving. In general here is where you can change the state of the actor depending on the received message. It's useful to note how the reference of the **channel** is implicitly available in the block of the actor.

4. You implement a simple loop, which offers 10 values into the channel for the actor.

5. You sent all your values and you can close the actor.

6. In order to see the output you can use a Thread.sleep().

If you run the code, you'll get an output like the following:

```
5
4
19
10
8
15
5
6
0
8
Completed!
```

As you can see, you'll get 10 random values and the **Completed!** message as expected.

Delegating actor workload

The actor model, however, relies on delegating excess work to others. So, for example, if you're building a robot-powered-storage system, where everything is organized by robots, you have to find a way to optimize the workload.

If a certain robot has too much to carry around, it can pass some of its work on to a different robot. And if that second robot has too much work, it can pass it to a third one, and so forth.

See how this would look in code. Select everything in **Actor.kt**, and replace with the following code:

```kotlin
fun main() {

  val items = listOf(
      Package(1, "coffee"),
      Package(2, "chair"),
      Package(3, "sugar"),
      Package(4, "t-shirts"),
      Package(5, "pillowcases"),
      Package(6, "cellphones"),
      Package(7, "skateboard"),
      Package(8, "cactus plants"),
      Package(9, "lamps"),
      Package(10, "ice cream"),
      Package(11, "rubber duckies"),
      Package(12, "blankets"),
      Package(13, "glass")
  )

  val initialRobot = WarehouseRobot(1, items)
```

```
    initialRobot.organizeItems()
    Thread.sleep(5000)
}
```

Here we're using two pre-baked classes: the **Package.kt** and the **WarehouseRobot.kt**. **Package.kt** is pretty simple; it's just a model holding some data. However, **WarehouseRobot.kt** is where the party's at. Open up **WarehouseRobot.kt**. First you see the constructor with its parameters, and the **companion object**:

```kotlin
class WarehouseRobot(private val id: Int,
                     private var packages: List<Package>) {

    companion object {
        private const val ROBOT_CAPACITY = 3
    }
    ...
}
```

Each robot will have an **id** and a set of **packages** it needs to organize around. Furthermore, each robot has the same package capacity, which is three packages per robot. Of course, each robot can process the items given to it:

```kotlin
private fun processItems(items: List<Package>) {
    val actor = GlobalScope.actor<Package>(
    capacity = ROBOT_CAPACITY) {

        var hasProcessedItems = false

        while (!packages.isEmpty()) {
            val currentPackage = poll()

            currentPackage?.run {
                organize(this)

                packages -= currentPackage
                hasProcessedItems = true
            }

            if (hasProcessedItems && currentPackage == null) {
                cancel()
            }
        }
    }

    items.forEach { actor.offer(it) }
}

private fun organize(warehousePackage: Package) =
```

```
            println("Organized package " +
                "${warehousePackage.id}:" +
                warehousePackage.name)
```

In this function, the robot creates a new actor, which uses the ROBOT_CAPACITY as the maximum number of items in the queue. The actor also has to use the hasProcessedItems flag, otherwise it'd close early, before there are any items processed. This happens because poll() returns a null item if the actor didn't receive any items yet.

Once the robot processes an item, it changes its inner state, or packages, by removing the processed item from the list. Only the actor can change this private state internally.

But the key function, here, which makes this class an actor is organizeItems():

```
fun organizeItems() {
  val itemsToProcess = packages.take(ROBOT_CAPACITY)
  val leftoverItems = packages.drop(ROBOT_CAPACITY)

  packages = itemsToProcess

  val packageIds = packages.map { it.id }
      .fold("") { acc, item -> "$acc$item " }

  processItems(itemsToProcess)

  if (leftoverItems.isNotEmpty()) {
    GlobalScope.launch {
      val helperRobot = WarehouseRobot(id.inc(), leftoverItems)

      helperRobot.organizeItems()
    }
  }

  println("Robot #$id processed following packages:$packageIds")
}
```

Initially, the robot has to divide the items up into those it has to process and the ones that it doesn't have the capacity for. Once it processes its items and if there are leftovers, it sends them to another robot. Finally, it returns to its station, waiting for more work. This looks a bit like **recursion**, since robots are creating robots within themselves. But effectively, the helper robots are created in the GlobalScope, so their **parents** can finish and be cleared from memory before they finish themselves.

If you build and run `main()` in **Actor.kt**, you should see the following output:

```
Organized package 1:coffee
Organized package 2:chair
Organized package 3:sugar
Robot #2 processed following packages:4 5 6
Robot #1 processed following packages:1 2 3
Organized package 7:skateboard
Organized package 8:cactus plants
Organized package 9:lamps
Robot #3 processed following packages:7 8 9
Organized package 4:t-shirts
Organized package 5:pillowcases
Organized package 6:cellphones
Robot #4 processed following packages:10 11 12
Organized package 10:ice cream
Organized package 11:rubber duckies
Organized package 12:blankets
Organized package 13:glass
Robot #5 processed following packages:13
```

The robot organizing system works!

Acting in parallel

Right now, the packages are mostly ordered, with a few exceptions to the rule. This means that, usually, once the first robot finishes its work, the helper robot starts on its packages. However, you're building recursion-like work, which doesn't suffer from the `StackOverflowException` or `OutOfMemory` exception, since the actors get cleaned up one by one.

To make them run in parallel, simply change the order of `processItems()`, with the check for creating a new actor. The order should be like this:

```
fun organizeItems() {
  ...
  if (leftoverItems.isNotEmpty()) {
    GlobalScope.launch {
      val helperRobot = WarehouseRobot(id.inc(), leftoverItems)

      helperRobot.organizeItems()
    }
  }

  processItems(itemsToProcess)
  ...
}
```

This will first create all the actors, and then run the item processing. If you run the code now, the output should be different. It should be something similar to this:

```
Robot #3 processed following packages:7 8 9
Robot #1 processed following packages:1 2 3
Robot #5 processed following packages:13
Robot #2 processed following packages:4 5 6
Robot #4 processed following packages:10 11 12
Organized package 10:ice cream
Organized package 4:t-shirts
Organized package 11:rubber duckies
Organized package 5:pillowcases
Organized package 1:coffee
Organized package 13:glass
Organized package 2:chair
Organized package 6:cellphones
Organized package 12:blankets
Organized package 3:sugar
Organized package 7:skateboard
Organized package 8:cactus plants
Organized package 9:lamps
```

First, the actors are created and their processing prints out. Then the packages are organized depending on how fast each actor can consume the items. This can be much faster than having to run actors one-by-one, but it could also mean that if you have a large number of items left to organize, there will be a higher amount of memory allocation, and many more objects created.

For best performance, when building such systems, you should tweak the capacity of each actor, optimize their workload and data structures. You could also build tree-like structures, where you'd have both sequential and parallel actor computation.

Key points

- **Produce-consumer** pattern and the **actor model** are tried and tested mechanisms for multi-threading.

- Producer-consumer relationships are **one-to-many**, where you can consume the events from multiple places.

- The **actor model** is a way to share data in a multithread environment using a dedicated queue.

- The **actor model** allows you to offload large amounts of work to many smaller constructs.

- Actors have a **many-to-one** relationship, since you can send events from multiple places, but they all end up in one actor.

- Each actor can **create new actors**, delegating and offloading work.

- Building actors using **threads** can be expensive, which is where coroutines come in handy.

- Actors can be arranged to run in **sequential** order, or to run in **parallel**.

Where to go from here?

You now know how to build effective communication mechanisms, using `produce()` and `actor()`. You've got everything you need to connect multiple threads, or to fan out a large workload. In the next few chapters, you'll see how to build a different kind of mechanism of communication like broadcasting. You'll also see how channels' data can be transformed and combined.

So let's *channel* this positive energy and head over to the next chapter!

Chapter 14: Beginning with Coroutines Flow

By Filip Babić

Coroutines are amazing when it comes to bridging the synchronous and asynchronous worlds, to return values and communicate between threads. Most of the time that's what you want and need, but sometimes, computer systems require you to consume multiple values over a period of time.

And there are two different ways you can do this - using **sequences** and **streams**. However there are certain limitations to both approaches. You've already learned about sequences, but they force you to block the calling thread when you're observing values. So let's see what streams have to offer, and how they behave in code.

Streams of data

One of the key similarities between sequences and streams is that both constructs can generate an infinite amount of elements. Sequences usually do this by defining an operation which you run behind the scenes to build a value.

This is also the key difference between streams and sequences, as you usually build streams using a function or their constructor. You then have an **interface** between the provider of values and a consumer, exposing a different part of the interface to each side.

Take this snippet for example, which uses the **Reactive Extensions**, or **Rx**, version of observable streams of data:

```
val subject = BehaviorSubject.create<String>()

subject.subscribe(observer)
subject.onNext("one")
subject.onNext("two")
subject.onNext("three")
```

You create a `Subject`, which implements both sides of the stream interface. The provider can use functions such as `offer()`, `onNext()`, and `send()`, to fill the queue for the stream with values to consume. In this case it's using `onNext()` from Rx.

Every `Observer` which subscribes to this stream will receive all its events, from the moment they subscribed, until they unsubscribe, or the stream closes. The observer in Rx will look like this:

```
val observer = object: Observer<String> {

  override fun onNext(value: String) {
    // consume the value
  }

  override fun onError(throwable: Throwable) {
    // handle the error
  }

  override fun onComplete() {
    // the stream completed
  }
}
```

Every time you send any of the events to the `Observable` side of the `Subject`, it will send all those events to all of its `Observers`. It acts as a relay of data from one central point to multiple observing nodes. This is the general idea of streams. Being **observable** and sending the events to every single `Observer` which is listening to its data.

But, depending on the implementation of streams, you might have a different setup. One of the things each stream mechanism and implementation shares is the type of streams and **when** their values are propagated. As such, there are **hot** and **cold** streams of data. Let's consume them one at a time.

Hot streams

Hot streams behave just like TV channels, or radio stations. They keep sending events, and emitting their data, even though no one may be listening or watching the show. It's why they are called **hot**. As they don't care if there are any observers, they will keep on working and computing no matter what, from the moment you create them, until they close.

This is really good when you want values computed in the background fast, preparing them for multiple observers you already have waiting. But if you're going to be adding observers after the fact, then you could lose the data a hot stream might emit between the computation and the observers starting to listen to events.

Additionally, if the producer of values is hot, it can keep on producing values, even though there are no consumers. This effectively wastes resources, and you have to manually close the stream if you stop using it.

If you were to use coroutines to build such hot streams, you'd use the **Channel API**. They are hot by default and also support coroutines, making them a bit less leak-prone. But even if you used **structured concurrency** and coroutines within the Channels, you could potentially leak some resources until the CoroutineScope cancels.

This is why the idea of having a cold stream is important.

Cold streams

It makes sense that, if hot streams are computed right away, and work even without any observers, **cold** streams do the opposite. They are like the **builder pattern**, where you define a set of behaviors for a construct, upfront, and only when you call a *finalizing* function, does it become live and active.

Given that, cold streams are like a social event. You can prepare everything upfront, think of each specific detail you have to fulfill and organize, and only when you're certain that people are coming, does the event happen. Following the analogy, cold streams won't produce or send values, until they have an active Observer, to whom they can emit the events.

This is much better, because if there are no observers, there is no need to execute a potentaily heavy operation to produce a value. But if there is at least one observer, then you will compute the value and pass it down the stream, to any amount of consumers.

It sounds too good to be true, and there's a reason why hot and cold streams aren't used everywhere, and for every occasion. It's because streams have a lot of internal limitations, and there are a lot of features a good stream should support to be versatile.

Limitations of streams

In every-day programming, there are certain limitations to the way things should operate for optimal use. You don't want to waste resources, freeze the UI, lose data and so on. Some of these concepts apply to streams, as well. These limitations revolve around the same problem - the speed of producing and consuming the values.

If your producer is sending out too many values, and the consumer cannot process them fast enough, then you're bound to lose some data. To effectively process the values, you have to apply **backpresure**. This is the technical term for eliminating the bottleneck in the producer-consumer pair.

When the producer queue fills up, and the consumer can't process the values fast enough, you become bottlenecked from the consumer side. If however, the consumer is eating the values too fast, and it keeps waiting for more to be produced, you're bottlenecked on the producer side. Either way, one side has to halt - **block**, until the pair is balanced again.

Supporting backpressure

As you've learned, if one side of the producer-consumer pair is too fast or too slow in its job, you will lose data, or end up blocking the non-bottlenecked side. Unless you add backpressure support.

Backpressure can be achieved in different ways, such as using buffered underlying streams with a fixed capacity. This is the easiest solution, but also the most error prone, because you can easily use up a lot of computer memory, or even overflow the buffer. This, again, will cause a bottleneck, and you'll lose data. You could have the capacitiy of *unlimited*, but then you risk overflowing the memory.

Another way is to build a synchronization mechanism, where you'd pause and resume threads as bottlenecks occur, but this may be even worse, as you could be freezing threads for a long time, which is a waste of resources in the end. This is why it's important to **avoid blocking threads**, when building streams with backpressure. Because of this design requirement, the **Flow API** is a fresh new take on streams.

A new approach to streams

Having the best of both worlds, the **Flow API** supports cold, asynchronously-built streams of values, where the thread communication and backpressure support is implemented through the use of coroutines. When you think about it, it's the perfect combination.

Having coroutines at its foundation allows for **backpressure-by-design**. If your producer is overflowing the consumer, then you can **suspend the producer**, until you free up the queue of events you need to process. On the other hand, if your consumer is really fast, and you need to slow it down - introduce a delay, or a debounce period, all you have to do is apply the same logic - suspend the consumer, until it meets your conditions.

The other happy coincidence of coroutines is the **built-in context switching**. By abstracting away threading and dispatching, through the use of `CoroutineContexts`, you can easily switch the consumption of events from one thread to another, by passing in a different `CoroutineContext` from a `Dispatchers`. And it's performant, because you don't have to worry about thread allocation, since coroutines use predefined thread pools.

This seems a bit too good to be true, right? It feels as if the API will be very complicated, because it has to handle all those details a regular stream cannot intrinsically implement.

Well that's where the fun kicks in. Weirdly enough, Flow works based on only two interfaces - the `Flow` and the `FlowCollector`. For the sake of comparison, if you're coming from a reactive-driven world, the `Flow` would be like an `Observable`, whereas the `FlowCollector` would be something similar to an `Observer` - a **subscriber to events**.

Let's examine how they work.

Building Flows

To create a `Flow`, just like with standard coroutines, you have to use a **builder**. But first open up **Main.kt**, in the **starter project**, which you can find by navigating to the project files, the **starter** folder, and opening the **beginning_with_coroutines_flow** folder.

Next, find `main()`. It should be empty, but you're about to add the code it needs to build a `Flow`. Add the following snippet to `main()`, so it doesn't look so empty. Conveniently enough, `Flow`'s builder function is called `flow`:

```
val flowOfStrings = flow {
  for (number in 0..100) {
    emit("Emitting: $number")
  }
}
```

This snippet of code will build a `Flow<String>`, which calls `emit()` a hundred times, sending a `String` value to every observer which starts listening to the data. And to do that, you must call `collect()`. Add the following snippet under the `flow()` call:

```
GlobalScope.launch {
  flowOfStrings.collect { value ->
    println(value)
  }
}

Thread.sleep(1000)
```

`collect()` is a suspending function, and as such needs to be called from a coroutine, or another suspending function. From within, you have access to every single value you emit from within the `Flow` builder. In this case, you're consuming each value by printing it out.

Now, to understand how `Flow`s work from within, check the builder definition:

```
public fun <T> flow(@BuilderInference block: suspend
FlowCollector<T>.() -> Unit): Flow<T>
  = SafeFlow(block)
```

You create a `Flow<T>`, with `BuilderInference`, meaning that, just like with producers and actors, you devise the generic type from within the function constructor. Futhermore, the lambda `block` is of the type `FlowCollector<T>.() -> Unit`, meaning that the internal scope of the lambda will be a `FlowCollector`. This is great as you can both create a `Flow`, and `emit()` values directly to the collector. You have the entire API connected in one place, making it very simple and clean to use.

In one of the previous snippets, you collected the values from a `Flow`, but there's much more you can do with the `Flow`, before you consume the data.

Collecting and transforming values

Once you build a Flow, you can do many things with the stream, before the values reach the FlowCollector. Just like with Rx, or with collections in Kotlin, you can transform the values using operators like map(), flatMap(), reduce() and much more. Additionally, you can use operators like debounce(), delayFlow() and delayEach() to apply backpressure or delays manually for each item, or the entire Flow.

Take the following snippet for example:

```
GlobalScope.launch {
  flowOfStrings
    .map { it.split(" ") }
    .map { it.last() }
    .delayEach(100)
    .collect { value ->
      println(value)
    }
}
```

If you replace the previous way of consuming the Flow, and run main() again, you'll now see the values are mapped back to the actual numbers, after the String is split. Furthermore, you print each value with a small delay, ultimately suspending the Flow until the consumer is ready.

> **Note**: All of the operators above are marked with suspend, so you have to call them from within a coroutine or another suspending function. This keeps the API uniform, as Flows are built upon coroutines.

Switching the context

Another thing you can do with Flow events, is switch the context in which you'll consume them. To do that, you have to call flowOn(context: CoroutineContext), just like this:

```
GlobalScope.launch {
  flowOfStrings
    .map { it.split(" ") }
    .map { it.last() }
    .flowOn(Dispatchers.IO)
    .delayEach(100)
    .flowOn(Dispatchers.Default)
```

```
      .collect { value ->
        println(value)
      }
  }
```

In this snippet, you're calling `flowOn()` twice. The first time after defining the mapping operations, and then the second time after delaying every item for a hundred miliseconds. The real power of applying context switch's is that you can do it as many times as you want, for each operator you're calling on the `Flow`. However, whenever you call `flowOn()`, you're applying the context switch only on the preceding operators, as the documentation states:

```
/**
 * Changes the context where this flow is executed to
 * the given [context]. This operator is composable
 * and affects only preceding operators that do not have
 * its own context.
 * This operator is context preserving: [context] **does not**
 * leak into the downstream flow.
 * ...
 **/
```

Additionally, as the docs state, the context is not leaked into the downstream flow, and the rest of the `Flow` operators and chained calls do not know about the context switch, nor can they abuse the previous `CoroutineContext`.

Ultimately, it's important to know that the final consumption of events can happen only on the **original context**. This means that no matter how many context switches you apply to the `Flow`, the last context will be the same as the original one.

So if you create a `Flow` on the **main thread**, you'll have to consume the events on it, as well. This is something you have to be careful about, because otherwise, you'll get an exception, if you try to produce values in a different context than the one you're consuming events in.

Flow Constraints

Since `Flow` is really easy to use as-is, there have to be some constraints in order to keep people from abusing or breaking the API. There are two main things which each `Flow` should adhere to, and each use case should enforce - **preserving the context** and **being transparent with exceptions**.

Preserving the Flow context

As mentioned above, you have to be clean when using `CoroutineContexts` with the Flow API. The producing and consuming contexts have to be the same. This effectively means that you cannot have concurrent value production, because the `Flow` itself is **not thread safe**, and doesn't allow for such emmisions.

So if you try to run the following snippet:

```
val flowOfStrings = flow {
  for (number in 0..100) {

    GlobalScope.launch {
      emit("Emitting: $number")
    }
  }
}

GlobalScope.launch {
  flowOfStrings.collect()
}
```

You will receive an exception, saying you can't change the `Flow` concurrently.

If you want coroutines to be synchronized, and have the ability to concurrently produce values in the `Flow`, you can use `channelFlow()` instead, and `offer()` or `send()` to emit the values to the `FlowCollector`. Changing the code to the following snippet will work:

```
val flowOfStrings = channelFlow {
  for (number in 0..100) {

    withContext(Dispatchers.IO) {
      offer("Emitting: $number")
    }
  }
}

GlobalScope.launch {
  flowOfStrings.collect()
}
```

If not, then you should create the `Flow` values in a non-concurrent way, and then use `flowOn()`, to switch the `Flow` to any `CoroutineContext` you want, if you want to avoid using `channelFlow()`.

Additionally, the `Flow`'s `CoroutineContext` cannot be bound to a `Job`, and as such you shouldn't combine any `Jobs` with the context you're trying to switch the `Flow` to.

This is because the Flow shouldn't be something that's lifecycle-aware, and something which can be cancelled. Especially because you can effectively mix multiple CoroutineContexts using flowOn(), and introducing a Job can only break things, or make them unsafe.

Being transparent with exceptions

When dealing with exceptions in coroutines, it's relatively easy to bury them down. For example, by using async(), you could effectively receive an exception, but if you never call await(), you're not going to throw it for the coroutines to catch. Additionally, if you add a CoroutineExceptionHandler, when exceptions occur in coroutines they get propagated to it, ending the coroutine.

This is why Flow exposes a convenient function which behaves similar to flowOn(). You can use catch(), providing a lambda which will catch any exception you produce in the stream and any of its previous operators. Examine the snippet below:

```
flowOfStrings
  .map { it.split(" ") }
  .map { it[1] }
  .catch { it.printStackTrace() }
  .flowOn(Dispatchers.Default)
  .collect { println(it) }
```

Instead of mapping to it.last(), you're using indices. In case you receive an empty string, this will cause an IndexOutOfBoundsException. But because you're calling catch(), after map(), if an exception occurs, you'll catch it, and print its stack trace. This way, you'll be able to handle any exceptions from the original stream and the operators alike.

Change the way you build Flow, to this:

```
val flowOfStrings = flow {
  emit("")

  for (number in 0..100) {
    emit("Emitting: $number")
  }
}
```

You will now cause an exception to be thrown, but you'll see that the program doesn't crash. This is because catch() will stop the exception from throwing all the way up to cause your app to crash.

You will still get a stack trace from the exception. Add this line of code under `collect()` and within the coroutine, to be certain the program continues normally:

```
println("The code still works!")
```

Run the code once again. You should now see an exception's stack trace, and right after that `The code still works!`. This means `catch()` has stopped the exception from one of the stream operators from breaking the entire program. And the rest of the coroutine still runs and works like a charm.

In case you'd want to continue emitting values if an exception occurs, you have access to the original `FlowCollector` within `catch()`, and it's advised to simply call `emitAll()`, with the fallback values. Change the `GlobalScope.launch()` code to the following:

```
flowOfStrings
  .map { it.split(" ") }
  .map { it[1] }
  .catch {
    it.printStackTrace()
    // send the fallback value or values
    emit("Fallback")
  }
  .flowOn(Dispatchers.Default)
  .collect { println(it) }

println("The code still works!")
```

You should now see the exception stack trace printed out, as well as `Fallback` and `The code still works!`. This shows you that you can catch exceptions in streams, handle them correctly, and continue the stream with some fallback values. You won't break the outer coroutine, even if an exception occurs and is caught with `catch()`!

Key Points

- Sometimes you need to build more than one value asynchronously, this is usually done with **sequences** or **streams**.
- **Sequences** are **lazy and cold**, but blocking when you need to consume events. It's better to use and suspend coroutines instead.
- If you build **streams** using `Channels`, then you have coroutine support and suspendability, but they are **hot** by default.

- Being cold means the data isn't computed, **until you start observing**. As opposed to being cold, being hot means the data is computed right away, **with, or without any observers**.
- As such, streams have two sides - the **producer**, or **observable** construct, and a **consumer**, or the **observer** construct.
- The main limitations of streams are they are **blocking and use backpressure**.
- Blocking happens when a stream needs to produce or consume events.
- **Backpressure** is when a stream is producing or consuming events too fast, and one side has to be slowed down, to balance the stream.
- Backpressure is usually done through **blocking the thread** of a producer or a consumer.
- A good stream **avoids blocking**, supports **context switching** while still allowing for backpressure.
- The Flow API is built upon coroutines, allowing for **suspending**.
- Because you can **suspend a consumer or a producer**, you get intrinsic backpressure support.
- Additionally, you're **avoiding blocking**, which is what a good stream should do.
- To create a Flow, simply call flow(), and provide a way to emit values to the FlowCollectors which decide to process the values.
- To attach a FlowCollector to a Flow, you have to call collect(), with a lambda in which you will consume each of the values.
- collect() is a suspending function, so it has to be within a coroutine or another suspending function.
- You have the access to a FlowCollector from within collect(), so you can emit values.
- Flows can be transformed and mutated by various operators like map(), flatMap().
- You can apply manual backpressure using debounce(), delayEach() and delayFlow().
- Switching the context of a Flow allows you to change the threads in which you consume each piece of data, or perform each operator.

- To switch context, call `flowOn(context)` after the operators you wish to switch the context of.

- The `Flow` collects the values always in the context of the `CoroutineScope` it is located in. So if you call `collect()` on the main thread, you'll also consume the values there.

- `Flow`s don't allow you to produce values concurrently. If you try to do that, an exception will occur.

- If you do need to produce values from multiple threads, you can use `channelFlow()`.

- It's better to use `flowOn()` to switch contexts of the `Flow`, than to bury them down in coroutines.

- `Flow`s should be transparent when it comes to exceptions.

- To handle exceptions with `Flow`s, use the `catch()` operator.

- `catch()` will intercept any uncaught exceptions, from all the operators you called before `catch()` itself.

Chapter 15: Testing Coroutines

By Filip Babić

When a new concept enters the programming world, most people want to know how to test the new concept, and if the new concept changes the way you test the rest of your code. Testing asynchronous code to make sure it runs and functions correction is a good thing. Naturally, people started asking how do you test coroutines, when it's such a *different* mechanism, compared to what used to be used in the JVM world.

The process of testing code is usually tied with writing **Unit and Integration tests**. This is code which you can run fast, debug, and use to confirm that a piece of software you've written is still working properly after you apply some changes to the code. Or rather that it doesn't work, because you've changed it, and now you should update the tests to reflect all the remaining cases.

Unit tests run a single **unit of code**, which should be as small as possible - like a small function's **input and output**. Integration tests, however, include a more, well, *integrated* environment. They usually test multiple classes working together. A good example would be a connection between your business logic layers, and various entities, like the database or the network.

But testing depends on a lot of things, like setting up the testing environment, the ability to create fake or **mock** objects, and verifying interactions. Let's see how to do some of those things with coroutines.

Getting started

To start with writing tests, you have to have a piece of code that you will test out! Open up this chapter's folder, named **testing-coroutines** and find the **starter** project. Import the project, and you can explore the code and the project structure.

First, within the **contextProvider** folder, you have the `CoroutineContextProvider`, and its implementation. This is a vital part of the testing setup because you'll use this to provide a test `CoroutineContext`, for your coroutines.

```kotlin
class CoroutineContextProviderImpl(
    private val context: CoroutineContext
) : CoroutineContextProvider {

    override fun context(): CoroutineContext = context
}
```

Next, the **model** package simply holds the `User` which you'll fetch and display in code, and use to test if the code is working properly.

```kotlin
data class User(val id: String, val name: String)
```

Next, the **presentation** package holds a simple class to represent the **business logic** layer of the code. You'll use **MainPresenter.kt** to imitate the fetching of a piece of data.

```kotlin
class MainPresenter {

    suspend fun getUser(userId: String): User {
        delay(1000)

        return User(userId, "Filip")
    }
}
```

Finally, you'll pass the data you fetch to the **view layer**, which will then print it out.

```kotlin
class MainView(
    private val presenter: MainPresenter
) {

    var userData: User? = null

    fun fetchUserData() {
        GlobalScope.launch(Dispatchers.IO) {
            userData = presenter.getUser("101")
        }
    }
```

```
  }
  fun printUserData() {
    println(userData)
  }
}
```

One last thing you have to add, to be able to test code and coroutines, are the Gradle dependencies. If you open up **build.gradle**, you'll see these two lines of code:

```
    testImplementation "org.jetbrains.kotlinx:kotlinx-coroutines-test:
      $kotlin_coroutines_version"
    testImplementation 'junit:junit:4.12'
```

The former introduces helper functions and classes, specifically to test coroutines, and the latter gives you the ability to use the **JUnit4** testing framework, for the JVM.

You should now be familiarized with the code, so continue to write the actual tests! :]

Writing tests for Coroutines

If you've never written tests on the JVM, know that there's a couple of different frameworks you can use and many different approaches to testing. For the sake of simplicity, you'll write a simple, **value-asserting** test, using the JUnit4 framework for the JVM test suite.

The name states what the test will do - assert and compare some values. This is one of the most basic test types you could write. In the **Project View**, open the **MainViewTest** file under the **test** -> **view** package. This is where you will begin writing your tests. Next, add the following code:

```
package view

import org.junit.Assert.assertEquals
import org.junit.Assert.assertNull
import org.junit.Test
import presentation.MainPresenter

class MainViewTest {

  private val mainPresenter by lazy { MainPresenter() }
  private val mainView by lazy { MainView(mainPresenter) }

  @Test
  fun testFetchUserData() {
```

```
    // todo add test code
  }
}
```

This is a basic example of what a test class should look like. You should have all the dependencies you need to be declared above, and set up, with the tests following after the declarations.

But your test is still empty. To make it do something, you have to fill it with the code you need to verify and the values you need to assert and check. You'll do this with a slightly modified **AAA** approach. AAA stands for **Arrange, Act and Assert**. Let's examine each of the steps:

- **Arrange** - Prepare all the data and dependencies you need, before you execute your tests. A good example would be prefilling the database with some values you're trying to fetch and compare.

- **Act** - Call the functions which produce results or achieve some behavior, which you will test or compare later on.

- **Assert** - Verify function calls, and if the code behavior is correct, or compare the received values with the expected results.

By doing so, you're splitting the test code into three sections, making it more readable, and clear, as to what you're testing and why.

Change the `testFetchUserData()` code to the following:

```
@Test
fun testFetchUserData() {
  // initial state
  assertNull(mainView.userData)

  // updating the state
  mainView.fetchUserData()

  // checking the new state, and printing it out
  assertEquals("Filip", mainView.userData?.name)
  mainView.printUserData()
}
```

It's fairly easy to follow the code, as not much is going on. You have to first assume the initial state within `MainView` is `null`, and then proceed to fetch the data. Once the data fetching finishes, you should check the state again, to see if the data matches what you returned in code. If that's fine, you can print out the data and see the output in the test console.

> **Note**: You're using `assertEquals()` and `assertNull()` from the JUnit framework, but there are many other functions in the framework to compare values.

To run this test click on the green run button that shows up in the gutter next to your `testFetchUserData()` method.

```
java.lang.AssertionError:
Expected :Filip
Actual   :null
<Click to see difference>
```

You should see a similar output. If everything's so straightforward, then why did the test fail? Well, it's because of how coroutines are built internally, that the underlying code didn't execute properly, to update the data. Since multi-threading is involved, and this is only a simple test environment, the runner doesn't know how to launch coroutines as it would in a real-world app, and as such, you don't get a result back. This, in turn, causes the assertion to fail, ultimately failing your entire test! But there is a way to mitigate this, by **setting up the test environment to be coroutine-friendly**.

Setting up the test environment

The problem you're facing when running the test is because of the way coroutines and test environments work internally. Because you're hardcoding the `MainPresenter` and `MainView` calls to the `GlobalScope` and `Dispatchers.IO`, you're losing the ability for the test JVM environment to adapt to coroutines.

To avoid this, you have to be explicit about your threading rules in tests, when testing coroutine-related code. There are a couple of small steps you have to take, to fully achieve this, so let's start with the simplest - **forcing coroutines to block**.

Running the tests as blocking

One of the greatest benefits of coroutines is the ability to **suspend instead of block**. This proves to be a powerful mechanism, which allows for things like simple context switching and thread synchronization, parallelism and much more.

However, when dealing with unit tests, you don't want the code to suspend. Because if it does, you're effectively losing valuable time, which you could otherwise use for writing or running more tests! To avoid the suspension of code, and force the coroutines to be blocking, you have to wrap the test in `runBlocking()` or a `runBlockingTest()`. They are special coroutine builders, which are built just for this occasion.

There is a difference between them though. You should use `runBlocking()` when it's a piece of code that has to bridge the non-coroutine to coroutine-power code, such as when dealing with external libraries.

`runBlockingTest`, however, is specifically useful when it comes to tests. It uses `runBlocking` underneath, but it's an extension function on `TestCoroutineScope`, which is a special type of `CoroutineScope`. You'll learn more about it later on.

```
/**
 * Convenience method for calling [runBlockingTest]
 * on an existing [TestCoroutineScope].
 */
@ExperimentalCoroutinesApi // Since 1.2.1, tentatively till
1.3.0
public fun TestCoroutineScope.runBlockingTest(
block: suspend TestCoroutineScope.() -> Unit) =
runBlockingTest(coroutineContext, block)
```

It's still experimental, but should be out with the `1.3.0` version of coroutines, just as the documentation above states. There's not much to see here, other than it calls to a global function with the same name. If you check out the documentation of that function, by using right-clicking, and selecting to **Go To -> Declaration**, you should see a bit more documentation.

Simply put, the function takes in all the `async()` and `launch()` calls which you do within your test code, which contain `delay()` calls, and advances the time for you, so that you can retrieve the values immediately, instead of waiting for the suspension to end. So if you have an example test, like the snippet in the documentation:

```
@Test
fun exampleTest() = runBlockingTest {
  val deferred = async {
    delay(1_000)
    async {
      delay(1_000)
    }.await()
  }

  deferred.await() // result available immediately
}
```

You can add any delays between the code, and they should be **fast-forwarded**. But all of this works with the TestCoroutineScope, so you have to also learn what that is.

Using test CoroutineScope and CoroutineContext

To start using runBlockingTest(), you have to integrate the rest of the test environment, for coroutines. Two things will ultimately help you control and affect the coroutines and other suspending functions within your test code. The TestCoroutineScope and TestCoroutineContext. Add the following declarations above your testFetchUserData() method:

```
// 1
private val testCoroutineDispatcher = TestCoroutineDispatcher()

// 2
private val testCoroutineScope =
  TestCoroutineScope(testCoroutineDispatcher)
```

These two values will help you dispatch the coroutines in the right contexts and within correct scopes so that you can test them cleanly and correctly. The first is the TestCoroutineDispatcher, which helps coroutines run immediately, and with the ability to control internal system clocks. You can also choose to pauseDispatcher() if you need to pause the execution, and to resumeDispatcher() when you're ready again.

The second is the TestCoroutineScope, which exposes all the functions to control the CoroutineDispatcher, and thus changing the execution flow of coroutines. If you pass in a TestCoroutineScope to the function call, you effectively fully set up the environment you need, to test coroutines.

But you're still using hardcoded scopes, and contexts, within the MainView, which in turn affect the execution and how well the concurrency is structured. Change **MainView.kt** to the following:

```
class MainView(
    private val presenter: MainPresenter,
    private val contextProvider: CoroutineContextProvider,
    private val coroutineScope: CoroutineScope
) {

  var userData: User? = null
```

```kotlin
  fun fetchUserData() {
    coroutineScope.launch(contextProvider.context()) {
      userData = presenter.getUser("101")
    }
  }

  fun printUserData() {
    println(userData)
  }
}
```

Instead of hardcoding those two components, you're now providing them through the constructor, and using the provided values to launch the coroutines. Next, change up the declarations in **MainViewTest.kt** to the following:

```kotlin
// 1
private val testCoroutineDispatcher = TestCoroutineDispatcher()
// 2
private val testCoroutineScope =
  TestCoroutineScope(testCoroutineDispatcher)
// 3
private val testCoroutineContextProvider =
  CoroutineContextProviderImpl(testCoroutineDispatcher)

// 4
private val mainPresenter by lazy { MainPresenter() }
private val mainView by lazy {
  MainView(
    mainPresenter,
    testCoroutineContextProvider,
    testCoroutineScope
  )
}
```

Now, you're using the `TestCoroutineScope` and `TestCoroutineContext`, to govern the way `MainView` is going to start and run coroutines. Finally, you can start using `runBlockingTest()`:

```kotlin
@Test
fun testFetchUserData() = testCoroutineScope.runBlockingTest {
  assertNull(mainView.userData)
  mainView.fetchUserData()

  assertEquals("Filip", mainView.userData?.name)
  mainView.printUserData()
}
```

Build and run the test again. It still fails to compare the values, because the actual value is `null` again. Why does this happen? Well, the test scope context helps you speed up all the `delay()` calls within nested coroutines, which you start with `launch()` or `async()`. But you're calling `mainPresenter.getUser()` which doesn't use those coroutine builders. It's only marked with `suspend` so it can use `delay()` internally.

In this case, you need to advance time by yourself, however, this doesn't mean you can time travel! :]

Advancing time

When you delay a coroutine, you're effectively stating how long it will wait until it resumes again. If you want to *skip* the wait, all you have to do, within a coroutine, is to advance the time by the same amount you're delaying.

The `TestCoroutineScope` exposes a handy function for that, called `advancedTimeBy(milis: Long)`. It advances the internal test clock, so you can skip any amount of delaying you have within your code. To fix the broken test, and fully enable testing of your code, change the test snippet to the following:

```
@Test
fun testFetchUserData() = testCoroutineScope.runBlockingTest {
  assertNull(mainView.userData)
  mainView.fetchUserData()

  // advance the test clock
  advanceTimeBy(1000)

  assertEquals("Filip", mainView.userData?.name)
  mainView.printUserData()
}
```

By calling `advanceTimeBy(1000)`, you can skip the `delay()` from within `MainPresenters getUser()` code. Try running the tests now, you should see a positive result! :]

You first check the value to be `null`, fetching data next, advancing the time so that the value is properly set, finally comparing the value to an expected result, and printing it for the sake of clarity. All in all, a good way to check your code works! You should now be ready to test the rest of your coroutine-related code, in your applications.

Summing it up

Testing coroutines may not be completely straightforward as it is with regular code which uses callbacks, or blocking calls, but there's a lot of documentation available, and it's fairly easy to set up. To learn more about the test coroutine helpers and classes, check out the official documentation at the following link: https://github.com/Kotlin/kotlinx.coroutines/tree/master/kotlinx-coroutines-test.

Key points

- Testing code is extremely useful to prove the **stability** of the software you write.
- Testing usually involves writing **unit** and **integration** tests.
- Commonly, unit tests validate input and output of functions.
- Each unit test should cover one *unit of code*, and be as small as possible.
- Integration tests, on the other hand, validate **interaction between layers** and dependencies - the **behavior of code**.
- **Value-asserting** tests are most common and simple to write, as they rely on comparing the result with expected values.
- A common testing approach is the **AAA** testing.
- AAA stands for **Arrange, Act and Assert**.
- **Arrange** sets up all the dependencies and values you need to start testing a unit of code.
- **Act** calls the necessary functions to change the data or cause some code behavior, which you will test.
- **Assert** compares the behavior or results provided by acting and checks its validity.
- To test coroutines, you have to set up a **coroutine-friendly environment**.
- To set up such an environment, you need to provide a **TestCoroutineScope** and **TestCoroutineContext**.
- `TestCoroutineScope` takes care of the lifecycle and delays within `launch()` and `async()` blocks, making it easier to execute coroutines.

- `TestCoroutineContext` gives you the ability to advance time, and pause and stop coroutine execution if needed.

- Unit tests should run fast and give results very quickly, without delays.

- Because of that, you need to force coroutines to be **blocking instead of suspending** in tests.

- To force coroutines to be blocking, you can use `runBlockingTest()`, on a `TestCoroutineScope`.

- If you have `delay()` calls outside of `async()` or `launch()` blocks, you have to **manually advance time**.

- To advance time in a test, call `advanceTimeBy(milis: Long)`, from within a `TestCoroutineScope`.

Section III: Coroutines & Android

Coroutines are becoming a very important tool for any Kotlin application and in particular for Android applications. They allow the creation of applications that are more readable and use simpler code. In this section, you'll learn how to use coroutines as a valid option for running background tasks which interact with the UI thread.

- **Chapter 16: Android Concurrency Before Coroutines**: The Android platform allows you to run background tasks in many different ways. In this chapter, you'll see and implement examples for all of them. You'll learn what Looper and Handler are and when to use an AsyncTask. You'll finally see how coroutines can make the code more readable and efficient.

- **Chapter 17: Coroutine on Android - Part 1**: This chapter covers using Kotlin Coroutines in an Android app, covering working with various context; i.e., UI and background to simplify and manage code sequentially. It will cover converting async callbacks for long-running tasks, such as a database or network access into sequential tasks while also keeping track and handling of the app lifecycle.

- **Chapter 18: Coroutine on Android - Part 2**: This chapter covers fortifying the use of Kotlin Coroutines in an Android app; i.e., enabling logging, exception handling, debugging and testing of code that uses Kotlin Coroutines. You will also discover the Anko library.

Chapter 16: Android Concurrency Before Coroutines

By Nishant Srivastava

The importance of concurrency was discovered quite early on by people who started with Android development. Android is inherently asynchronous and event-driven, with strict requirements as to which threads certain things can happen. Add to this the often-cumbersome Java callback interfaces, and you will be trapped in spaghetti code pretty quickly (aptly termed as "Callback Hell"). No matter how many coding patterns you use to avoid it, you will encounter state changes across multiple threads in one way or the other.

The only way to create a responsive app is by leaving the UI thread as free as possible, letting all the hard work be done asynchronously by background threads.

> **Note**: You've already met the term "Callback Hell" in the first chapter. It's the situation in which you have to serially execute and process the results of asynchronous services by nesting callbacks, often several layers deep.

The purpose of coroutines is to take care of the complications of working with asynchronous programming. You write code sequentially, like you usually would, and then leave the hard asynchronous work up to coroutines.

Using coroutines in Android provides some of the following benefits:

- Coroutines are a feature provided by a Kotlin library and, thus, can be updated independently from the Android platform releases.

- Coroutines make asynchronous code look synchronous, making the code more readable. Also, since a synchronous sequence of steps is much easier to manage than asynchronous code, coroutines enable greater confidence in changing the flow when needed.
- Thanks to coroutines, getting rid of any callbacks and the need to pass around state information is fairly easy, i.e., storing temporary state in a Presenter/ViewModel is simplified. State is not passed across multiple methods any longer.
- Coroutines are a language feature provided out of the box by Kotlin and, thus, they can be updated independently from the Android platform releases.
- Coroutines enable better, concise and testable code.

In this chapter, you'll learn about what different mechanisms already exist for asynchronous programming on the Android platform and why coroutines are a much better replacement for all of them. You'll see what Kotlin coroutines bring to the table and how they simplify various facets of Android development.

Getting started

Async Wars

For this chapter, you will use a basic app called **Async Wars** to learn about various async primitives in Android and coroutines at a high level. If you have already downloaded the starter project, then import it into Android Studio.

The project consists of some pre-written utility classes under the package `utils`. Let's go over them one by one:

1. `DownloaderUtil`: A **singleton** which has a method called `downloadImage()` that fetches an image from a pre-setup URL returning a `Bitmap`. This is done on the main thread and it will be your goal to execute this method on a background thread, and then you will display the image on the screen.

2. `ImageDownloadListener`: Interface which is used as a listener for images being downloaded.

3. `BroadcasterUtil`: A **singleton** which is used to abstract away the calls made using `LocalBroadcastManager`.

4. `MyBroadcastReceiver`: Implementation of `BroadcastReceiver` class used as an **adapter** between the sender and an `ImageDownloadListener`.

5. `Extensions.kt`: Utility Kotlin extension methods.

Under the package `async`, you will find `GetImageAsyncTask` and `MyIntentService` classes, which will be used and discussed at a later stage in this chapter.

Apart from that, there is `MainActivity` class where everything is wired up for making calls to download images using various async constructs in Android and to display them in the UI. Almost all the code is pre-written to make it easier for you to switch between these async constructs and see the results. There are two important sections inside `MainActivity` class that you should take note of:

1. `MethodToDownloadImage`: This is an enum class defined inside the `MainActivity` class, which enumerates all the various types of async construct types in Android.

2. Inside the `onCreate()` is a code region marked to be modified:

```
//region
val doProcessingOnUiThread = true
val methodToUse = MethodToDownloadImage.Thread
//endregion
```

This is where you will make the changes to trigger the right kind of async construct for downloading an image and displaying it in the UI. Here, when working with async constructs, you will have to set `doProcessingOnUiThread = false`. After that, the value of `methodToUse`, which will be one of the items from the `MethodToDownloadImage` enum class, will be used later to trigger the specific async method.

When not dealing with async constructs, simply set back to `doProcessingOnUiThread = true`.

Run the app. You will see a UI like below with a button and an animating spinner. The spinner is there to show the impact of calls on the UI thread while a widget is animating. The button will trigger a calculation of a Fibonacci sequence number on the main thread when the flag `doProcessingOnUiThread` is set to `true`.

Starter Project

Does Android need coroutines?

When you start an Android application, the first thread spawned by its process is the main thread, also known as the UI thread. This is the most important thread of an application. It is responsible for handling all the user interface logic, user interaction and also tying the application's moving parts together.

Android takes this very seriously; if your UI thread is stuck working on a task for more than a few seconds, the Android framework will throw an **Application Not Responding** (ANR) error and the app will crash. Most importantly, even small work on the UI/Main thread can lead to your UI freezing, i.e., animations will stop, and the UI will become non-responsive to the user interaction; everything will stop until the work is finished.

To demonstrate this behavior, inside the `MainActivity.kt` of the starter app, make sure that the value of the flag `doProcessingOnUiThread` is set to `true`. If it is, then simply run the app.

You will see the below app state:

UI blocking processing

Now, click the Start button in the UI. This will trigger a call to `runUiBlockingProcessing()` method. Here is the method definition:

```
fun runUiBlockingProcessing() {
  // Processing
  showToast("Result: ${fibonacci(40)}")
}
```

Here, `fibonacci(number)` method is a helper method and has the below naive implementation:

```
// ------------- Helper Methods -------------//
fun fibonacci(number: Int): Long {
  return if (number == 1 || number == 2) {
    1
  } else fibonacci(number - 1) + fibonacci(number - 2)
}
```

Here, the `runUiBlockingProcessing()` method starts a calculation of the 40th

Fibonacci sequence number. Since the processing is done on the UI thread, you will see that the animating spinner stops until the calculation has completed.

You will see a toast message with the result value when the calculation completes, after which the spinner start animating again.

UI blocking processing

Now, here is the problem: almost all code in an Android application will be executed on the UI thread by default. Since the tasks on a thread are executed sequentially, this means that your user interface could become unresponsive while it is processing some other work.

Long-running tasks called on the UI thread could be fatal to your application, leading to an ANR dialog, which allows the user to force-quit the application. Even small tasks can compromise the user experience; hence, the correct approach is to move as much work off the UI thread onto a background thread.

Android comes with some pre-built solutions to handle such situations, but, due to its design, it has proven to be difficult for many. Using the low-level threading packages with Android means that you have to worry about a lot of tricky synchronization to avoid race conditions or, worse, deadlocks.

The good news is that the folks working on the Android framework noticed this and provided a better API to deal with such situations. **AsyncTask**, **IntentService**,

ExecutorService, etc. are some of the very useful classes, as well as the **HaMeR** classes: **Handler**, **Message** and **Runnable**. Each comes with its own pros and cons.

Take a quick look at each one of them.

> **Note**: Before you continue with the chapter, from here onwards, inside the `MainActivity.kt` of the starter app, ensure that the value of the flag `doProcessingOnUiThread` is set to `false`. You will not be needed to set it to `true` anymore.

Threads

A thread is an independent path of execution within a program. Every thread in Java is created and controlled by a `java.lang.Thread` instance. A Java program can have many threads, and these threads can run concurrently, either asynchronously or synchronously.

Every Android developer, at one point or another, needs to deal with threads in their application. The main thread is responsible for dispatching events to the appropriate user-interface widget, as well as communicating with components from the Android UI toolkit. To keep your application responsive, it is essential to avoid using the main thread to perform operations that may last for long.

Network operations and database calls, as well as the loading of certain components, are common examples of operations that should not run in the main thread. When they are called in the main thread, they are called synchronously, which means that the UI will remain completely unresponsive until the operation completes.

For this reason, they are usually performed in separate threads, which thereby avoids blocking the UI while they are being performed (i.e., they run asynchronously from the UI).

Sample usage

You can create a thread in two ways:

1. Extending the `Thread` class:

```
// Creation
class MyThread : Thread() {

  override fun run() {
    doSomeWork()
  }
}
```

```kotlin
// Usage
val thread = MyThread()
thread.start()
```

2. Passing a `Runnable` interface implementation as the `Thread` constructor parameter:

```kotlin
// Creation
class MyRunnable : Runnable {
  override fun run() {
    doSomeWork()
  }
}

// Usage
val runnable = MyRunnable()
val thread = Thread(runnable)
thread.start()
```

To see a working example, in your **MainActivity.kt** under `onCreate()`, set `methodToUse = MethodToDownloadImage.Thread`. This makes sure that, when the button is clicked, the method `getImageUsingThread()` is called. Here is the method definition:

```kotlin
fun getImageUsingThread() {
// Download image
val thread = Thread(myRunnable)
thread.start()
}
```

Where `myRunnable` has the below implementation:

```kotlin
inner class MyRunnable : Runnable {
  override fun run() {
    // Download Image
    val bmp = DownloaderUtil.downloadImage()

    // Update UI on the UI/Main Thread with downloaded bitmap
    runOnUiThread {
      imageView?.setImageBitmap(bmp)
    }
  }
}
```

Run the app.

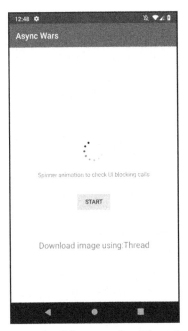

Download image using Thread

When you click the Start button, you will see that the image is downloaded and displayed in the `ImageView` without blocking the UI; the spinner animates while the image is being downloaded.

It's important to note how the downloaded image has been passed to the UI thread using the `runOnUiThread()` function that you inherit from the `Activity` class.

> **Note**: The animation will stop now just for a brief time. Passing an image from one thread to another never comes free.

```
inner class MyRunnable : Runnable {
  override fun run() {
    // Download Image
    val bmp = DownloaderUtil.downloadImage()

    // Update UI on the UI/Main Thread with downloaded bitmap
    runOnUiThread {
      imageView?.setImageBitmap(bmp)
    }
  }
}
```

Interacting with UI components from a background thread would have caused an error like this:

```
E/AndroidRuntime: FATAL EXCEPTION: Thread-4
    Process: com.raywenderlich.android.asyncwars, PID: 3127
    android.view.ViewRootImpl$CalledFromWrongThreadException:
      Only the original thread that created a view hierarchy can
 touch its views.
```

The operating system's scheduler is responsible for the management of the lifecycle of each thread. It can execute, suspend and resume threads depending on its state and some synchronization requirement. This is an expensive job and, if you try to launch a high number of threads — a million, for example — your processor will spend more time changing from one thread to another than executing the code you want it to execute. This is called **context switch**. Every Thread you instantiate in Java (or Kotlin) corresponds to a thread of the operating system (either physical or virtual), and, therefore, it is the scheduler of the operating system that is in charge of prioritizing which thread should be executed in every moment.

In a nutshell, threads might be:

- **Expensive**: Context switching and having upper limits in the number of threads that can be spawned.

- **Difficult**: Creating a multithreaded program is quite complex, requiring a lot of ceremonies around how the code is referenced and executed across the threads.

Taking that into account, engineers working on the Android framework came up with a solution to handle this scenario of doing work on the background thread to then publish it to the UI thread; it is called **AsyncTask**.

AsyncTask

In Java, you usually put the code you want to run asynchronously into the run method of a class, which implements the Runnable interface. This works well if all you need to do is offload work to another thread. However, it becomes cumbersome when you need to relay the results of that thread back to the UI thread.

When Google adopted Java for Android, it released a new type of class called AsyncTask that made it easier to offload long-running tasks to a background thread, then update the UI thread with the result if there was one. Using AsyncTask instances certainly was easier than Runnable, but it came with its own set of issues.

AsyncTask is the most basic Android component for threading. It's simple to use and can be good for basic scenarios. The only important thing you should know here is that only one method of this class is running on another thread: `doInBackground`. The other methods are running on UI thread.

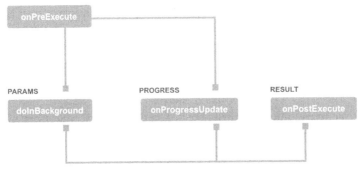

AsyncTask Process Flow

Sample usage

```kotlin
class ExampleActivity : Activity() {

  override fun onCreate(savedInstanceState: Bundle?) {
    super.onCreate(savedInstanceState)

    MyTask().execute(url)
  }

  private inner class MyTask : AsyncTask<String, Void, String>() {

    override fun doInBackground(vararg params: String): String {
      val url = params[0]
      return doSomeWork(url)
    }

    override fun onPostExecute(result: String) {
      super.onPostExecute(result)
      // do something with result
    }
  }
}
```

To see a working example, in your **MainActivity.kt** file under the `onCreate()` function, set `methodToUse = MethodToDownloadImage.AsyncTask`.

This makes sure that, when the button is clicked, the method `getImageUsingAsyncTask()` is called. Here is the method definition:

```
fun getImageUsingAsyncTask() {
  // Download image
  val myAsyncTask = GetImageAsyncTask(imageDownloadListener)
  myAsyncTask.execute()
}
```

Here, `GetImageAsyncTask` has the below implementation:

```
class GetImageAsyncTask(val imageDownloadListener:
ImageDownloadListener) :
    AsyncTask<String, Void, Bitmap>() {

    // This executes on the background thread
    override fun doInBackground(vararg p0: String?): Bitmap? {
        // Download Image
        return DownloaderUtil.downloadImage()
    }

    // This executes on the UI thread
    override fun onPostExecute(bmp: Bitmap?) {
        super.onPostExecute(bmp)
        if (isCancelled) {
            return
        }

        // Pass it to the listener
        imageDownloadListener.onSuccess(bmp)

        // Cancel this async task after everything is done.
        cancel(false)
    }
}
```

`ImageDownloadListener` is used to set up a listener, which will return the bitmap once it is downloaded. In the `MainActivity.kt`, an instance of this is created and used inside the `getImageUsingAsyncTask()` method while creating the `GetImageAsyncTask`, which, in turn, is used to update the UI:

```
private val imageDownloadListener = object :
ImageDownloadListener {
  override fun onSuccess(bitmap: Bitmap?) {
    // Update UI with downloaded bitmap
    imageView?.setImageBitmap(bitmap)
```

```
    }
}
```

Run the app.

Download image using AsyncTask

When you click the Start button, you will see that the image is downloaded and displayed in the `ImageView` without blocking the UI; the spinner animates while the image is being downloaded.

The image downloads:

Download image using AsyncTask

The `AsyncTask` defines some callback methods to simplify the way cancellation and the progression of the task are communicated to the UI; however, it does not play out well when it comes to doing complex operations based on an Android component's lifecycle. It is actually unaware of the Activity's lifecycle; in other words, if the activity is destroyed, the `AsyncTask` doesn't know about it in the `onPostExecute()` method unless you tell it.

It is worth noting that even something as simple as screen rotation can cause the activity to be destroyed. Also, canceling an AsyncTask just puts it in a canceled state — it's up to you to check whether it's been canceled and halt operations.

Handlers

Handler is part of the **HaMeR Framework** (`Handler`, `Message` & `Runnable`), which is the recommended framework for communication between threads in Android. This is the one used, under the hood, by the `AsyncTask` class.

As you have seen in the previous chapters, threads can share data using queues, which usually have a **producer** and a **consumer**. The producer is the object that puts data into the queue, and the consumer is the object that reads the data from the queue when available.

If the producer runs on thread A and the consumer on thread B, you can use the queue as a communication channel between different threads. This is the idea behind the HaMeR framework. The queue is actually a `MessageQueue`, and the data you pass are encapsulated into a `Message` object. Each `Message` can contain some data or the reference to a `Runnable` implementation that defines the code to execute in the thread of the consumer.

If you had to implement the consumer of the queue on your own, you would probably implement it with a cycle that waits for a `Message` and, when available, reads and uses the information into it or else run the code into the `Runnable` object if available. That cycle would be in the `run` implementation of the related `Thread` class. Android defines this cycle in a class called `Looper`. It's important to note that you decide the destination thread putting the message into the related queue. This also implies that there is only one `Looper` per `Thread`.

What's the role of the `Handler` in all of this? Each `Handler` instance is associated with a specific `Thread` through its `Looper`. You can bind a `Looper` to a `Handler`, passing it as the constructor parameter or by simply creating the `Handler` instance into the `Looper`'s thread. You can then use a `Handler` in two different ways:

1. You can use it in order to put a `Message` into the queue that its `Looper` will read into the associated `Thread`.

2. You can also use `Handler` as the object containing the actual consumer logic. In this case, you usually override the `handleMessage(Message?)` method like this:

```
object handler: Handler(){
  override fun handleMessage(msg: Message?) {
    // Consume the message
  }
}
```

This is possible because, when a thread reads a message from its queue, it delegates the actual usage of the data to its handlers.

How can you use all this in order to send data from a background thread to the UI? You just need a `Handler` associated with the main looper that is available by calling `Looper.getMainLooper()` and then post an action as a `Runnable`:

```
val runnable = Runnable {
    // update the ui from here
}
val handler = Handler(Looper.getMainLooper())
handler.post(runnable)
```

You can summarize the responsibilities of the different objects as:

- **Looper**: Runs a loop on its `Thread`, waiting for `Message` instances on its `MessageQueue`.

- **MessageQueue**: Holds a list of messages for a given `Thread`.

- **Handler**: Allows the sending and processing of `Message` and `Runnable` to the `MessageQueue`. It can be used to send and process messages between threads.

- **Message**: Contains the description and data that can be created and sent using a `Handler`.

- **Runnable**: Represents a task to be executed.

Handler is then the HaMeR workhorse. It's responsible for sending `Message` (data message) and post `Runnable` (task message) objects to the `MessageQueue` associated with a `Thread`.

After delivering the tasks to the queue, the handler receives the objects from the looper and processes the messages at the appropriate time. It can be used to send or post some message or runnable objects between threads, as long as such threads share the same process. Otherwise, it will be necessary to use an **Inter Process Communication** (IPC) mechanism, like the `Messenger` class or some **Android Interface Definition Language** (AIDL) implementation.

To see a working example, in your **MainActivity.kt** file under the `onCreate()` function, set `methodToUse = MethodToDownloadImage.Handler`. This makes sure that, when you click the button, the method `getImageUsingHandler()` is called. Here is the method definition:

```kotlin
fun getImageUsingHandler() {
    // Create a Handler using the main Looper
    val uiHandler = Handler(Looper.getMainLooper())

    // Create a new thread
    Thread {
        // Download image
        val bmp = DownloaderUtil.downloadImage()

        // Using the uiHandler update the UI
        uiHandler.post {
            imageView?.setImageBitmap(bmp)
        }
    }.start()
}
```

Run the app.

Download image using Handler

When you click the Start button, you will see that the image is downloaded and displayed in the `ImageView` without blocking the UI; the spinner animates while the image is being downloaded.

HandlerThreads

The UI thread already comes with a `Looper` and a `MessageQueue`. For other threads, you need to create the same objects if you want to leverage the HaMeR framework. You can do this by extending the `Thread` class as follows:

```kotlin
// Preparing a Thread for HaMeR
class MyLooperThread : Thread() {

  lateinit var handler: Handler

  override fun run() {
    // adding and preparing the Looper
    Looper.prepare()

    // the Handler instance will be associated with Thread's Looper
    handler = object : Handler() {
      override fun handleMessage(msg: Message) {
        // process incoming messages here
```

```
      }
    }
    // Starting the message queue loop using the Looper
    Looper.loop()
  }
}
```

However, it's more straightforward to use a helper class called `HandlerThread`, which creates a `Looper` and a `MessageQueue` for you. Check out the implementation of `getImageUsingHandlerThread()` method inside `MainActivity.kt` of the starter app:

```
var handlerThread: HandlerThread? = null
fun getImageUsingHandlerThread() {
  // Download image
  // Create a HandlerThread
  handlerThread = HandlerThread("MyHandlerThread")

  handlerThread?.let{
    // Start the HandlerThread
    it.start()
    // Get the Looper
    val looper = it.looper
    // Create a Handler using the obtained Looper
    val handler = Handler(looper)
    // Execute the Handler
    handler.post {
      // Download Image
      val bmp = DownloaderUtil.downloadImage()

      // Send local broadcast with the bitmap as payload
      BroadcasterUtil.sendBitmap(applicationContext, bmp)
    }
  }
}

override fun onDestroy() {
  super.onDestroy()

  // Quit and cleanup any instance of dangling HandlerThread
  handlerThread?.quit()
}
```

Here, you create an instance of the `HandlerThread`, passing a name that is useful for debugging purposes. The `HandlerThread` extends the `Thread` class and you have to start it to use its `Looper`. You then access the `looper` property and pass it as the constructor parameter of the `Handler`. You can then use the handler that you have created for sending `Runnable` objects to the `HandlerThread`.

All of the code you encapsulate into the `Runnable` object will then be executed in the `HandlerThread`.

> **Note**: You must call `quit()` on the `HandlerThread` instance when the work is done, possibly in the `onDestroy()` method of the activity to release resources it would be holding.

All of the code you encapsulate into the `Runnable` object will be then executed into the `HandlerThread`.

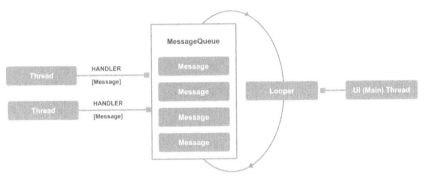

HandlerThread

> **Note**: When the `Activity` is destroyed, it's important to terminate the `HandlerThread`. This also terminates the `Looper`.

To see a working example, in your **MainActivity.kt** file under the `onCreate()` function, set `methodToUse = MethodToDownloadImage.HandlerThread`. This makes sure that, when you click the button, the method `getImageUsingHandlerThread()` is called.

Run the app.

When you click the Start button, you will see that the image is downloaded and displayed in the `ImageView` without blocking the UI.

The spinner animates while the image is being downloaded:

Download image using HandlerThread

Service

The definition of a **component** implies the existence of a **container**. You usually describe all your components to the container using some document; the container will create, suspend, resume and destroy components depending on the state of the application or on the available resources on the device.

You would say that the container is responsible for the component's lifecycle. You can apply the same concept to Android when you describe all your components to the system using the `AndroidManifest.xml` file.

In the example you've seen earlier, the component is an `Activity` whose lifecycle depends mainly on the application usage and the available resources. For instance, when the user rotates the device, the activity is destroyed and then re-created — unless you don't configure it differently.

What happens when you start a task in the background from an `Activity` and then rotate the device? In the case of the `HandlerThread`, you should make it aware of the lifecycle and cancel any tasks, if any, and execute them again. This is not always the best solution — especially in cases of very long tasks like downloading a file.

For situations like these, Android provides a different component whose lifecycle doesn't depend on what's happening on the UI but that can only depend on the available resources: the **service**. It's an Android component and, as such, you have to declare it in the `AndroidManifest.xml` file, and it has a lifecycle different from the activity's lifecycle.

The `Service` is a component that you can use as the owner of a very long task because the system will change its state only if it needs resources. You can think of it as a safe place to put your long-running code. It's important to note that a service does not create its thread and does not run in a separate process unless you explicitly say so.

Sample usage

```kotlin
class ExampleService : Service() {

  fun onStartCommand(intent: Intent, flags: Int, startId: Int): Int {
    doSomeLongProccesingWork()
    return START_NOT_STICKY
  }

  fun onBind(intent: Intent): IBinder? {
    return null
  }

  fun doSomeLongProccesingWork(){
    // Do some work
    // Stop service when required
    stopSelf()
  }
}
```

It is your responsibility to stop a `Service` when its work is completed by calling either the `stopSelf()` or the `stopService()` method. The `Service` doesn't know what is going on in the code running in your thread or executor task — it is your responsibility to let it know when you've started and when you've finished.

A basic service can exist in two flavors:

- A **started** service is initiated by a component in your application and remains active in the background of the device, even if the original component is destroyed. When a started service finishes running its task, the service will stop itself. A standard started service is generally used for long-running background tasks that do not need to communicate with the rest of the app.

- A **bound** service provides a client/server communication paradigm. The service is usually thought of as the server and an Android context, usually an activity, is the client. This type of service is similar to a started service, and it also provides callbacks for various app components that can bind to it. When all bound components have unbound themselves from the service, the service will stop itself.

It is important to note that these two ways to run a service aren't mutually exclusive so you can start a service that will run indefinitely and have components bound to it.

However, since **Api Level 26 (Android 8.0)**, the Service usage as you might know it today, has been deprecated. It is no longer allowed to fulfill its primary purpose, namely to execute a long-running task in the background. Calling startService() method when your app has been put in background throws an IllegalStateException. The only way one can use services now is as a **foreground service**.

Intent service

As stated previously, Service components, by default, are started in the main thread like any other Android component. If you need the service to run a task as a background task, then it's up to you to create a separate thread and move your work to that thread. The Android frameworks also offers a sub-class of Service that can do all the threading work for you: IntentService.

It runs on a separate thread and stops itself automatically after it completes its work. IntentService is usually used for short tasks that don't need to be attached to any UI. Since IntentService doesn't attach to any activity and it runs on a non-UI thread, it serves that need perfectly. Moreover, IntentService stops itself automatically, so there is no need to manually manage it, either.

One of the biggest issues with a standard **started** service is that it cannot handle multiple requests at a time, but that is not the case with an IntentService. It creates a default worker thread for executing all intents that are received in onStartCommand(), so all operations can happen off the main thread. It then creates a work queue for sending each intent to onHandleIntent() one at a time so that you don't need to worry about multi-threading issues.

Essentially, there is always only one instance of your IntentService implementation at any given time and it has only one HandlerThread. This means that if you need more than one thing to happen at the same time, IntentServices may not be a good option.

Sample usage

```kotlin
// Required constructor with a name for the service
class MyIntentService : IntentService("MyIntentService") {

  override fun onHandleIntent(intent: Intent?) {
    //Perform your tasks here
    doSomeWork();
  }
}
```

To see a working example, in your **MainActivity.kt** file under the `onCreate()` function, set `methodToUse = MethodToDownloadImage.IntentService`. This makes sure that when the button is clicked, the method `getImageUsingIntentService()` is called. Here is the method definition:

```kotlin
fun getImageUsingIntentService() {
  // Download image
  val intent = Intent(this@MainActivity,
MyIntentService::class.java)
  startService(intent)
}
```

Here, `MyIntentService` has the below implementation:

```kotlin
// Required constructor with a name for the service
class MyIntentService : IntentService("MyIntentService") {

  override fun onHandleIntent(intent: Intent?) {
    // Download Image
    val bmp = DownloaderUtil.downloadImage()

    // Send local broadcast with the bitmap as payload
    BroadcasterUtil.sendBitmap(applicationContext, bmp)
  }
}
```

Here, `BroadcasterUtil` is a utility class that internally uses LocalBroadcastManager. It is used here to easily send the image back to the UI thread. You will learn more about this process in the next section. Run the app.

When you click the Start button, you will see that the image is downloaded and displayed in the `ImageView` without blocking the UI; the spinner animates while the image is being downloaded.

Download image using IntentService

Sending data from a Service to the UI

You learned that a started `Service` is an Android component that is not bound to the UI. If you need to send some data from a service to a different component, like an `Activity`, you need some other mechanisms like the `LocalBroadcastManager` that you used via the `BroadcasterUtil` in the previous example. You can see how to send data from a service in the `onHandleIntent()` method of the `MyIntentService` class:

```
override fun onHandleIntent(intent: Intent?) {
  // Download Image
  val bmp = DownloaderUtil.downloadImage()

  // Send local broadcast with the bitmap as payload
  BroadcasterUtil.sendBitmap(applicationContext, bmp)
}
```

Here, `sendBitmap(applicationContext, bmp)` is a method defined inside `BroadcasterUtil` class as shown below:

```
/**
 * Send local broadcast with the bitmap as payload
 * @param context Context
 * @param bmp Bitmap
 * @return Unit
 */
fun sendBitmap(context: Context, bmp: Bitmap?) {
    val newIntent = Intent()
    bmp?.let {
        newIntent.putExtra("bitmap", it)
        newIntent.action = MainActivity.FILTER_ACTION_KEY

LocalBroadcastManager.getInstance(context).sendBroadcast(newInte
nt)
    }
}
```

As you can see, it uses `LocalBroadcastManager` to send a broadcast using an intent, which has a payload of the passed bitmap. A `LocalBroadcastManager` needs a `BroadcastReceiver` to be registered using the `registerReceiver()` method. In the starter app, there is an implementation for a `BroadcastReceiver` already provided named `MyBroadcastReceiver`, which is shown below:

```
class MyBroadcastReceiver(val imageDownloadListener:
ImageDownloadListener) : BroadcastReceiver() {
    override fun onReceive(context: Context, intent: Intent) {
        val bmp = intent.getParcelableExtra<Bitmap>("bitmap")

        // Pass it to the listener
        imageDownloadListener.onSuccess(bmp)
    }
}
```

`ImageDownloadListener` is used here to set up a listener, which will return the bitmap once it is downloaded. In the `MainActivity.kt`, you've already created an instance of this during the AsyncTask section of this chapter.

`BroadcasterUtil` abstracts the register and unregister methods of `MyBroadcastReceiver` for the `LocalBroadcastManager` by defining helper methods:

```
/**
 * Register Local Broadcast Manager with the receiver
 * @param context Context
 * @param myBroadcastReceiver MyBroadcastReceiver
```

```
 * @return Unit
 */
fun registerReceiver(context: Context, myBroadcastReceiver:
MyBroadcastReceiver?) {
    myBroadcastReceiver?.let {
        val intentFilter = IntentFilter()
        intentFilter.addAction(MainActivity.FILTER_ACTION_KEY)

LocalBroadcastManager.getInstance(context).registerReceiver(it,
intentFilter)
    }
}

/**
 * Unregister Local Broadcast Manager from the receiver
 * @param context Context
 * @param myBroadcastReceiver MyBroadcastReceiver
 * @return Unit
 */
fun unregisterReceiver(context: Context, myBroadcastReceiver:
MyBroadcastReceiver?) {
    myBroadcastReceiver?.let {

LocalBroadcastManager.getInstance(context).unregisterReceiver(it
)
    }
}
```

You use these helper methods later to register and unregister an instance of `MyBroadcastReceiver` to the `LocalBroadcastManager` in `onStart()` and `onStop()` respectively, of the `MainActivity`:

```
// ------------ Lifecycle Methods -----------//
override fun onStart() {
  super.onStart()
  BroadcasterUtil.registerReceiver(this, myReceiver)
}

override fun onStop() {
  super.onStop()
  BroadcasterUtil.unregisterReceiver(this, myReceiver)
}
```

Important points to note, here:

- If there's no `BroadcastReceiver` registered, there won't be any update in the UI.

- The thread that will perform the `ImageView` update is the UI thread.

- IntentService uses HandlerThread internally.

Executors

You've seen that you can encapsulate code into a `Runnable` implementation in order to eventually run it in some given `Thread`. Every object that can execute what's defined as a `Runnable` can be abstracted using the `Executor` interface, introduced in Java 5.0 as part of the concurrent APIs.

```
interface Executor {
    fun execute(command: Runnable)
}
```

You can execute a `Runnable` in many different ways. You can, for instance, simply invoke directly the `run()` method or pass the `Runnable` object as a constructor parameter of the `Thread` class and start it, as seen previously. In the former case, you're executing the runnable code in the caller thread. In the latter, you're executing the same code into a different thread. This depends on the particular `Executor` implementation.

Creating a thread is simple in code but expensive in practice. Every time you create a `Thread` instance you need to request resources from the operative system and every time the thread completes its job — when its `run()` method ends — it must be garbage collected. The typical solution is the usage of a **thread pools**, which need some kind of **lifecycle**.

The pool needs to be initialized with a minimum number of threads. When the application ends, the pools should shut down and release all their resources. Even when the pool is active, you can have a different policy for the minimum number of instances of threads to keep alive or how to manage the creation of new instances when needed. You could limit the number of threads, forcing the client to wait, or create a new thread every time you need to run something. There is more than the simple `Executor` interface and that is the `ExecutorService` interface.

The `ExecutorService` is then the abstraction for a specific `Executor`, which needs to be initialized and shut down to allow for the execution of `Runnable` objects in an efficient and optimized way. The way this happens depends on the specific implementation. One of the most important classes is the `ThreadPoolExecutor`. It manages a pool of worker threads and a queue of tasks to execute.

Depending on the configured policy, it reuses an available thread or creates a new one to consume the tasks from a queue.

The concurrent APIs provide different implementations that are available through some **static factory methods** of the `Executors` class. The most common is

Executors.newSingleThreadExecutor(), which create an executor that will process a single task at a time, and Executors.newFixedThreadPool(N), which creates an executor with an internal pool of N threads.

It's important to note that an ExecutorService also provides the option of executing Callable<T> implementations. While the Runnable interface defines a run() method, which returns Unit, a Callable<T> is a generic interface, which defines the call() method that returns an object of type T:

```
interface Callable<T> {
    fun call(): T
}
```

You can think of a Callable<T> as a Runnable that returns an object of type T at the end of the task. You can ask the ExecutorService to run the given Callable<T> using the invoke() method, getting a Future<T> in return. The Future<T> provides a get() method, which blocks until the result of type T is available or throws an exception in case of error or interruption.

Sample usage

```
val executor = Executors.newFixedThreadPool(4)
(1..10).forEach {
  executor.submit {
    print("[Iteration $it] Hello from Kotlin Coroutines! ")
    println("Thread: ${Thread.currentThread()}")
  }
}
```

To see a working example, in your **MainActivity.kt** file under the onCreate() function, set methodToUse = MethodToDownloadImage.Executor. This makes sure that, when you click the button, the method getImageUsingExecutors() is called. Here is the method definition:

```
fun getImageUsingExecutors() {
    // Download image
    val executor = Executors.newFixedThreadPool(4)
    executor.submit(myRunnable)
}
```

Here, myRunnable in the MainActivity.kt is an instance of MyRunnable, which you've already created during the Thread section of this chapter.

Run the app.

When you click the Start button, you will see that the image is downloaded and displayed in the `ImageView` without blocking the UI; the spinner animates while the image is being downloaded.

Download image using Executor

The main advantages of using `ThreadPoolExecutor` in an Android application are:

- Powerful task execution framework as it supports task addition in a queue, task cancellation, and task prioritization.

- Reduces the overhead associated with thread creation as it manages a required number of threads in its thread pool.

- Reduces boilerplate code as it abstracts most of the codebase behind factory methods with sane defaults.

However, although `ExecutorService` implementations provide an optimized usage of threads in terms of creation and reuse, they don't solve the problems related to context switching between threads.

WorkManager

Announced at Google I/O 2018 as part of Jetpack, **WorkManager** aims to simplify the developer experience by providing a first-class API for system-driven background processing. The WorkManager API makes it easy to specify deferrable, asynchronous tasks and when they should run. It is intended for background jobs that should run even if the app is no longer in the foreground. Where possible, it delegates its work to a JobScheduler, Firebase JobDispatcher, or Alarm Manager + Broadcast receivers depending on the Android version. If your app is in the foreground, it will even try to do the work directly in your process. The task is still guaranteed to run, even if your app is force-quit or the device is rebooted.

WorkManager chooses the appropriate way to run your task based on such factors as the device API level and the app state.

By default, WorkManager runs each task immediately, but you can also specify the conditions the device needs to fulfill before the task can proceed, including network conditions, charging status and the amount of storage space available on the device. If WorkManager executes one of your tasks while the app is running, it can run your task in a new thread in your app's process.

If your app is not running, WorkManager chooses an appropriate way to schedule a background task — depending on the device API level and included dependencies. You don't need to write device logic to figure out what capabilities the device has and choose an appropriate API; instead, you can just hand your task off to WorkManager and let it choose the best option.

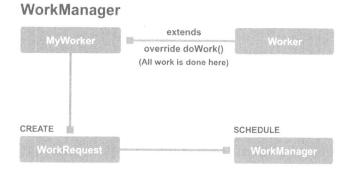

WorkManager Process Flow

Sample usage

```
// A simple Worker
class DoSomeWorker : Worker() {
    // This method will run in background thread and WorkManger
    // will take care of it
    override fun doWork() : WorkerRequest() {
        doSomeWork()
        return WorkResult.SUCCESS
    }
}

// Usage
// Create the request
val request : WorkRequest =
OneTimeWorkRequestBuilder<DoSomeWorker>()
                            .build()
// Enqueue the request
val workManager : WorkManager = WorkManager.getInstance()
workManager.enqueue(request)
```

In short, the WorkManager is another library that is trying to solve the old problem of executing long-running jobs on the Android platform. It delegates the logic to different components that are available only on specific versions of the platform. If you decide to use this library, you accept all the fallbacks and workarounds used to enable support for older platforms/APIs. WorkManager is seen as the third attempt by Google to solve the job management problem on the Android Platform and will probably not be the last.

RxJava + RxAndroid

Reactive programming is an asynchronous programming paradigm concerned with data streams and the propagation of change. The essence of reactive programming is the **observer pattern**.

> **Note**: The observer pattern is a software design pattern wherein data sources or streams, called observables, emit data and one or more observers, who are interested in getting the data, subscribe to the observable.

In reactive programming, you are allowed to create data streams from anything including `Array`, `ArrayList`, etc. These data streams can be observed, modified, filtered or operated upon. You can use a stream as an input to another one. You can even use multiple streams as inputs to another stream.

You can merge two streams. You can filter a stream to get another one that has only those events you are interested in. You can map data values from one stream to another.

A typical data stream can emit three different values: one when the event occurs, one when an error occurs or one when the event is completed.

RxJava is a library that makes it easier for you to implement reactive programming principles on any JVM-based platform, including Android. To manage threads, RxJava has a helper class called `Schedulers`. Schedulers are how you tell where the observer and observables should run.

Some general use Schedulers to observe:

- `Schedulers.computation()`: Used for CPU intensive tasks.
- `Schedulers.io()`: Used for IO bound tasks.
- `Schedulers.from(Executor)`: Used with custom ExecutorService.
- `Schedulers.newThread()`: It always creates a new thread when a worker is needed.

This is where RxAndroid library comes into the picture, which plays a major role in supporting multi-threading concepts in Android applications. It provides a `Scheduler` that schedules on the main thread or any given `Looper`.

Sample usage

```
Observable.just("Hello", "from", "RxJava")
        .subscribeOn(Schedulers.newThread())
        .observeOn(AndroidSchedulers.mainThread())
        .subscribe(/* an Observer */);
```

This will execute the `Observable` on a new thread and emit results through `onNext()` on the main thread.

To see a working example, in your **MainActivity.kt** file under the `onCreate()` function, set `methodToUse = MethodToDownloadImage.RxJava`. This makes sure that when you click the button, the method `getImageUsingRx()` is called. Here is the method definition:

```
var single: Disposable? = null
fun getImageUsingRx() {
    // Download image
    single = Single.create<Bitmap> { emitter ->
```

```
      DownloaderUtil.downloadImage()?.let { bmp ->
        emitter.onSuccess(bmp)
      }
  }.observeOn(AndroidSchedulers.mainThread())
    .subscribeOn(Schedulers.io())
    .subscribe { bmp ->
        // Update UI with downloaded bitmap
        imageView?.setImageBitmap(bmp)
    }
}

override fun onDestroy() {
  super.onDestroy()

  // Cleanup disposable if it was created i.e. not null
  single?.dispose()
}
```

> **Note**: It is important that you call `dispose()` on the `Single` instance when the work is done, possibly in the `onDestroy()` of the activity to release resources it would be holding and close the stream.
>
> Also note that the topic of reactive extensions is pretty vast; covering the mechanics of its functionalities is out of the scope of this book.

Run the app.

Download image using RxJava

When you click the Start button, you will see that the image is downloaded and displayed in the `ImageView` without blocking the UI; the spinner animates while the image is being downloaded.

Download image using RxJava

Although reactive programming is a compelling tool and solves a lot of complex concurrency problems, the learning curve for RxJava is very steep and complex. It is a different approach towards programming and can lead to some confusion when programming larger apps.

Coroutines

Now that you have a clear idea about various ways of doing asynchronous work in Android, as well as the pros and cons, let's come back to Kotlin coroutines. Kotlin coroutines are a way of doing things asynchronously in a sequential manner. Creating coroutines is cheap versus creating threads.

> **Note**: Coroutines are completely implemented through a compilation technique (no support from the VM or OS side is required), and suspension works through code transformation.

Coroutines are based on the idea of suspending functions: functions that can stop the execution when they are called and make it continue once it has finished running their own task. Enabling Kotlin coroutines in Android involves just a few simple steps. To show how easy it is to enable coroutines, head back to the starter project and add the Android coroutine library dependency into your app's **build.gradle** file under dependencies block, replacing the line `// TODO: Add Kotlin Coroutine Dependencies here` with the following:

```
dependencies {
  ..
  // Coroutines
  final def coroutineVer = "1.3.0"
  implementation "org.jetbrains.kotlinx:kotlinx-coroutines-core:$coroutineVer"
  implementation "org.jetbrains.kotlinx:kotlinx-coroutines-android:$coroutineVer"
}
```

> **Note**: To use Coroutines v1.3.0, make sure that the Kotlin standard library is at least v1.3.50.

Next, inside your **MainActivity.kt** file, add the implementation for the method `getImageUsingCoroutines()` by replacing `// TODO: add implementation here` with the below code snippet:

```
GlobalScope.launch {
  // Download Image in background
  val deferredJob = async(Dispatchers.IO) {
    DownloaderUtil.downloadImage()
  }
  withContext(Dispatchers.Main) {
    val bmp = deferredJob.await()
    // Update UI with downloaded bitmap
    imageView?.setImageBitmap(bmp)
  }
}
```

To see a working example, in your **MainActivity.kt** file under the `onCreate()` function, set `methodToUse = MethodToDownloadImage.Coroutine`.

This makes sure that when you click the button, the method `getImageUsingCoroutines()` is called.

Run the app.

Download image using Coroutine

When you click the Start button, you will see that the image is downloaded and displayed in the `ImageView` without blocking the UI; the spinner animates while the image is being downloaded.

A lot has already been explained about the mechanics of Kotlin coroutines in the previous chapters; in the subsequent chapters, you will mostly cover the usage of Kotlin coroutines in Android apps.

Introducing Anko

While Kotlin does remove much of the verbosity and complexity typically associated with Java, no programming language is perfect and, thus, libraries that build on top of the language are born. Anko is one such library that uses Kotlin and provides a lot of extension functions to make your Android development easier.

> **Note:** That's how Anko got its name: (An)droid (Ko)tlin.

Anko was originally designed as a single library. As the project grew, adding Anko as a dependency began to have a significant impact on the size of the APK (Android Application Package).

Today, Anko is split across several modules:

- **Commons**: Helps you perform the most common Android tasks, including displaying dialogs and launching new Activities.

- **Layouts**: Provides a Domain Specific Language (DSL) for defining Android layouts.

- **SQLite**: A query DSL and parser that makes it easier to interact with SQLite databases.

- **Coroutines**: Supplies utilities based on the kotlinx.coroutines library.

You can see the differences in a sample comparison, below.

Using language provided coroutines:

```
button.setOnClickListener {
  launch(UI){
    val userId = fetchUserString("user_id_1").await()
    val user = deserializeUser(userId).await()
    showUserData(user)
  }
}
```

Using an Anko-provided coroutine helper:

```
button.onClick {
  val userId= bg { fetchUserString("user_id_1").await() }
  val user = bg { deserializeUser(userId).await() }
  showUserData(user)
}
```

onClick and bg are some of the many helper functions Anko provides for making the process of handling coroutines even simpler, which will be covered in depth in later chapters.

Key points

- Android is inherently **asynchronous and event-driven**, with strict requirements as to which thread certain things can happen on.

- The **UI thread** — a.k.a., main thread — is responsible for interacting with the UI components and is the most important thread of an Android application.

- Almost all code in an Android application will be executed on the **UI thread** by default; blocking it would result in a non-responsive application state.

- **Thread** is an independent path of execution within a program allowing for asynchronous code execution, but it is highly complex to maintain and has limits on usage.

- **AsyncTask** is a helper class that simplifies asynchronous programming between UI thread and background threads on Android. It does not work well with complex operations based on Android Lifecycle.

- **Handler** is another helper class provided by Android SDK to simplify asynchronous programming but requires a lot of moving parts to set up and get running.

- **HandlerThread** is a thread that is ready to receive a `Handler` because it has a `Looper` and a `MessageQueue` built into it.

- **Service** is a component that is useful for performing long (or potentially long) operations without any UI, and it runs in the main thread of its hosting process.

- **IntentService** is a service that runs on a separate thread and stops itself automatically after it completes its work; however, it cannot handle multiple requests at a time.

- **Executors** is a manager class that allows running many different tasks concurrently while sharing limited CPU time, used mainly to manage thread(s) efficiently.

- **WorkManager** is a fairly new API developed as part of JetPack libraries provided by Google, which makes it easy to specify deferrable, asynchronous tasks and when they should run.

- **RxJava + RxAndroid** are libraries that make it easier to implement reactive programming principles in the Android platform.

- **Coroutines** make asynchronous code look synchronous and work pretty well with the Android platform out of the box.

- **Anko** is a library that uses Kotlin and provides a lot of extension functions to make our Android development easier.

Where to go from here?

Phew! That was a lot of background on asynchronous programming in Android! But the good thing is that you made it!

In the upcoming chapters, you will dive deeper into how you can leverage coroutines in Android apps to handle async operations while keeping in sync with various nuances of the Android platform, such as respecting lifecycles of an app and efficient context switching to facilitate the various use cases of apps to fetch-process-display data.

Chapter 17: Coroutines on Android - Part 1

By Nishant Srivastava

Most Android apps are data-consuming apps, meaning that, most of the time, these apps are requesting data from some other source, usually a web service. Android apps run by default on the **main** thread. When it comes to consuming data either from local or remote locations, they use multiple approaches to switch context from the **main (or UI)** thread to a **background** thread in order to offload heavy processing and/or long-running tasks, and then back to the **main** thread to convey the result in the UI (you read about many of these approaches in the previous chapter).

Of those many approaches, coroutines stand out as a completely different approach to handling async operations. As was made clear in the previous chapter, coroutines turn out to be the simplest of them all. They make context switching clear, easy and sequential, which, in turn, leads to a lean and readable implementation.

In this chapter, you will learn how to use Kotlin Coroutines in an Android app. Also, you will learn about coroutine concepts such as dispatchers, coroutine scopes and how they enable working with various lifecycle events in an Android app.

Getting started

Coroutines on Android: Part 2

Android apps mainly involve **CRUD** operations on information (i.e., Create, Read, Update, Delete). The information can be accessed either from the local database or from a remote server via network calls, which can be a long-running task. Since the Android OS executes tasks by default on the main/UI thread, executing such long-running tasks can freeze your app, or crash the app and show an ANR (Application Not Responding) error.

Coroutines are a Kotlin feature that allows you to write asynchronous code in a sequential manner while still ensuring that long-running operations, such as database or network access, are properly dispatched to run in the background, which keeps the UI thread from being blocked. Once the long-running or high-processing task complete, the result is dispatched to the main/UI thread in an obvious manner.

For this chapter, you will use a simple Android app called **StarSync**, which is an offline first **MVP** (Model-View-Presenter) app. There is a repository that takes care of fetching data from the **SWAPI** API, which is a public *Star Wars* API. You can access the documentation for the same at https://swapi.co. The SWAPI API is pretty straight forward and completely public. You don't even need to set up a token. Once fetched, the data is saved to the local database using the Room architecture components library.

The starter app uses a callback style for long-running tasks. The app uses the MVP architecture to separate the UI code in **MainActivity** from the app logic in **MainActivityPresenter**. Take a moment to familiarize yourself with the structure of the project.

If you have already downloaded the starter project, open it in Android Studio.

The project consists of pre-setup MVP architecture, with classes under their respective packages:

1. **contract**: This package consists of contracts/interfaces defining the methods concrete implementations should be following.

2. **repository**: This package contains the local and remote repository sub packages. It also contains the model sub package, which, in turn, contains the POJO (Plain Old Java Object) model classes.

3. **ui**: This package contains the main and splash screen sub packages, which, in turn, contain the Activity and the Presenter associated with them.

4. **utils**: This package contains some helper classes in order to help in writing clean code.

Some important classes to look at include:

1. `RemoteRepo`: This class takes care of defining methods used for fetching data from the remote server using the Retrofit library.

2. `LocalRepo`: This class takes care of defining methods used for fetching from and saving to a local database using the Room library.

3. `DataRepository`: This class implements the repository pattern to implement logic around fetching from a remote server or local database.

4. `RemoteApi`: This is a singleton class, which defines the base URL for SWAPI API, the people's route path and the retrofit service with pre-setup with the Moshi Converter and Coroutine Adapter.

5. `RetrofitService`: This interface defines the retrofit service routes used for making the GET requests to the SWAPI API.

6. `MainActivityPresenter`: This class is the presenter for the `MainActivity.kt` file implementing the main business logic. This is where you will be working mostly. Notice that the presenter is initialized in the onCreate() and uses the `getData()` method to fetch data when the **FloatingActionButton** is clicked, and in `onResume()`. Later in `onDestroy()` the presenter calls `cleanup()` to avoid memory leak.

7. `RemoteRepo`: This class takes care of defining methods used for fetching data from the remote server using Retrofit library.

8. `LocalRepo`: This class takes care of defining methods used for fetching from and saving to local database using Room library.

9. `DataRepository`: This class implements the repository pattern to implement logic around fetching from a remote server or local database.

10. `RemoteApi`: This is a singleton class, which defines the base URL for SWAPI API, the people's route path and the retrofit service with pre-setup Moshi Converter and Coroutine Adapter.

> **Note**: The starter app includes both a callback and a coroutine-based implementation. To use the right kind, inside the `MainActivityPresenter`, a value is passed to the property `processingUsing` as `ProcessUsing.BackgroundThread` by default. This means that the app uses callback based implementation. To switch to the coroutine-based implementation, simply change the value of `processingUsing` to `ProcessUsing.Coroutines`.

Run the starter app now and you will see the following:

Starter App

When the app loads for the first time, because it is an offline-first Android app, it tries to load data from the local database first. It then goes on to fetch from the remote server via a GET call to the SWAPI API.

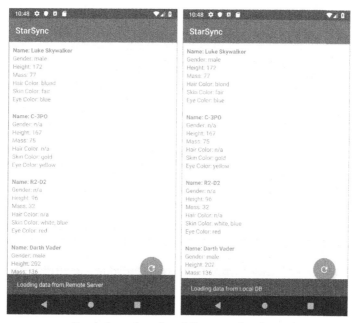

Fetch from Local and Remote database

After the first remote fetch, data is saved to a local database. To verify the offline-first approach, simply switch to **Airplane Mode** and re-launch the app. Data will be fetched from the local database and populated in the list on the screen.

To simplify and focus on coroutines, you will notice everything is mostly wired up. You will, however, be implementing the important parts. So get ready to get your feet wet!

> **Note**: It is expected that you know about the usage of Retrofit and Room libraries, as well as the implementation of the MVP architecture. The parts covered here will focus mostly on the implementation of coroutines in a practical real-world Android app.

What's in the context?

When talking about Android apps, one cannot ignore the pain around multi-threading. Android apps are limited to a single main thread for all processing and this makes it difficult to build highly responsive and performant apps. If a lot of processing is done on the main thread, the UI can become non-responsive and eventually lead to an app crash. To avoid that, do all heavy processing on a background thread. This is easy to achieve because one can simply start a thread or a pool of threads to offload the heavy processing.

It becomes tricky when the heavy processing completes and the result needs to be updated in the UI — i.e., back in the main thread. Switching back to the main thread isn't as easy it sounds. Passing values across threads is very painful and this is the reason Android has constructs like AsyncTask, which switch from background thread to the main thread automatically.

CoroutineDispatcher

The CoroutineDispatcher determines what thread or threads the corresponding coroutine uses for its execution. It can confine (restrict) coroutine execution to a specific thread, dispatch it to a thread pool, or let it run unconfined (unrestricted).

In the simplest terms, it defines where your piece of code executes — i.e., on the main thread, background thread or a pool of threads.

The standard coroutine library provides the following dispatchers:

1. **Dispatchers.Default**: Used by all standard builders if no dispatcher is specified. It uses a common pool of shared background threads. This is an appropriate choice for compute-intensive coroutines that consume CPU resources.

2. **Dispatchers.IO**: Uses a shared pool of on-demand created threads and is designed for offloading of IO-intensive blocking operations (like file I/O and blocking socket I/O).

3. **Dispatchers.Unconfined**: Unrestricted to any specific thread or pool and should not be used normally in code. There will be certain use-cases in which you might need to use this.

4. **newSingleThreadContext**: Use to create a new private single-threaded coroutine context.

5. **newFixedThreadPoolContext**: To create a private thread pool of fixed size.

6. **asCoroutineDispatcher**: Extension function to convert an Executor to a dispatcher.

7. **Dispatchers.IO**: Uses a shared pool of on-demand created threads and is designed for offloading of IO-intensive blocking operations (like file I/O and blocking socket I/O).

8. **Dispatchers.Unconfined**: Unrestricted to any specific thread or pool and should not be used normally in code. There will be certain use-cases in which you might need to use this.

9. **newSingleThreadContext**: To create new private single-threaded coroutine context.

All coroutines builders like **launch** and **async** accept an optional CoroutineContext parameter that can be used to explicitly specify the dispatcher for new coroutine and other context elements. There is, however, another coroutine builder called **withContext** that takes in a CoroutineContext parameter, which is not optional. The usage, however, is pretty similar to the **async** coroutines builder:

```
withContext(Dispatchers.IO) {
    // Code to execute
}
```

> **Note**: launch(Dispatchers.Default) { ... } uses the same dispatcher as GlobalScope.launch { ... }.

A coroutine can switch dispatchers any time after it is started. For example, a coroutine can start on the main dispatcher then use another dispatcher to process a long-running task off the main thread. This is typically called **context switching** in coroutines. Kotlin Coroutines typically make this very easy to achieve.

In Android, we need a coroutine dispatcher context that restricts the coroutine execution to the main UI thread. The core coroutines library provides the **Dispatchers.Main** context that uses a service loader behind the scenes to pick the correct main-thread dispatcher implementation. The dispatcher implementation you want is provided via an Android specific `kotlinx-coroutines-android` library dependency, which should be added alongside the core coroutines library. The `kotlinx-coroutines-android` library provides a concrete implementation of a **Dispatchers.Main** context for Android applications, which allows you to start coroutines confined to the main thread.

Coroutines, during execution, can easily switch context from **Dispatcher.IO** or **Dispatcher.Default** to **Dispatchers.Main**, thereby enabling processing in a background thread without blocking the main thread and, when the result is ready, switching back to the main thread to display it in the UI.

The dispatcher implementation you want is provided via an Android specific `kotlinx-coroutines-android` library dependency, which should be added alongside the core coroutines library.

The `kotlinx-coroutines-android` library provides a concrete implementation of a **Dispatchers.Main** context for Android apps, which allows you to start coroutines confined to the main thread. A coroutine started on the main won't block the main thread while suspended.

To add `kotlinx-coroutines-android` library, simply add the library below to your app's `build.gradle` file in the dependencies section, replacing `//TODO: add Kotlin Coroutines Android dependency here` and sync your project:

```
dependencies {
    // Other dependencies

    // Kotlin Coroutines Android
    implementation 'org.jetbrains.kotlinx:kotlinx-coroutines-android:1.3.0'
}
```

Now, that the dependency is added to the project, calls like demonstrateUsingMainDispatcher, shown below, are possible:

```
private fun demonstrateUsingMainDispatcher() {
    GlobalScope.launch(Dispatchers.Main) {

        //1 Runs on Main Thread
        var stringToShow = "Luke"
        prompt(stringToShow)

        //2 Runs on Background Thread
        withContext(Dispatchers.IO) {
            delay(5000)
            stringToShow = "Darth Vader"
        }

        //3 Runs on Main Thread
        prompt(stringToShow)
    }
}
```

Here's what this code does:

1. When demonstrateUsingMainDispatcher() is called, the prompt method is called on the main thread with the string "Luke". Next, the context is switched to IO thread (i.e., background thread) and the coroutine now suspends. After a delay of five seconds (using the delay call), the value for stringToShow is updated to "Darth Vader" and then finishes.

2. Next, the context is switched to IO thread (i.e., background thread) and the coroutine now suspends. After a delay of five seconds, the value for stringToShow is updated to "Darth Vader" and then finishes.

3. Finally, once done, the coroutine switches back to the main thread and calls the prompt method with the updated value for stringToShow, which is now "Darth Vader".

Navigate to `MainActivity.kt` file. The above method is pre-written and exists inside the `MainActivity.kt` file. If you check the code under the `onClickListener` on the **FloatingActionButton** called `fab`, you will see:

```
// Setup FAB
fab.setOnClickListener {
    // 1
    presenter?.getData()

    // 2
    // demonstrateUsingMainDispatcher()
}
```

Uncomment `demonstrateUsingMainDispatcher()` and comment out `presenter?.getData()`. Now, run the app.

When you press the **FloatingActionButton**, you will see that at first a snackbar with the text "Luke" shows up. Then, after a delay of five seconds, another snackbar shows with the text "Darth Vader." You will also notice that, during the delay of five seconds, you can scroll the list of items on the screen because the main thread is not blocked at all.

> **Note**: You will not be using this code anymore in the future, so you can delete `demonstrateUsingMainDispatcher()` called inside the onClickListener for the fab. Make sure you uncomment `presenter?.getData()` after removing `demonstrateUsingMainDispatcher()`.

CoroutineScope

Each coroutine runs inside a scope defined by you, so you can make it app-wide or specific for an Android component with a well-defined life cycle, such as an Activity or Fragment. The scope here is represented by the class name **CoroutineScope**. Each coroutine waits for all the coroutines inside their block/scope to complete before completing themselves. A scope controls the lifetime of coroutines through its job. When you cancel the scope's job, it cancels all coroutines started in that scope, i.e. when the user navigates away from an Activity or Fragment.

> **Note**: Every coroutine builder is an extension of CoroutineScope and inherits its coroutineContext to automatically propagate both context elements and cancellation.

CoroutineScope provides properties like **coroutineContext**, and it is a set of various elements like the Job of the coroutine and its dispatcher. You can also check whether a coroutine is active or not using the **isActive** property of Job.

> **Note**: **GlobalScope** is used to launch a coroutine that corresponds to the lifetime of the whole app.

Setting up a **CoroutineScope** is pretty straightforward in Android because you almost always want to update the UI on the main thread. Starting coroutines on the main thread is a reasonable default. To create a scope that is dispatched to the UI thread, you first define a job and then pass it along with `Dispatchers.Main` to CoroutineScope constructor as shown below:

```
private val coroutineJob = Job()

private val uiScope = CoroutineScope(Dispatchers.Main + coroutineJob)
```

Since `coroutineJob` is passed as the job to `uiScope`, when `coroutineJob` is canceled, every coroutine started with `uiScope` will be canceled as well.

To cancel coroutines on a job object, simply call `cancel()` on the job instance:

```
coroutineJob.cancel()
```

The same code is being called inside the `MainActivityPresenter` class under the method `cleanup()`. It means that, when the presenter calls the `cleanup()` method, it will cancel all ongoing coroutine jobs.

> **Note**: You **must** pass CoroutineScope a Job in order to cancel all coroutines started in the scope. If you don't, the `cancel` function will throw an `IllegalStateException` when you try to cancel the scope.

Scopes created with the CoroutineScope constructor add an implicit job, which you can cancel using `uiScope.coroutineContext.cancel()`, which is another way of canceling coroutines running inside a CoroutineScope.

Another step that is required for creating Scopes: implement the **CoroutineScope** interface. When you do that, you need to override the `coroutineContext` and assign it the right dispatchers.

Implement `CoroutineScope` on `MainActivityPresenter`, as shown below:

```
class MainActivityPresenter(var view: ViewContract?, var
repository: DataRepositoryContract?) :
    PresenterContract, CoroutineScope {
}
```

Next, replace `coroutineScope` with the below snippet:

```
override val coroutineContext: CoroutineContext =
Dispatchers.Main + coroutineJob
```

Here, by default, the scope is set on the main thread. When required, the coroutines will switch to a different dispatcher such as `Dispatcher.IO`. You can find an example under the `saveDataUsingCoroutines()` method inside the `MainActivityPresenter` class.

Now that you have implemented the **CoroutineScope** interface, you do not need to use the `coroutineScope` property that is defined in `MainActivityPresenter` directly, so you can remove all calls to it.

For all calls like:

```
coroutineScope.launch {
    ...
}
```

Simply becomes:

```
launch {
    ...
}
```

Delete the `coroutineScope` property and update your `MainActivityPresenter` class with the above changes to fix the errors created after deletion of the property.

Note that you can directly call `cancel()` on the `coroutineContext` inside the `cleanup()` method instead of calling it on the `coroutineJob`.

Inside `MainActivityPresenter` class under `cleanup()` method, the call:

```
override fun cleanup() {
    // Cancel all coroutines running in this context
    coroutineJob.cancel()

    ...
}
```

Now becomes:

```
override fun cleanup() {
    // Cancel all coroutines running in this context
    coroutineContext.cancel()

    ...
}
```

Converting existing API call to use coroutines

On Android, to guarantee a great and smooth user experience, the app needs to function without any visible pauses. Most pauses are usually noticeable when the device cannot refresh the screen at 60 frames per second. On Android, the main thread is a single thread responsible for handling all updates to the UI, calls to all click handlers and other UI callbacks. Common tasks, such as writing data to a database or fetching data from the network, usually take longer than 16ms to do and this long processing time makes it hard to keep screen refresh rates at 60 frames per second. Therefore, calling code like this from the main thread can cause the app to pause, stutter, or even freeze. Moreover, if you block the main thread for too long, the app may even crash and present an Application Not Responding dialog.

For performing long-running tasks without blocking the main thread, callbacks are a common pattern you can use. By using callbacks, you can start long-running tasks on a background thread. When the task completes, the callback is called to inform you of the result on the main thread.

If you look at the implementation of the `getData()` method inside the `MainActivityPresenter` class, you will find:

```
override fun getData() {
    // Start loading animation
    view?.showLoading()

    // Fetch Data
    fetchData()
}

private fun fetchData() {
    when (processingUsing) {
        // 1
        ProcessUsing.BackgroundThread ->
```

```
        fetchUsingBackgroundThreads()

            // 2
            ProcessUsing.Coroutines -> fetchUsingCoroutines()
      }
}
```

Inside the getData() method, a call to fetchData() is made, and based on the value of processingUsing, calls the corresponding method. In the current case, since processingUsing is equal to ProcessUsing.BackgroundThread, the fetchUsingBackgroundThreads() method is called.

Diving deeper inside the method implementation of fetchUsingBackgroundThreads(), you can find the implementation calls an AsyncTask called FetchFromLocalDbTask and passes a callback called ItemListCallback to the AsyncTask in the constructor as shown below:

```
class FetchFromLocalDbTask(val repository: DataRepositoryContract?,
    private val itemListCallback: ItemListCallback) :
AsyncTask<Void, Void, List<People>>() {

  override fun onPostExecute(result: List<People>?) {
    super.onPostExecute(result)

    // Return callback
    itemListCallback.onSuccess(result)

    // Stop the task
    cancel(true)
  }

  override fun doInBackground(vararg params: Void?):
List<People> {
    return repository?.getDataFromLocal() ?: emptyList()
  }
}
```

The call itemListCallback.onSuccess(result) is called when the AsyncTask has finished and is called on the main thread while doInBackground executes on the background thread.

Back inside the fetchUsingBackgroundThreads() method implementation, inside the MainActivityPresenter class, under onSuccess the view is updated when AsyncTask has finished on the main thread.

This is the usual way of using a callback pattern to pass the data around. However, it eventually leads to Callback Hell and is not very efficient nor readable. A lot of jumping back and forth is required to follow the code flow.

Using coroutines, you can avoid this callback hell and make the code more readable. Kotlin coroutines let you convert callback-based code to sequential code. To do this, change the value of processingUsing to ProcessUsing.Coroutines inside the MainActivityPresenter class.

Now, whenever the getData() method is called, it will call fetchData(), which will then call fetchUsingCoroutines() method.

Take a look at the implementation of the fetchUsingCoroutines() method:

```
private fun fetchUsingCoroutines() {
    launch {
        try {
            //1
            var itemList = withContext(Dispatchers.IO) {
                repository?.getDataFromLocal()
            }

            //2
            updateData(itemList, "Local DB")

            //3
            itemList = withContext(Dispatchers.IO) {
                repository?.getDataFromRemoteUsingCoroutines()
            }

            //4
            updateData(itemList, "Remote Server")
        } catch (e: Exception) {
            handleError(e)
        }
    }
}
```

Notice, how the code flow is defined, here:

1. Fetch from local first, using a background thread — i.e., Dispatcher.IO.

2. When done, update the UI (set to Dispatcher.Main in the coroutineScope).

3. Try fetching from remote next, using a background thread — i.e., Dispatcher.IO.

4. When done, update the UI (set to Dispatcher.Main in the coroutineScope).

As is visible, the code flow is pretty straightforward and can be read sequentially.

In the end, they do the same thing: wait until a result is available from a long-running task and continue execution. However, in code, they look very different.

Coroutines and Android lifecycle

Android apps consists of various components, which have a lifecycle of their own such as Activities, Fragments, Services, etc. Processing done outside the lifecycle of these components can lead to memory leaks or crashes in general. For example, if the Activity is destroyed and an async processing task — after finishing its work — tries to update the UI of the Activity, it will lead to a crash. This is a serious problem when it comes to configuration changes, such as when the phone is rotated.

Coroutines are not free from such issues; however, they are well prepared to handle them. One of the important concepts that can be used to combat these lifecycle issues is to confine the CoroutineScope to the lifecycle of the Android component.

To do that, you will need to observe the lifecycle of the Android component. Such functionality is available via the Architecture Components Libraries. These libraries consist of a **LifecycleObserver** and **DefaultLifecycleObserver** interfaces to enable observing the lifecycle of a lifecycle owner.

You already set up a CoroutineScope for the presenter. All you need to do now is to make sure the presenter adheres to the lifecycle of the Activity. When the Activity goes to the `onDestroy()` state, it will call the presenters `cleanup()` method, thus canceling all the coroutines within the presenters CoroutineScope and its siblings. This process makes sure there are no coroutines running once the Activity is destroyed. This concurrency mechanism is called **Structured Concurrency**.

To implement this functionality, go to your app's `build.gradle` file and replace `// TODO: add lifecycle dependencies here` under the dependencies section with the following, and sync your project:

```
dependencies {
    // Other dependencies

    //region Lifecycle
    final lifecycleVersion = "2.0.0"
    implementation "androidx.lifecycle:lifecycle-runtime:$lifecycleVersion"
    implementation "androidx.lifecycle:lifecycle-common-java8:$lifecycleVersion"
    //endregion
}
```

Now, simply implement the interface **DefaultLifecycleObserver** on your MainActivityPresenter class, as below:

```
class MainActivityPresenter(var view: ViewContract?, var repository: DataRepositoryContract?) :
    PresenterContract, CoroutineScope, DefaultLifecycleObserver
{
    ...
}
```

Once implemented, you can override the onResume() and onDestroy() methods inside MainActivityPresenter class:

```
override fun onResume(owner: LifecycleOwner) {
    super.onResume(owner)
    getData()
}

override fun onDestroy(owner: LifecycleOwner) {
    cleanup()
    super.onDestroy(owner)
}
```

Notice the call to cleanup() inside the onDestroy() and the call to getData() inside onResume(). Now, all that is required is to wire this presenter to the lifecycle of the MainActivity.

To do that, navigate to `MainActivity.kt` and, inside the `onCreate()` method, add the presenter as the observer on the lifecycle by replacing the `//TODO: Observe the lifecycle` line as shown below:

```kotlin
override fun onCreate(savedInstanceState: Bundle?) {
...

    // Setup the presenter
    val presenter = MainActivityPresenter(this, repository)

    //TODO: Observe the lifecycle
    lifecycle.addObserver(presenter)

    ...
}
```

Notice that the presenter is now a local `val` inside the `onCreate()`. Because you already react to the lifecycle of the Activity and call `getData()` when the Activity goes through `onResume()`, and you also react to the call `cleanup()` when the Activity goes through `onDestroy()`, you no longer need those methods inside the `MainActivity.kt` file itself. So you can safely delete those methods inside the `MainActivity.kt` file:

```kotlin
// Delete the below from within MainActivity.kt file

private var presenter: PresenterContract? = null
...
override fun onResume() {
    super.onResume()
    presenter?.getData()
}

override fun onDestroy() {
    presenter?.cleanup()
    super.onDestroy()
}
```

Another way to handle the lifecycle is to make your CoroutineScope lifecycle aware. The implementation of such a CoroutineScope would look like below:

```kotlin
class LifecycleScope : DefaultLifecycleObserver, CoroutineScope
{
  private val job = Job()

  override val coroutineContext: CoroutineContext = job + Dispatchers.Main

  override fun onDestroy(owner: LifecycleOwner) {
    coroutineContext.cancel()
```

```
      super.onDestroy(owner)
    }
}
```

In such a case, the CoroutineScope, in itself, calls cancel on its coroutineContext when the lifecycle owner goes through the `onDestroy()` state.

> **Note**: You can find the implementation of such a lifecycle aware CoroutineScope in the final app, under the utils package in the file named `LifecycleScope.kt`.

Coroutines and WorkManager

WorkManager is a simple library that is a part of Android Jetpack, used for deferrable background work. It enables a combination of **opportunistic** and **guaranteed** executions. Opportunistic execution means that WorkManager will do your background work as soon as it can. Guaranteed execution means that WorkManager will take care of the logic to start your work under a variety of situations, even if you navigate away from your app.

Some examples of tasks that are a good use of WorkManager include:

- Uploading logs
- Periodically syncing local data with the network
- Applying filters to images and saving the image

To enable coroutine support in WorkManager, you need the dependency shown below, which is already added to the starter project.

```
dependencies {
    // Other dependencies

    final workManagerVersion = "2.1.0"
    implementation "androidx.work:work-runtime-ktx:
$workManagerVersion"
}
```

To define background work in WorkManager, you extend **Worker** and implement **doWork()**. However, when dealing with Coroutines, you would extend from **CoroutineWorker** and implement the **doWork()** method, which is a suspend marked method; thus, it will not block the main thread when called.

You can find the existing implementation for the same inside the file named `RefreshRemoteRepo.kt`. Under the `doWork()` method implementation, a call to `refreshData()` is made, which is another suspend coroutine.

Here, data is fetched from the network using the repository, and the local database is updated with the latest information fetched:

```
// Refresh data from the network using [DataRepository]
@WorkerThread
suspend fun refreshData(): Result {

    // 1
    val localRepo = LocalRepo(applicationContext)
    val remoteRepo = RemoteRepo(applicationContext)
    val repository = DataRepository(localRepo, remoteRepo)

    return try {
            //2
            val itemLists =
    repository.getDataFromRemoteUsingCoroutines()

            //3
            repository.saveData(itemLists)

            //4
            Result.success()
    } catch (error: Exception) {

            //5
            Result.failure()
        }
}
```

The code flow is as follows:

1. Initialize the repository.

2. Fetch from remote first using coroutines.

3. Once the updated data is fetched, update the local database with the refreshed data.

4. Signal successful completion of the work to WorkManager.

5. Signal failed work to WorkManager.

WorkManager is typically wired inside a custom Application class, extending from Application class. The implementation can be checked out inside the StarSyncApp.kt file:

```kotlin
class StarSyncApp : Application() {

  override fun onCreate() {
    super.onCreate()

    setupWorkManagerJob()
  }

  private fun setupWorkManagerJob() {
    // 1
    val constraints = Constraints.Builder()
        .setRequiresCharging(true)
        .setRequiredNetworkType(UNMETERED)
        .build()

    //2
    val work = PeriodicWorkRequest
        .Builder(RefreshRemoteRepo::class.java, 1, TimeUnit.DAYS)
        .setConstraints(constraints)
        .build()

    //3 Enqueue it work WorkManager, keeping any previously scheduled jobs for the same work.
    WorkManager.getInstance()
        .enqueueUniquePeriodicWork(RefreshRemoteRepo::class.java.name, KEEP, work)
  }
}
```

The code flow is pretty straightforward:

1. Set up conditions/constraints on the WorkManager to execute the worker jobs, such as the phone needs to be plugged in and charging while being on the unmetered (wifi) network before executing the worker jobs.

2. Set up a periodic job, which will be attempted to run every day.

3. Enqueue the work to WorkManager, keeping any previously scheduled jobs for the same work.

This custom Application class needs to be wired in the **AndroidManifest.xml** too for this to work. Navigate to **AndroidManifest.xml** and you will see it is pre-wired in the <application> as a value to the name attribute:

```xml
<application
    android:name=".StarSyncApp"
    ...
    >
    ...
</application>
```

Run the app. The worker jobs will be scheduled to run in the background every day and refresh the data in the local database with updated data fetched from the remote server, i.e., SWAPI API.

Final App

Key points

1. **CoroutineDispatcher** determines what thread or threads the corresponding coroutine uses for its execution.

2. A coroutine can switch dispatchers any time after it is started.

3. **Dispatchers.Main** context for Android apps, allows starting coroutines confined to the main thread.

4. Each coroutine runs inside a defined scope.

5. A Job **must** be passed to CoroutineScope in order to cancel all coroutines started in the scope.

6. Coroutines can replace callbacks for more readable and clear code implementation.

7. Making **CoroutineScope** lifecycle aware helps to adhere to the lifecycle of android components and avoid memory leaks.

8. Coroutines seamlessly integrate with WorkManager to run background jobs efficiently.

Where to go from here?

This chapter introduced the concept of using coroutines in an Android app. The concept of various contexts was also covered and how to switch between them when required, all while being able to react to lifecycle events in an Android app.

In the next chapters, you will be working your way through the topics testing, debugging and logging with Coroutines, which are the most important aspects of building a solid Android app.

Chapter 18: Coroutines on Android - Part 2

By Nishant Srivastava

Developing Android apps can get complex when dealing with asynchronous tasks. It is not immediately clear on what thread the code is executing, and trying to figure it out usually involves adding logging statements and debugging the code flow. More importantly, it is the best practice to be able to test the business logic of complex asynchronous tasks. It gets fairly more complex when coroutines are added to the system.

As you know by now, there could be hundreds of coroutines, and they can be executed easily because they are very lightweight. Now, imagine trying to debug a codebase wherein hundreds of these coroutines are executing. Thankfully, there are ways to handle those and the tooling/libraries are built to address such situations.

All of this and more will be covered in this chapter while working with an Android app. Without much ado, jump over to the next section in this chapter.

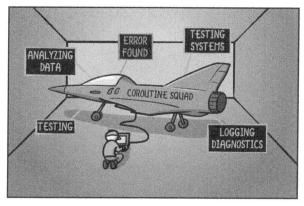

Coroutines on Android: Part 3

Getting started

For this chapter, you will start from where you left off in the last chapter, with the Android app called **StarSync**. As you already know, the app is an offline first MVP app. There is a repository that takes care of fetching data from the **SWAPI** API, which is a public Star Wars API. You can access the documentation for the same at https://swapi.co/. Once fetched, the data is saved to the local database using the Room architecture components library.

If you have already downloaded the starter project, then import it into Android Studio.

Run the starter app now and you will see the following:

Starter App

Because this is an offline-first Android app, when the app loads for the first time, it tries to load data from the local database first. It then goes on to fetch from the remote server via a GET call to the SWAPI API:

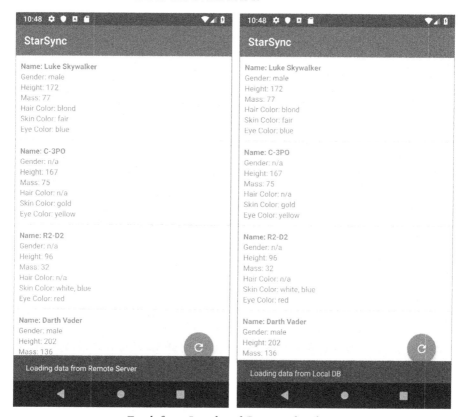

Fetch from Local and Remote database

After the first remote fetch, data is saved to the local database. To verify the offline-first approach, simply switch to **Airplane Mode** and re-launch the app. Data will be fetched from the local database and populated in the list on the screen.

Some important classes to look at:

1. `Extensions.kt`: This class includes custom Kotlin Extension methods to be used in the app.

2. `StarSyncApp.kt`: This class extends the **Application** class and is the main entry point of the Android app. This class is used to set up configurations for the app when it loads up.

You will pick up where you left off from the last chapter — i.e., the app was set up to use coroutines to be able to function as intended. Next, you will enable logging capabilities in the app for coroutines.

Debugging coroutines

When you run the app, the various processes of fetching data from the local and remote repository's are fired up using multiple coroutines. At the same time, there is context switching from executing a fetch operation on the background and then switching to the main thread to display the result when it is available.

While developing your app, you often need to know the name of the coroutine in which your code is executed, mostly in order to debug the app. Having that functionality makes visualizing the coroutines while they are executing much easier to follow. There is a utility method `logCoroutineInfo` already setup in **Extensions.kt** file:

```
// Log Coroutines
fun logCoroutineInfo(msg: String) = println("Running on: [$
{Thread.currentThread().name}] | $msg")
```

All it does is simply print to the standard output with a formatted text that includes the name of the thread. You can use this right away in the starter project.

Go to `RemoteRepo.kt` first, under package `repository/remote`. Now, find the method `getDataUsingCoroutines()` and replace the line with comment `// TODO: Add a log with msg 'Fetching from remote'` with line of code as below:

```
logCoroutineInfo("Fetching from remote")
```

Next, go to `MainActivityPresenter.kt` under `ui/mainscreen` package and find the method `fetchUsingCoroutines()`. You will now add a couple of log statements by replacing TODO comments as below

Replace `// TODO: Add a log with msg 'launch executed'` with:

```
logCoroutineInfo("launch executed")
```

Replace `// TODO: Add a log with msg 'Fetching from local'` with:

```
logCoroutineInfo("Fetching from local")
```

Replace // TODO: Add a log with msg 'Got items from local' with:

```
logCoroutineInfo("Got items from local")
```

Replace // TODO: Add a log with msg 'Got items from remote' with:

```
logCoroutineInfo("Got items from remote")
```

Once done, run the app. Now open **Logcat** and filter for "Running on." You will see the below output:

```
I/System.out: Running on: [main] | launch executed
I/System.out: Running on: [DefaultDispatcher-worker-1] |
Fetching from local
I/System.out: Running on: [main] | Got items from local
I/System.out: Running on: [DefaultDispatcher-worker-2] |
Fetching from remote
I/System.out: Running on: [main] | Got items from remote
```

Nice — now you have logs in order. But wait: If you take a closer look at the logs printed on the screen, the string between [] contains the thread name such as DefaultDispatcher-worker-2, and that is not very helpful. When using coroutines, the thread name alone does not give much of a context. It would be nice to be able to log the coroutines themselves as they are executing instead of the thread they are running on.

For the same reason, kotlinx.coroutines includes debugging facilities, but it needs to be enabled upfront by setting the -Dkotlinx.coroutines.debug to on as a JVM property.

In an Android app, you would typically do this inside the custom Application class. In the starter app, that would be inside the StarSyncApp.kt file.

Replace the comment // TODO: Enable Debugging for Kotlin Coroutines with:

```
System.setProperty("kotlinx.coroutines.debug", if
(BuildConfig.DEBUG) "on" else "off")
```

That is it. Now, run the app, again. The output now changes to:

```
I/System.out: Running on: [main @coroutine#1] | launch executed
I/System.out: Running on: [DefaultDispatcher-worker-1
@coroutine#1] | Fetching from local
I/System.out: Running on: [main @coroutine#1] | Got items from
local
```

```
I/System.out: Running on: [DefaultDispatcher-worker-3
@coroutine#1] | Fetching from remote
I/System.out: Running on: [main @coroutine#1] | Got items from
remote
```

You will notice that the log statements now include a section pertaining to the coroutine with a number appended to it.

In debug mode, every coroutine is assigned a unique consecutive identifier. Every thread that executes a coroutine has its name modified to include the name and identifier of the currently running coroutine. When one coroutine is suspended and resumes another coroutine is dispatched in the same thread, then the thread name displays the whole stack of coroutine descriptions that are being executed on this thread.

However, this can be improved even more. When coroutines are tied to the processing of the specific request or doing some background-specific task, it is better to name it explicitly for debugging purposes. Automatically assigned IDs are usually good when you want to log coroutines often, and you just need to correlate log records coming from the same coroutine — but having a named coroutine just makes logs easy to consume and more focused.

To facilitate that functionality, kotlinx.coroutines provides a class called CoroutineName. This class allows you to specify a name for the coroutine and is typically passed to the coroutine as a context:

```
withContext(CoroutineName("CustomName")) {
    // body
}
```

In this case, a coroutine already has a **Dispatcher** being passed as a context, one can add CoroutineName to the existing **Dispatcher** using the + operator like below:

```
withContext(Dispatchers.IO + CoroutineName("CustomName")) {
    // body
}
```

You will make the same change to provide a name to the coroutine used for fetching from the local database. In the MainActivityPresenter.kt, under ui/mainscreen package, change it to the following:

```
var itemList = withContext(Dispatchers.IO +
CoroutineName("Coroutine for Local")) {
    logCoroutineInfo("Fetching from local")
    repository?.getDataFromLocal()
}
```

Now, run the app and open the **Logcat** to track the logs. You will be able to see something like below:

```
I/System.out: Running on: [main @coroutine#1] | launch executed
I/System.out: Running on: [DefaultDispatcher-worker-1 @Coroutine
for Local#1] | Fetching from local
I/System.out: Running on: [main @coroutine#1] | Got items from
local
I/System.out: Running on: [DefaultDispatcher-worker-3
@coroutine#1] | Fetching from remote
I/System.out: Running on: [main @coroutine#1] | Got items from
remote
```

Notice the second log statement, which now contains the name for the coroutine as @Coroutine for Local#1. This looks much better.

Note: **CoroutineName** context element is displayed in the thread name that is executing this coroutine only when debugging mode is turned on.

Exception handling

Exception handling in coroutines was covered in previous chapters extensively, thus our focus here will be on their behavior on the Android platform.

Before you look into how exceptions are handled by coroutines on Android, understand what actually happens when an exception is thrown in a coroutine:

1. The exception is caught and then resumed through a **Continuation**.

2. If your code doesn't handle the exception, and it isn't a **CancellationException**, the first **CoroutineExceptionHandler** is requested through the current **CoroutineContext**.

3. If a handler isn't found or it errors, the exception is sent to platform-specific code.

4. On the JVM, a **ServiceLoader** is used to locate global handlers.

5. Once all handlers have been invoked, or one of them has errors, the current thread's exception handler gets invoked.

6. If the current thread doesn't handle the exception, it bubbles up to the thread group and then finally to the default exception handler.

7. Crash!

Android, as a platform, has many ways by which an exception can be handled. The most common one being **try-catch**. Coroutines use the same to handle exceptions. To see how it looks like in practice, navigate to `MainActivityPresenter.kt` under `ui/mainscreen` package.

Inside `fetchUsingCoroutines()` method, a `try-catch` is already setup around the body of the method. You will need to trigger a **RuntimeException** to force an exception.

Replace `// TODO: Force a Runtime crash here (for demonstrating try catch behavior)` with:

```
throw RuntimeException("My Runtime Exception: The Darkforce is strong with this one")
```

Notice that the `catch` inside the `fetchUsingCoroutines()` method calls `handleError(e: Exception)` method:

```
try{
    // Method body
}catch (e: Exception) {
    handleError(e)
}
```

Where `handleError(e: Exception)` is defined as inside the `MainActivityPresenter.kt` file itself:

```
override fun handleError(e: Exception) {
    // Hide loading animation
    view?.hideLoading()

    // prompt in view
    view?.prompt(e.message)
}
```

This means that, when the **RuntimeException** is thrown, you should see a prompt on the screen and the loading state will be hidden. Now, run the app.

You will see a snackbar show up with the RuntimeException message you set earlier: "My Runtime Exception: The Darkforce is strong with this one."

Handling My Runtime Exception using try-catch

In the case of exceptions that are not handled on Android, there exists an UncaughtExceptionHandler, which can be configured in the Application class. By default, coroutines use the default Android policy on uncaught exception handling if no try-catch is set up for exception handling.

To set up your own UncaughtExceptionHandler, you will need to define a new UncaughtExceptionHandler and set it as the default UncaughtExceptionHandler, as shown below:

```
// Setup handler for uncaught exceptions.
Thread.setDefaultUncaughtExceptionHandler { _, e ->
    Log.e("UncaughtExpHandler", e.message)
}
```

> **Note**: This is already defined and set up in the **StarSyncApp.kt** file in the starter app.

Now, to see this functioning in practice, you will need to remove the `try-catch` inside the `fetchUsingCoroutines()` method and run the app. This time, the app will start and will be stuck in the loading state. Open the **Logcat** window inside Android Studio. You will notice a stacktrace of a `RuntimeException`, as well as the log statement you added to your `UncaughtExceptionHandler`:

```
com.raywenderlich.android.starsync E/AndroidRuntime: FATAL EXCEPTION: main
    Process: com.raywenderlich.android.starsync, PID: 12774
    java.lang.RuntimeException: My Runtime Exception: The Darkforce is strong with this one
        at com.raywenderlich.android.starsync.ui.mainscreen.MainActivityPresenter$fetchUsingCoroutines$1.invokeSuspend(MainActivityPresenter.kt:67)
        at kotlin.coroutines.jvm.internal.BaseContinuationImpl.resumeWith(ContinuationImpl.kt:32)
        at kotlinx.coroutines.DispatchedTask.run(Dispatched.kt:233)
        at android.os.Handler.handleCallback(Handler.java:873)
        at android.os.Handler.dispatchMessage(Handler.java:99)
        at android.os.Looper.loop(Looper.java:193)
        at android.app.ActivityThread.main(ActivityThread.java:6669)
        at java.lang.reflect.Method.invoke(Native Method)
        at com.android.internal.os.RuntimeInit$MethodAndArgsCaller.run(RuntimeInit.java:493)
        at com.android.internal.os.ZygoteInit.main(ZygoteInit.java:858)

com.raywenderlich.android.starsync E/UncaughtExpHandler: My Runtime Exception: The Darkforce is strong with this one
```

Why didn't the app crash, though? Although you removed the `try-catch` earlier, you also setup a default `UncaughtExceptionHandler`, which consumes all uncaught exceptions and logs them to the **Logcat** as per the definition you set up.

Another way to handle exceptions is to create a `CoroutineExceptionHandler` that logs the exception directly. A `CoroutineExceptionHandler` is already defined inside the `MainActivityPresenter.kt` under `ui/mainscreen` package named as `handler`:

```
private val handler = CoroutineExceptionHandler { _, throwable ->
    handleError(Exception(throwable.message))
}
```

To use the handler with a coroutine, simply pass it along with the context using the + operator as shown below:

```
launch(Dispatchers.IO + handler) {
    //body
}
```

You can set it up in the starter app right away. Do as follows: Go to `// TODO: Setup CoroutineExceptionHandler for launch coroutine` here and update the launch coroutine to:

```
launch(Dispatchers.IO + handler){
    ...
}
```

Next, replace `// TODO: Force a Runtime crash here (for demonstrating CoroutineExceptionHandler behavior)` and with a RuntimeException as shown below:

```
launch(Dispatchers.IO + handler){
    throw RuntimeException("My Runtime Exception: The Darkforce is strong with this one")
    ...
}
```

Run the app, now. You will see the app show a snackbar with the error message you defined in the `RuntimeException`:

Handling My Runtime Exception using CoroutineExceptionHandler

When a launch coroutine crashes, its parent is canceled, which in turn cancels all the parent's children. Once coroutines throughout the tree have finished canceling, the exception is sent to the current context's exception handler. On Android, that means your app will crash, regardless of what dispatcher you were using if the exception was not handled.

On the other hand, `async` holds on to its exceptions. What that means is that `await()` explicitly handles all exceptions and installing a `CoroutineExceptionHandler` will have no effect.

All these exceptions and errors need to be handled, but if you wrote tests for your app you can always be sure these situations are not unexpectedly rising up.

Don't forget testing

Tests in an Android app are one of the most important aspects of building a quality app. Having tests in place makes sure that the business logic is correct and the app executes as expected. When it comes to asynchronous programming, it becomes even more important to have tests in place. Because of complex timing and execution states, the multi-threaded nature of async operations on the Android platform increases the chances of errors.

One can spawn multiple Kotlin coroutines on a background thread or the main thread. But when it comes to testing, you want to set a specific thread on which your tests run, thereby removing ambiguity around where the coroutines are executing and eliminating context switching completely. To enable that kind of functionality, you will need to make sure you can specify the **Dispatchers** your coroutines run on.

In the starter app, you will notice all the coroutines are executing inside the MainActivityPresenter class with each having their own **Dispatcher** defined to execute on. You need to now modify the MainActivityPresenter class under ui/mainscreen package so that its constructor can take in two more arguments as below:

```
class MainActivityPresenter(var view: ViewContract?,
    var repository: DataRepositoryContract?,
    uiDispatcher: CoroutineDispatcher = Dispatchers.Main,
    val ioDispatcher: CoroutineDispatcher = Dispatchers.IO)
```

Notice the two new arguments now being passed to the primary constructor of the MainActivityPresenter class. To make sure the API does not break, default values are provided.

This means if you do not pass in arguments, the default values will be passed in — i.e., inside the MainActivity.kt file, the call to initialize MainActivityPresenter does not need to be changed:

```
// Setup the presenter
val presenter = MainActivityPresenter(this, repository)
```

The above initialization of presenter is completely valid, and, since no third or fourth arguments are provided, the default ones will be used to initialize the presenter.

Navigate back to the MainActivityPresenter.kt file under ui/mainscreen package and replace all occurrences of Dispatchers.Main with uiDispatcher and Dispatchers.IO with ioDispatcher.

This makes sure that when you do pass in values to those arguments, the set **Dispatchers** will be used for executing the coroutines. Now, the **MainActivityPresenter** class is testable.

However, the constructor for MainActivityPresenter class also accepts arguments such as instances of ViewContract and DataRepositoryContract. These are dependencies that need to be defined when writing tests.

That is a problem because these can change and writing tests with dependencies that can change makes the tests flaky — i.e., not reliable. To fix this issue, these dependencies should be **mocked** out.

> **Note**: Mocked objects are simulated objects that mimic the behavior of real objects in controlled ways. Mocking for tests is vast subject and is out of the bounds of this book.

There is a helper **MockData** class under the test/<app_packagename>/repository that provides a simple method called generateFakeData(), which simply returns a list of fake People objects. This list will be used to validate against in our tests. Typically, this a mocked out version of a list of People objects.

You are going to use one of the mocking libraries for Kotlin called **Mockk**. This library is written specifically for Kotlin and enables mocking final classes, which are the default in Kotlin as well as providing many helper DSLs (Domain Specific Language) to write tests in a more idiomatic manner.

To add it to the starter project, navigate to your build.gradle file for the **app** module and replace // TODO: add Mockk dependency here with below:

```
testImplementation "io.mockk:mockk:1.9"
```

> **Note**: To be able to mock and verify coroutines, you need to have the kotlinx-coroutines-core dependency, which, in our case, is already added in the **build.gradle** for the app module.

Now, sync your project. Once your project is synced and the **Mockk** dependency is available during runtime, you will have access to various methods such as mockk, verify, every, verifyOrder, etc. methods, which allow mocking Kotlin classes and coroutines behavior.

As a short primer about using Mockk, you need to understand the flow of how the tests are written. You will most likely mock out the classes you want to define a set behavior for when running under your tests. Then, you will need to define what happens on every call to a certain method on those classes. This is where the every{} DSL from **Mockk** comes into play. It basically allows you to define what to return immediately when a call to a certain method on a mocked object is made — for example:

```
// 1
val repository: DataRepositoryContract = mockk(relaxUnitFun =
true)

// 2
every { repository.getDataFromLocal() } returns mockedItemList
```

Here:

1. Initializes the repository variable, which is of type DataRepositoryContract class with a mocked version of DataRepositoryContract. The part relaxUnitFun = true passed to the mockk() method only means that Mockk library will not throw an error when trying to Mockk methods that return nothing, i.e., Unit. It relaxes the strict behavior.

2. Defines on every call of getDataFromLocal() method on the mocked repository instance return a list of mocked out list items. Where mockedItemList is an ArrayList of mocked out list items defined as below:

```
val mockData = MockData()
val mockedItemList= mockData.generateFakeData()
```

Using this knowledge, you will now update the Unit Test file created against the MainActivityPresenter class called MainActivityPresenterTest. Navigate to MainActivityPresenterTest.kt file under tests package.

Next, implement the setUp and tearDown methods replacing // TODO comments as below:

```
@Before
fun setUp() {
    // 1
    repository = mockk(relaxUnitFun = true)
    //2
    view = mockk(relaxUnitFun = true)

    // 3
    presenter = MainActivityPresenter(view, repository,
Dispatchers.Unconfined, Dispatchers.Unconfined)
}

@After
fun tearDown() {
    // 4
    unmockkAll()
}
```

Here:

1. Mock the repository.

2. Mock the view.

3. Initialize the presenter, by passing in the mocked-out view and repository as arguments to the constructor. For the **uiDispatcher** and **ioDispatcher**, you pass in Dispatchers.Unconfined. It is the dispatcher that is not confined to any specific thread; i.e., it runs on the same thread as the one on which the coroutine was launched.

4. Finally, when the tests all finish executing, simply reset the mocks so as to create a clean slate for the next time the tests are run.

Now that the setup is done, you only need to write the tests to validate the business logic for the **MainActivityPresenter** class.

The first test you will write is to validate the logic for updateData() method inside the presenter.

Inside the MainActivityPresenterTest.kt file under tests package, a test stub already exists called presenter_updateData(). Simply replace the // TODO: Add presenter_updateData() implementation here with:

```
// When
// 1
presenter.updateData(mockedItemList, "Repo")

// Then
// 2
verify {
    view.prompt(any())
}

// 3
coVerify {
    repository.saveData(mockedItemList)
}

// 4
verifyOrder {
    view.hideLoading()
    view.updateWithData(mockedItemList)
}
```

Going through the code step by step:

1. At the start of the test, call the presenter.updateData(mockedItemList, "Repo").

2. Then, verify that the view.prompt() method with any() argument passed to it is called.

3. Then coVerify checks if the coroutine repository.saveData(mockedItemList) was called.

4. Next verify that view.hideLoading() and view.updateWithData(mockedItemList) are called one after the other in order.

If all of these hold true, then the test would pass. This is the happy path that you just implemented, and the test will pass in our case because the starter app is written with the correct business logic. Try running the test by right-clicking on the test and selecting **Run 'presenter_updateData()'**.

To validate if the tests are functional, try to change the business logic in the app. Navigate to MainActivityPresenter.kt file under ui/mainscreen and comment the saveDataUsingCoroutines(it) inside the updateData() method definition:

```
// saveDataUsingCoroutines(it)
```

Now, go back to MainActivityPresenterTest.kt file under the tests package and execute the test called presenter_updateData() once again. This time the test will fail denoting that the business logic is not correct and needs to be fixed. You will be looking at a stacktrace:

```
ava.lang.AssertionError: Verification failed: call 1 of 1:
DataRepositoryContract(#1).saveData(eq([People(name=Luke
Skywalker, height=172, mass=77, hair_color=blond,
skin_color=fair, eye_color=blue, gender=male), People(name=Darth
Vader, height=202, mass=136, hair_color=none, skin_color=white,
eye_color=yellow, gender=male), People(name=Leia Organa,
height=150, mass=49, hair_color=brown, skin_color=light,
eye_color=brown, gender=female)]))) was not called

    at
io.mockk.impl.recording.states.VerifyingState.failIfNotPassed(Ve
rifyingState.kt:66)
    at
io.mockk.impl.recording.states.VerifyingState.recordingDone(Veri
fyingState.kt:42)
    at
io.mockk.impl.recording.CommonCallRecorder.done(CommonCallRecord
er.kt:48)
```

```
        at
io.mockk.impl.eval.RecordedBlockEvaluator.record(RecordedBlockEv
aluator.kt:60)
        at
io.mockk.impl.eval.VerifyBlockEvaluator.verify(VerifyBlockEvalua
tor.kt:27)
        at io.mockk.MockKDsl.internalCoVerify(API.kt:143)
        at io.mockk.MockKKt.coVerify(MockK.kt:162)
        at io.mockk.MockKKt.coVerify$default(MockK.kt:159)
        at
com.raywenderlich.android.starsync.ui.mainscreen.MainActivityPre
senterTest.presenter_updateData(MainActivityPresenterTest.kt:99)
```

Uncomment the saveDataUsingCoroutines(it) inside the updateData() method definition in MainActivityPresenter.kt file to get back to a functional business logic and re-run the test to validate it.

The second test you will write is to validate the logic for the getData() method inside the presenter.

Inside the MainActivityPresenterTest.kt file under the tests package, a test stub already exists called presenter_getData(). Simply replace the // TODO: Add presenter_getData() implementation here with:

```
// Given
every { repository.getDataFromLocal() } returns mockedItemList
coEvery { repository.getDataFromRemoteUsingCoroutines()} returns
mockedItemList

// When
presenter.getData()


// Then
verifyOrder {
    view.hideLoading()
    view.showLoading()
}

coVerify {
    repository.getDataFromLocal()
}

verify {
    view.prompt(any())
}

coVerify {
    repository.saveData(mockedItemList)
}
```

```
verifyOrder {
    view.hideLoading()
    view.updateWithData(mockedItemList)
}
coVerify {
    repository.getDataFromRemoteUsingCoroutines()
}
verify {
    view.prompt(any())
}
coVerify {
    repository.saveData(mockedItemList)
}
verifyOrder {
    view.hideLoading()
    view.updateWithData(mockedItemList)
}
```

This test is very similar to the one explained above. This is, again, the happy path and when you run this test, it will pass successfully. If, however, you change the business logic, the test will fail — thus, acting as a safeguard against unintended changes in future.

Anko: Simplified coroutines

Kotlin coroutines are essentially a language feature. Similar to how the standard `kotlin.coroutines` library builds upon them, **Anko (ANdroid KOtlin)** coroutines is another library that is based on the `kotlin.coroutines` library, providing simpler syntax and approach to async programing.

Anko is a helper library built by the folks at JetBrain. Anko was originally designed as a single library. As the project grew, adding Anko as a dependency began to have a significant impact on the size of the APK, hence it was split out into sub-libraries, namely:

- **Commons**: Helps you perform the most common Android tasks, including displaying dialogues and launching new Activities.

- **Layouts**: Provides a Domain Specific Language (DSL) for defining Android layouts.

- **SQLite**: A query DSL and parser that makes it easier to interact with SQLite databases.
- **Coroutines**: Supplies utilities based on the `kotlinx.coroutines` library.

Anko-Coroutines, as of writing this chapter, provides access to only one helper method called `asReference()`.

By default, a coroutine holds references to captured objects until it is finished or cancelled. That means in the Android world, it will capture/hold on to the instance of Activity or Fragment, until it is finished or cancelled. If not cancelled/finished, this might lead to memory leaks.

Consider a common use case of using a coroutine as an asynchronous API. Once called, the API would execute the coroutine to do the specific work, suspend it and then resume it back. Pretty simple :]

However there is a caveat here. If the asynchronous API does not support cancellation, your coroutine may be suspended for an indefinite time period. In Android world, the coroutine would hold a reference to the instance of the Activity/Fragment indefinitely, which is pretty bad as it leads to memory leaks.

To avoid such a situation, the `asReference()` function creates a weak reference wrapper around the instance of a Activity/Fragment to protect against memory leaks.

To start using `asReference()`, open the starter app and navigate to the `app/build.gradle` file and replace `// TODO: add Anko Coroutines dependency here` with the below:

```
// Anko Coroutines
implementation "org.jetbrains.anko:anko-coroutines:0.10.8"
```

Sync your project. Now, the `asReference()` function should be available to you. You will now implement a new function that fetches data from the remote repo and updates the result in the UI, called `fetchResultUsingAnkoCoroutine()`.

Navigate to `MainActivityPresenter.kt` file under the `ui/mainscreen` package and replace `//TODO: Anko implementation` with:

```
// Anko implementation
// 1
private lateinit var job: Job

private fun fetchResultUsingAnkoCoroutine() {
  // 2
  val ref = asReference()
```

```
    // 3
    job = launch(uiDispatcher) {
      try {

        // 4
        val deferred = async(ioDispatcher) {
          repository?.getDataFromRemoteUsingCoroutines()
        }

        // 5
        ref().apply {
          //  Prompt in view about the source of data
          view?.prompt("Loading data from Remote")

          // Hide loading animation
          view?.hideLoading()

          // Update view
          view?.updateWithData(deferred.await()?: emptyList())
        }
      } catch (e: Exception) {
        e.printStackTrace()
      }
    }
}
```

Here,

1. An instance of a Job class is declared with lateinit modifier so as to initialize it later.

2. Inside the function, a reference is acquired of the current class; i.e., the presenter class using asReference() function from the **Anko-Coroutines** library. This creates a weak reference around the presenter.

3. Assign the job instance with the job returned from the **launch()** coroutine builder.

4. Execute the async coroutine builder to handle call to repository?.getDataFromRemoteUsingCoroutines() function in background, returning a **Deferred** instance.

5. Using the ref instance defined earlier, reference the view and update the UI.

Next, navigate to the function fetchData() and replace the call to fetchUsingCoroutines() with fetchResultUsingAnkoCoroutine(). Also call job.cancel() inside the cleanup() function, which makes sure the coroutines are canceled when cleanup() function is called. The ref instance makes sure that no strong references are kept around.

Now, run the app and you will notice that the data is fetched from the remote repository and displayed in the UI as a list, as shown on the next page.

Fetch from Remote server

> **Note: Anko-Coroutines** has more helper methods such as `bg()` and `doAsync()`, which are now deprecated in favor of the standard `kotlin.coroutines` library's implementations.

Key points

Android is an ever-evolving platform, each year a new flavor of Android is released. The complexity with each new release around async processing also increases as new APIs are released. New devices with completely different setups are being released, such as foldable phones. Handling the Activity/Fragment lifecycles and managing the app states is going to become more complex. Thankfully, Kotlin coroutines are a step forward in simplification of async processes, enabling well testable apps.

1. Debugging coroutines is pretty easy since you can name them and also log the name of the thread they are running on.

2. To enable debugging logs in coroutines, -Dkotlinx.coroutines.debug flag needs to be set as a JVM property.

3. By default, coroutines use the default Android policy on uncaught exception handling if no **try-catch** is set up for exception handling.

4. Using CoroutineExceptionHandler, you can set up a custom handler for exceptions generated from coroutines.

5. Dispatchers.Unconfined dispatcher is not confined to any specific thread; i.e., it runs on the same thread as the one on which the coroutine was launched.

6. In order to make coroutines testable, the normal dispatchers need to be replaced by Dispatchers.Unconfined inside test methods.

7. **Mockk** is a Kotlin mocking library, which allows to mock coroutines as well and tests their execution points.

8. **Anko (ANdroid KOtlin)** is a set of helper libraries built by the folks at JetBrain. The Anko coroutines library is based on the standard kotlin.coroutines library.

Conclusion

Congratulations! After a long journey you learned a lot of new concepts about multithreading and concurrent programming with Kotlin. With coroutines, you can now execute tasks in the background using the proper data structure and the best coroutine launcher. You now have the fundamentals of coroutines, like context and dispatcher, flows, and you are able to learn all the new exciting APIs that the coroutine team is going to release in the future.

If you're an Android developer you've also learned how to use coroutines along with the Activity and Fragment lifecycles with better and more efficient use of the device resources.

Finally, you learned how to use coroutines in different environment like Java.

And, remember, if you want to further your understanding of Kotlin and Coroutine app development after working through *Kotlin Coroutines*, we suggest you read the *Android Apprentice*, available on our online store:

- https://store.raywenderlich.com/products/android-apprentice

If you have any questions or comments as you work through this book, please stop by our forums at http://forums.raywenderlich.com and look for the particular forum category for this book.

Thank you again for purchasing this book. Your continued support is what makes the tutorials, books, videos, conferences and other things we do at raywenderlich.com possible, and we truly appreciate it!

Wishing you all the best in your continued Kotlin and Coroutine adventures,

– The *Kotlin Coroutines by Tutorials* team

Made in the USA
Columbia, SC
02 December 2020